**Interbasin
Transfers
of
Water**

Interbasin Transfers of Water

Economic Issues and Impacts

Charles W. Howe
and
K. William Easter

Published for
Resources for the Future, Inc.
by
The Johns Hopkins Press
Baltimore and London

Resources for the Future, Inc.
1755 Massachusetts Avenue, N.W., Washington, D.C. 20036

Resources for the Future is a nonprofit corporation for research and education in the
development, conservation, and use of natural resources and the improvement of the
quality of the environment. It was established in 1952 with the cooperation of the Ford
Foundation. Part of the work of Resources for the Future is carried out by its resident
staff; part is supported by grants to universities and other nonprofit organizations.
Unless otherwise stated, interpretations and conclusions in RFF publications are those
of the authors; the organization takes responsibility for the selection of significant subjects for study, the competence of the researchers, and their freedom of inquiry.

This book is one of RFF's studies on water resources. Charles W. Howe, who served
as head of the water resources program until mid-1970, is now professor of economics
at the University of Colorado. K. William Easter, formerly with the U.S. Bureau of the
Budget, is associate professor, University of Minnesota, and Ford Foundation consultant.
Charts were drawn by Frank and Clare Ford.

RFF editors: Henry Jarrett, Vera W. Dodds, Nora E. Roots, Tadd Fisher.

The Johns Hopkins Press, Baltimore, Maryland 21218
The Johns Hopkins Press Ltd., London

Library of Congress Catalog Card Number 78–149241
International Standard Book Number 0-8018-1206-2

The rain is plenteous but, by God's decree,
Only a third is meant for you and me;
    Two-thirds are taken by the growing things
Or vanish Heavenward on vapour's wings:
    Nor does it mathematically fall
With social equity on one and all.
    The population's habit is to grow
In every region where the water's low:
    Nature is blamed for failings that are Man's,
And well-run rivers have to change their plans.

—A.P.H.

From the poem "Water" by Sir Alan Herbert, quoted with permission of the author.

Preface and Acknowledgments

This project originated at Resources for the Future in 1965 as a result of discussions with Irving K. Fox and Allen V. Kneese in an attempt to isolate top priority issues in the water resource field. An advisory group consisting of Harvey O. Banks, Emery N. Castle, and Maurice Kelso was set up to help in guiding the study. These persons cannot be held responsible for shortcomings of the book, but they contributed greatly to its strong points.

In the spring of 1968 the mutual interests of the two authors led to a collaboration which enabled the scope of the study to be expanded. Easter's work on the impacts of irrigated agriculture on other regions (now incorporated as chapter 6) complemented Howe's analyses of the economic impact on the regions directly importing or exporting water. Every chapter has been strengthened by this collaboration.

Special thanks are due the extensive efforts of Emery N. Castle of Oregon State University, Warren A. Hall of the Dry Lands Research Institute at the University of California at Riverside, Irving Hoch of RFF, and Maurice M. Kelso of the University of Arizona in reviewing earlier drafts. Many others also contributed: Blair T. Bower, Michael F. Brewer, Marion Clawson, Allen V. Kneese, John V. Krutilla, and Robert A. Young of RFF; Thomas Barry and other Bureau of the Budget staff members; James T. Bonnen, Michigan State University; Gardner M. Brown, University of Washington; Harold O. Carter, University of California at Davis; Melvin Cotner, Economic Research Service, U.S. Department of Agriculture; B. Delworth Gardner, Utah State; Donald C. Horton, Western Illinois University; Lionel Lerner, California Department of Water Resources; Arthur Madison; William E. Martin, University of Arizona; Kenneth Ruffing; Vernon W. Ruttan, University of Minnesota; and Charles L. Schultze, University of Maryland and the Brookings Institution. Clifford S. Russell of RFF contributed the proof in the appendix to Chapter 2.

We are grateful to Nora Roots who, in doing a superb job of editing, refused to let the authors obfuscate issues large or small; Mae Patterson Davis who typed the initial draft; and Dee Stell who typed, organized men and materials, and generally kept things running when they threatened to bog down.

CHARLES W. HOWE

K. WILLIAM EASTER

August, 1970

Contents

List of Tables

List of Figures

Interbasin
Transfers
of
Water

1

Introduction

Large-scale water development projects have been receiving increasing publicity and public attention in the past few years. The Northeastern drought of 1963 through 1966 and assertions of impending water crises in the Southwestern United States have attracted widespread attention to the very uneven distribution of the water resource, both geographically and through time. One type of prescription for alleviating these conditions has been the large-scale transfer of water from one river basin to another, from one region of the country to another, or even from one part of the North American continent to other distant parts. The public advocacy of these transfers by various groups and the rebuttal provided by others have frequently clouded basic questions that need to be asked and answered if water transfers are to receive the unbiased and informed evaluation required for wise policy formulation.

The objectives of the book are to sum up what is currently known about the direct and indirect benefits attributable to water, the potential costs of interbasin transfers, and the problems relating to such transfers; to present information on a range of alternatives to interbasin transfers; and to suggest methods of economic analysis appropriate to these large projects. The West receives the most attention simply because that is where interbasin transfers have been most frequently proposed and where the natural water deficit is greatest. Sufficient justification for this concentration is found in the region's water use patterns: withdrawals of 100 million acre-feet each year for irrigation compared to a national total of 140 million, and 55 million acre-feet consumed in irrigation each year out of a national total of 78 million (see table 1).

Table 1. Estimated Water Use Characteristics of the United States, 1965

Water use regions	1965 Population	1950–60 Decade rate of employment growth	Average annual runoff, 1931–60		Annual runoff available 90 percent of time	Public supply		Rural irrigation, domestic, and livestock			Self-supplied industrial water		
						Withdrawal	Consumptive use	Withdrawal	Consumptive use	Conveyance losses	Withdrawals Fresh	Other	Consumptive use
	millions	percent	inches	maf	maf	maf	maf	maf	maf	maf	maf	maf	maf
Eastern													
New England	10.5	13.2	23	75	54.9	1.3	0.2	0.1	0.1	*	2.4	4.1	0.1
Delaware and Hudson	25.8	13.1	21	37	31.4	3.5	0.7	0.3	0.1	*	10.3	13.4	0.4
Chesapeake Bay	9.5	13.9	16	48	33.6	1.1	0.1	0.2	0.1	*	5.6	3.7	0.2
South Atlantic and Eastern Gulf	23.7	20.3	15	229	142.2	2.4	0.4	4.4	2.2	0.6	15.9	8.9	0.4
Eastern Great Lakes	13.3	13.0	16	39	24.6	1.9	0.3	0.2	0.1	*	14.6	*	*
Central													
Western Great Lakes	13.5	13.1	11	45	32.5	2.4	0.3	0.2	0.1	*	17.9	*	0.2
Ohio River	18.3	5.9	16	121	68.3	1.9	0.2	0.3	0.3	*	31.4	*	0.5
Tennessee—Cumberland	4.5	6.5	21	66	44.8	0.4	0.1	0.2	0.1	*	8.6	*	0.2
Middle Western													
Upper Mississippi	13.2	6.7	7	66	35.8	1.3	0.2	0.7	0.5	*	15.7	*	0.1
Lower Mississippi	5.1	0.2	16	61	30.2	0.5	0.2	0.9	0.6	0.1	3.9	0.4	0.3
Upper Missouri–Hudson Bay	6.5	10.8	2	43	25.8	0.9	0.2	18.4	11.4	3.7	1.8	*	0.1
Lower Missouri	2.4	4.3	8	22	5.6	0.2	*	0.2	0.2	*	1.7	*	*
Upper Arkansas–Red	3.6	11.3	2	19	5.6	0.4	0.1	6.5	4.7	0.9	0.8	0.1	0.9
Lower Arkansas–White–Red	4.2	−0.6	15	89	35.8	0.3	0.1	1.3	0.9	0.1	2.0	*	0.3
Western													
Western Gulf	11.1	43.6	3	49	19.0	1.5	0.6	20.2	15.2	3.7	5.8	5.2	0.8
Colorado	2.4	65.2	2	19	10.1	0.5	0.2	18.1	9.0	3.4	0.3	*	0.1
Great Basin	1.3	34.0	1	11	4.5	0.3	0.1	7.1	4.1	1.5	0.5	*	*
Pacific Northwest	5.7	14.6	17	234	165.8	1.3	0.2	29.2	11.1	7.9	1.9	*	0.1
South Pacific	18.1	61.8	12	69	31.4	4.4	1.5	24.2	15.1	4.7	1.7	12.3	0.1
Coterminous United States	192.9	15.4		1,344	795.2	26.1	5.8	138.9	77.5	27.0	145.6	50.6	4.3

Sources: Employment growth and average runoff for 1931–60 in million acre-feet (maf) computed by Howe. Other data are from various tables in C. Richard Murray, Estimated Use of Water in the United States, 1965, U.S. Geological Survey Circular 556, Washington, D.C., 1968.

* Less than 0.1.

a Do not include water used for hydroelectric power generation.

The Water Problem

The economically useful water resources of the United States are quite unevenly distributed. The grossest division would be to specify those parts of the United States lying east of the 100th meridian as humid and moist with plentiful rainfall, and those west of the 100th meridian (with the exception of the Pacific Northwest) as semiarid with scant rainfall. The distributions of population, economic activity, and types of water use are also far from uniform.

Several important points can be observed from the data given in table 1 for nineteen water resource regions: (1) natural water availability in the West (except for the Northwest) as measured by reliable runoff is low relative to the rest of the country; (2) this low availability of natural water supply has not prevented the rapid growth of the western regions, among which are found the most rapidly growing regions of the country; (3) withdrawals by public supply systems (mostly urban) are small compared to those of agriculture and industry; (4) combined consumptive uses and conveyance losses in irrigated agriculture are more than ten times those in public (urban) and industrial systems; (5) irrigation uses are heavily concentrated in the West and Upper Great Plains regions.

It is thus seen that those sections of the country which have the smallest natural endowment of water have developed water-intensive types of activity of a highly water-consumptive nature. How it became possible and profitable to undertake such activity in an arid environment is a question answered only by a broad treatment of United States economic history and, in particular, the history of resource development policy. It is not surprising, at any rate, that the water problems of the West as perceived by many people should be problems of water availability for these water-intensive activities.

The Eastern, Central, and Middle Western regions also have water problems, but these are generally related to water quality. The growth of population and industry and the traditional reliance on watercourse disposal of waste (including heat) have overburdened many streams and estuaries. These regions also face the problem of infrequent, unpredictable drought—quite a different type of problem from that of perennial water deficit in the West. Natural rainfall provides frequent replenishment for surface and ground reservoirs and most of the water needed for agriculture and outside lawn and garden watering. The provision of supply systems having adequate inventories to meet the extreme demands of long droughts requires large investments which stand idle most of the time, in contrast to the western water systems which, while built large, are called upon to operate at near capacity most of the time.

Three types of water problems thus face various regions of the United States: water quantity, water quality, and infrequent but extreme drought. Whether these problems require immediate responses or whether there is time to study solutions over a longer period of time may be a matter for debate, but one point is clear: the West cannot maintain a rapid rate of economic growth without devising better ways of utilizing its present water resources or importing new supplies, and the East cannot continue to contaminate its water environment without serious impact on the quality of living.

There are many ways of dealing with these problems of water quantity and quality. Among the actions that have been proposed (particularly but not exclusively in connection with the water quantity problems of the West) is the large-scale interbasin transfer of water from "surplus" to "deficit" areas. The economic aspects of such water transfers constitute the subject matter of this book.

WHAT IS DIFFERENT ABOUT LARGE-SCALE INTERBASIN TRANSFERS?

An important distinction between existing transfers and those proposed for future implementation is size. New York City's diversions from the Delaware River Basin currently average less than 1 million acre-feet per year. By the mid-1960s the city had invested more than $500 million in reservoir and transmission facilities in that system over a thirty-year period.[1] The Colorado-Big Thompson diversion project carries an average of 230,000 acre-feet to the eastern slopes of Colorado and represents a total investment of $161.6 million. In contrast, current proposals for diverting water into the West vary from a Columbia River–Colorado River transfer of 2.4 million acre-feet per year with capital costs (including interest during construction) of $1.4 billion[2] to the North American Water and Power Alliance (NAWAPA) proposed by the Ralph M. Parsons Company of Los Angeles and designed to bring 110 million acre-feet of water (expandable to 250 million) from the far northwestern part of the continent to seven provinces of Canada, thirty-three states in the United States, and three states of Mexico at a capital cost of about $100 billion over a twenty-year construction period.[3] NAWAPA's proposed delivery of 78 million acre-feet annually to the United States would rep-

[1] City of New York, Board of Water Supply, *61st Annual Report, 1966*, Table A.

[2] Samuel B. Nelson, *Snake-Colorado Project: A Plan to Transport Surplus Columbia River Basin Water to the Arid Pacific Southwest*, Department of Water and Power, City of Los Angeles (1963).

[3] For a summary of NAWAPA's features, see The Ralph M. Parsons Company, *NAWAPA: North American Water and Power Alliance*, Brochure 606-2934-19, Los Angeles (no date).

resent about 50 percent of all current *withdrawals* of water from all sources in the regions that would be served.[4] The economic, hydrological, and ecological impacts of a project of this size would be profound, both during the construction period and throughout the operating lifetime.

For interbasin transfer projects of this size, institutional and political arrangements and agreements would have to be devised on a scale never before attempted. What type of agency could carry out the planning and management of a large interbasin project in a way that would be economically efficient from the nation's viewpoint and agreeable to the many states physically affected? How would such projects be financed? These institutional and political questions may have answers, but they will require innovation and invention beyond the presently existing federal-state agency framework.

Another differentiating factor stemming from large size is the indivisible or "lumpy" nature of the component parts of the system. There are such large construction economies in the building of reservoirs and transport facilities (canals, aqueducts, tunnels, piping) that these components would rationally be built with a greater capacity than needed at the beginning of the project. Thus very large commitments of capital must be made, only to stand idle until demand catches up. These indivisibilities tend to place large transfers at a cost disadvantage relative to alternative sources of supply unless the storage and transport facilities can be fitted into a larger systems plan which will permit fuller utilization early in the life of the project.

Interbasin transfer projects also tend to have irreversible effects on the environment as reservoirs innundate valleys and as regional water balances are changed.

Long life (current calculations of benefits and costs are typically based on an expectation of 100-year life) means a lack of flexibility in incorporating technological innovations in the water system. A desalting plant or a water reclamation system with an economic life of twenty or thirty years may be disassembled and replaced by new equipment if technological improvements warrant such a change, but once the storage and transport facilities of a transfer system are in place, it becomes physically difficult to remove the structures and probably impossible to regenerate the natural ecosystems of the reservoir areas. In general, longer life means greater uncertainty—economic, technological, and ecological—against which the investment bet is made.

To some degree, the physical indivisibilities, nonreversibilities, and political difficulties of these large projects may be offset by a greater flexi-

[4] This assumes total withdrawals of 125 million acre-feet per year in Eastern and Western Great Lakes, Upper Missouri, Colorado, Great Basin, and South Pacific regions.

bility in the use of present water resources which could follow from the prospect of new water supplies. Short-distance transfers among basins and uses might be more readily agreed to by the parties involved if replacement water could be promised. It has been suggested by Laycock[5] that the prospect of plentiful importations could alleviate regional fears, overcome political resistance, avoid the costs of litigation, and generally result in much more efficient utilization of existing supplies. The plausibility of this suggestion depends upon the economic viability of the smaller transfers and upon overcoming the same types of political and economic conflicts between the prospective large-scale importers and exporters.

BRIEF HISTORIES OF PAST PROJECTS

Interesting examples of currently operating interbasin transfers are described below to provide the reader with a picture of the types of transfers that currently exist.

California

The State of California has the earliest interbasin transfer project as well as the most recent and the largest one.[6] Although a proposal was made as early as 1873 to transfer water from the Sacramento Valley to the San Joaquin Valley, the earliest project executed was the Los Angeles Aqueduct, completed in 1913.[7] This project initially carried about 150,000 acre-feet per year from Owens Valley on the eastern slopes of the Sierra Nevada. Initial bond issues by the City of Los Angeles of $24.5 million financed the purchase of land and water rights in Owens Valley and the construction of the aqueduct. The aqueduct was extended to Mono Basin in the Sierras in 1940, expanding the safe yield[8] of the system to about 320,000 acre-feet per year, and was again expanded in 1968 to deliver a total of 472,000 acre-feet.

As the coastal metropolitan area of Southern California continued to grow, the desirability of obtaining additional water supplies on a centrally organized and large-scale basis was recognized. In 1928 the Metropolitan Water District (MWD) was organized by the cities in Los Angeles, Orange, and San Bernardino counties to build a 242-mile aque-

---

[5] Personal discussion with Arleigh Laycock, 24 November 1969.

[6] The descriptive materials on California diversions are taken from Smith and Brewer (1961) and Bulletin No. 160-66 of the California State Department of Water Resources (March 1966).

[7] For a fascinating story of the Owens Valley development, see Nadeau (1950).

[8] "Safe yield" traditionally has meant the rate of water production below which the system output would fall with a frequency equivalent to once in 100 years. However, the methods by which such calculations have been made differ so widely that the figures quoted here should be interpreted only as gross measures of system size.

duct from the Colorado River to the metropolitan area. This transfer system initially involved 92 miles of tunnels, 63 miles of concrete-lined canals, and 54 miles of concrete conduits.[9] An expansion program started in 1952 has increased the delivery capacity to more than 1 billion gallons per day, and the system delivers approximately 1.2 million acre-feet per year to the metropolitan coastal area. An interesting feature of the water-use pattern is that about one-third of the water delivered by the system in recent years has been used to replenish the groundwater in the coastal areas, a resource that was seriously overdrawn between 1950 and 1960.

A third notable system is the Hetch Hetchy Water Supply and Power System which developed the water resources of the Tuolumne watershed in Yosemite National Park for the provision of water and power to the City of San Francisco and other public agencies. Water is carried from O'Shaughnessy Dam, 150 miles from San Francisco's storage reservoir, via tunnels and pipelines across the San Joaquin Valley. The first dam of the system was completed in 1923, and the first project water was delivered to the City in 1934. The system currently delivers about 290,000 acre-feet per year. Financing has consisted of the issuance of general obligation and revenue bonds relating to the sale of power and water.

A statewide water study completed in 1923 and complemented by other studies resulted in a "Statewide Water Plan" of 1931, which was the basis of what is known as the Central Valley Project. Responsibility for this project was assumed by the U.S. Bureau of Reclamation in 1935 because the state could not sell its bonds in the depressed securities markets. The project consists primarily of Shasta and Keswick Dams on the Sacramento River, the natural river channel to the Delta Area, and the Contra Costa and Delta-Mendota canals carrying water into Contra Costa County for municipal and industrial purposes and into the San Joaquin Valley for irrigation. This system, supplemented by water from Friant Dam in the Sierra Nevada east of Fresno, delivers about 2.8 million acre-feet per year. Financing has followed the typical Bureau of Reclamation pattern: costs allocated to power and municipal-industrial uses plus interest are to be paid back from user charges; irrigation costs are adjusted to a measure of ability to pay for water over a fifty-year period without interest and are further subsidized by excess power revenues; and costs allocated to flood control, navigation, salinity repulsion, and fish and wildlife activities are not considered reimbursable. The Bureau of Reclamation is currently completing the San Luis project, a 2 million acre-foot dam and reservoir project which, by storing water drawn from the Delta-Mendota Canal during the nonirrigation seasons, will provide irrigation for an additional half-million acres.

[9] Again, see Nadeau (1950) for the exciting details of the struggle to control the lower Colorado River and the construction of the Colorado River aqueduct.

The largest of the state projects currently under construction is the State Water Project. The main component of the project is a 3.5 million acre-foot storage dam on the Feather River with transport facilities to carry water as far as Southern California. Total delivery of the system will be 4.23 million acre-feet per year of which 2 million will be delivered to the Metropolitan Water District, a feat that requires lifting the water some 3,500 feet over the Tehachapi Mountains. The total costs of the project were estimated in 1961 to be 2.5 billion dollars, of which 1.75 billion was to be financed through state general obligation bonds, and the remainder from other state and federal sources.

New York City

New York City established one of the early water transfer systems for the provision of city water: first developing the Croton River in steps from 1842 to 1904, then the Catskill system of Ashokan Reservoir in 1915 and Schoharie Reservoir in 1924. These systems in the Hudson Basin provided a safe yield of about 986,000 acre-feet per year.[10] A report of 1923 recommended development of sources in the Delaware Basin, but initial attempts were frustrated by court actions brought by New Jersey to prevent the transfers. A Supreme Court decree of 1931 granted the city the right to divert 440 million gallons per day, subject to provisions on water releases during certain periods of low flow. In 1936, the 85-mile Delaware tunnel aqueduct was started. The regular operation of Rondout Reservoir (safe yield approximately 135,000 acre-feet per year) was started in 1952 and that of Neversink Reservoir (130,000 acre-feet) in 1954. Pepacton (420,000 acre-feet) was completed in 1955, and the controversial Cannonsville Reservoir (350,000 acre-feet) in 1968. Thus the present New York City system consists of three major upland reservoir systems: the pre-1905 Croton system (364,000 acre-feet), the Catskill system (622,000 acre-feet) completed in 1924, and the Delaware system (1.03 million acre-feet) started in 1936 and now nearing completion. After the 1963–65 drought the estimated safe yield from the system was reduced from 2 million acre-feet per year to approximately 1.7 million acre-feet.

Colorado

The State of Colorado provides three examples of interbasin transfers. The topography of the state presents interesting water problems; the heaviest precipitation falls on the western slopes of the continental divide, while 60 percent of the land area and over 80 percent of the population are located east of the divide.

[10] Materials primarily from Hirshleifer, DeHaven, and Milliman (1960), chapter 10, and Dore (1962).

The first project to bring western slope water to the east was the Colorado–Big Thompson Project which collects water in the Upper Colorado River Basin and carries it via the Adams Tunnel to the Big Thompson, Poudre, and St. Vrain rivers and Boulder Creek—all tributaries of the South Platte. This water was intended to supplement natural surface and groundwater supplies for irrigation of 615,000 acres in eastern Colorado, but each year more water is being used for domestic, municipal, and other nonirrigation purposes as the urban centers and industry of eastern Colorado continue to grow. Deliveries of the system have averaged about 230,000 acre-feet per year, the first deliveries commencing in 1957.

Denver takes more than 50 percent of its water supply from the western slope. In 1936, the city began diverting water from the Fraser River, a Colorado tributary, through the mountains via the Moffat Tunnel. After water from the Williams Fork River was brought into the Moffat system through additional tunnels in 1959, diversions totaled about 100,000 acre-feet. Existing and planned facilities for diverting the Blue through the Roberts Tunnel will provide for as much as 150,000 additional acre-feet to serve future demands. The Denver system will, by 1975, have a yield of approximately 335,000 acre-feet per year, 250,000 being diverted from the western slope.

The third substantial diversion project in Colorado is the Frying-pan-Arkansas Project, diverting water from Roaring Fork River via the 7-mile Fryingpan-Arkansas Tunnel in the amount of about 75,000 acre-feet per year. This water is intended primarily for supplemental irrigation, but the project was planned for multipurpose benefits, including municipal and industrial water, power production, flood control, and fish and wildlife objectives.

THE CURRENT SETTING: ATTITUDES

Current attitudes towards large-scale interbasin diversions range widely. Some see them as the answer to a perceived crisis requiring immediate action; others condemn them. Typical of the "crisis school of thought" are the following statements, which appeared in a 1964 Senate Subcommittee report.

Water to develop the West and enrich the Nation is needed now. In the Pacific Southwest, further development of the economy depends on developing new sources of water. . . .

It is a well established fact that a serious water problem exists in the Western United States. This water crisis is a problem of serious and far-reaching implications. It will grow steadily worse until it reaches alarming proportions in the years 1980 and 2000. The existing and proposed Federal developments will help to alleviate the situation but it is doubtful if such piecemeal developments will completely solve the water shortage problem. It therefore becomes imperative that new sources of water supply for the arid and semi-arid West be explored at an early date.[11]

This analysis of the situation by the Senate Subcommittee on Western Water Development was based on projections of water demand which were, in turn, based on assumptions "that adequate water supplies will be made available under the present general pricing policies, that there will be relatively little change in presently known technical methods of water use, and that, with the exception of increased application of techniques for improving the efficiency of irrigation, present inefficient methods of using water will continue."[12] Naturally, such assumptions have been and should be called into question.

Prospective exporting regions, especially the Pacific Northwest and Canada, are trying to protect their interests by demanding careful study of the needs not only of their own regions but of the prospective importing regions. While many supporters of diverting Columbia River water into the Colorado quote the large flows of the Columbia which pour "unused" into the ocean each year,[13] a recent report of the State of Washington Water Research Center concludes that by 1980, "nearly half of the local streams will have deficiencies during the 92-day critical period in the residual flows required to maintain the maximum spawning potential of salmonoid fish. . . . there appears to be the likelihood that the flow in the lower Columbia will be drastically reduced by depletions from irrigation throughout the Pacific Northwest."[14]

A spokesman for the Pacific Northwest has said:

The people of the Northwest deeply believe that before any other region asks for a study of the diversion of the Columbia River, such region must first establish that it actually needs additional water and that it cannot obtain additional water by any reasonable means except diverting the Columbia. . . .

The country as well as the West must seek answers to many questions: Does the Southwest need more water? What does it need it for? How is it using existing supplies? Can sufficient water be secured through conservation and re-use to satisfy its needs? To what extent and under what criteria should the

[11] U.S. Senate, Subcommittee on Western Water Development of the Committee on Public Works, *Western Water Development* (1964), pp. 10–11.

[12] *Ibid.*, p. 7.

[13] The average flow of record at The Dalles (approximately 200 miles from the mouth) is about 140 million acre-feet per year with a minimum flow of record of about 90 million acre-feet in 1926. The lowest *rate* of flow of record is 25 million acre-feet.

[14] State of Washington Water Research Center, *An Initial Study of the Water Resources of the State of Washington: Digest*, Report No. 2, Pullman, Washington (1967), pp. II-2 and II-7.

Federal government assist local water conservation measures? What are the prospects for improving water supplies within the Southwest by desalinization, weather modifications, or other means? Are present irrigation practices wasteful? Does it make sense to transport water 800 to 1,000 miles for irrigation?

Many questions must be asked about the Northwest, for example: What are the needs of the Northwest? Is there water to "spare"? How will the economy of the Northwest be affected if large quantities of water are taken away? What are potential benefits and liabilities?[15]

The Northwestern United States has been cautious and not overly enthusiastic about exporting water to the Southwest. Canada, too, has stated quite clearly the basic principles that will guide the government in managing that nation's vast water resource. The Christian Science Monitor (21 December 1965) contained the following report of a speech by John N. Turner, Parliamentary Secretary to the Ministry of Northern Affairs, given at the U.S. Chamber of Commerce's National Water Conference in Washington, D.C., 8–9 December 1965:

> First, Canada does not agree that its water is a "continental" resource as often suggested by American officials. In Ottawa's opinion it is Canadian property to be used as Canada alone decides.
>
> Second, Canada alone will survey its water, find out exactly how much it owns and how much it is likely to need for a rapidly expanding population.
>
> Third, when these unknown facts are clarified and if a water surplus is revealed, Canada will discuss the possible sale of water with the United States.
>
> Fourth, as Mr. Turner put it, "We might wish to export water not for money but in return for access to your markets."
>
> Fifth, even if some water exports are arranged later on Canada must use its own resources to attract industry.
>
> Sound continental development, Mr. Turner argued, does not necessarily mean "increasing concentration in existing centers" but "should include the development of Canadian population and industry and its expansion into the empty northland. Why should not population and industry come where water is rather than sending water where the population now is."

THE CURRENT SETTING: PROPOSALS

Table 2 presents a summary of the projects that have been proposed. The most discussed type of transfer involves the diversion of water from the Columbia River or its tributaries to points in the Colorado Basin. Figure 1 indicates several possible routes. These projects as proposed could transport from 2.4 to 30.0 million acre-feet per year. It should be

15 From an address, "Water and the West," by Senator Henry M. Jackson, Chairman, Senate Committee on Interior and Insular Affairs, Antioch, California, 5 November 1965.

Table 2. Summary of Information on Plans Proposed for Regional Water Transfer

Project name and approximate date of proposal	Agency sponsor, company sponsor, author of plan	River basin(s) of source	River basin(s) of use	Countries and states involved	Literature citation
United Western (1950)	U.S. Bureau of Reclamation Rep. R. J. Welch-Calif.	Columbia River North Pacific coastal streams	Great Basin South Pacific Coastal Plain Colorado River	U.S. (11 Western States); Mexico	USDI 1950
California Water Plan (1957)	California Department of Water Resources	Northern California rivers	Central Valley South Pacific Coastal Plain	U.S. (California)	{Calif., 1957, 1965, 1966
*Pacific Southwest Water Plan (1963)	U.S. Bureau of Reclamation W. I. Palmer	Northern California streams Colorado River	Lower Colorado River South Pacific Coastal Plain	U.S. (California, Arizona, Nevada, Utah, New Mexico); Mexico	USDI 1963
*Snake-Colorado Project (1963)	Los Angeles Department of Water and Power S. B. Nelson	Snake River	Colorado River South Pacific Coastal Plain	U.S. (Idaho, Nevada, Arizona, California); Mexico	Nelson 1963
*North American Water and Power Alliance (NAWAPA) (1964)	Ralph M. Parsons Company	Alaskan and Canadian rivers, with Columbia River	Great Lakes Basin South Pacific Coastal Plain Colorado River Texas High Plains	U.S. (Western States, Texas, Lake States); Canada; Mexico	Parsons 1964
Yellowstone-Snake-Green Project (1964)	T. M. Stetson, Consulting Engineer	Yellowstone River Snake River	Green River Colorado River	U.S. (Montana, Idaho, Wyoming, Lower Colorado States)	Stetson 1964
*Pirkey's Plan Western Water Project (1964)	F. Z. Pirkey, Consulting Engineer	Columbia River	Colorado River Sacramento River South Pacific Coastal Plain	U.S. (Oregon, Washington, California, Utah, Arizona, Nevada); Mexico	Pirkey 1963
*Dunn Plan Modified Snake-Colorado Project (1965)	W. G. Dunn, Consulting Engineer	Snake and Columbia rivers	Great Basin Snake River South Pacific Coastal Plain Colorado River	U.S. (Idaho, Oregon, Washington, Utah, Arizona, Nevada, California); Mexico	Dunn 1965

Project	Proposed by	Source	Region served	States	Reference
*Sierra-Cascade Project (1965)	E. F. Miller, Consulting Engineer	Columbia River	Oregon Valleys, Central Valley, South Pacific Coastal Plain	U.S. (Oregon, Nevada, California)	ASCE 1967
Undersea Aqueduct System (1965)	National Engineering Science Company F. C. Lee	North Coast Pacific rivers	Central Valley South Pacific Coastal Plain	U.S. (Oregon, California)	Lee and Stern 1965 McCammon and Lee 1966
Southwest Idaho Development Project (1966)	U.S. Bureau of Reclamation, Region 1	Payette River Weiser River Bruneau River	Snake River	U.S. (Idaho)	USDI 1966
Canadian Water Export (1966)	E. Kuiper	Several Canadian rivers	Western States (indefinite)	U.S. (all Western States); Canada	Kuiper 1966
*Central Arizona Project (1948, 1967)	U.S. Bureau of Reclamation	Lower Colorado River Basin	Colorado River	U.S. (Utah, Nevada, Ariz., Calif.); Mexico	U.S. Congress 1968
Central North American Water Project C3 NAWP (1967)	E. R. Tinney, Washington State University	Canadian rivers	Great Lakes, Entire Western States	U.S. (Great Lakes States, Western States); Canada; Mexico	Tinney 1967
Smith Plan (1967)	L. G. Smith, Consulting Engineer	Liard River Mackenzie River	All river basins of 17 Western States	U.S. (17 Western States); Canada; Mexico	Smith 1968
*GRAND Canal Concept (1965)	T. W. Kierans, Sudbury, Ontario	Great Lakes and St. Lawrence River	Canadian rivers flowing to Hudson Bay	U.S. (Great Lakes States); Canada	Kierans 1964
Beck Plan (1967)	R. W. Beck Associates	Missouri River	Texas High Plains	U.S.(S.Dak.,Neb,Kans., Colo., Okla., Tex.)	Bathen et al. 1967
*West Texas and Eastern New Mexico Import Project (1967, due 1972)	U.S. Bureau of Reclamation and U.S. Corps of Engineers	Mississippi and Texas rivers	High Plains of Texas and New Mexico	U.S. (Oklahoma, Texas, New Mexico, Louisiana)	USDI, May 1968
Pacific-Mead Aqueduct Augmentation by Desalinization (1968)	U.S. Bureau of Reclamation	Pacific Ocean	Colorado River	U.S. (California, Arizona); Mexico	USDI 1968
Yukon-Taiya Project (1968)	Alaska Power Administration	Yukon River	Taiya River	U.S. (Alaska); Canada	Norwood 1963

* Plans and costs discussed at greater length in text.

Source: Warnick (1969). With permission of the author.

13

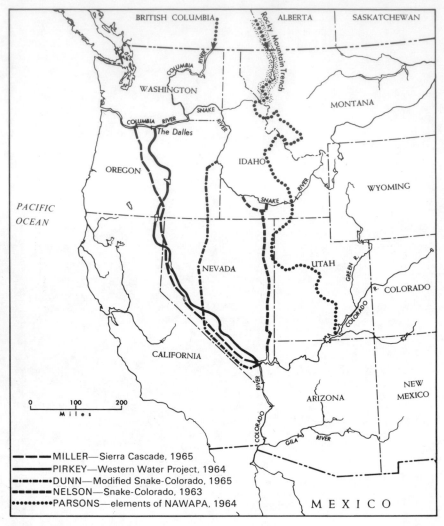

Figure 1. Five interbasin water transfer projects. (Adapted from a map by the Colorado River Association.)

noted that none of the presently proposed diversions has been designed in detail, so matters of size, cost, and detailed routes are not settled matters.

Another plan to provide more water for the Lower Colorado Basin was the Pacific Southwest Water Plan (1963). It called for diversions from northern California rivers to Southern California to make it possible to stop diversions from the Colorado into Southern California (see figure 2).

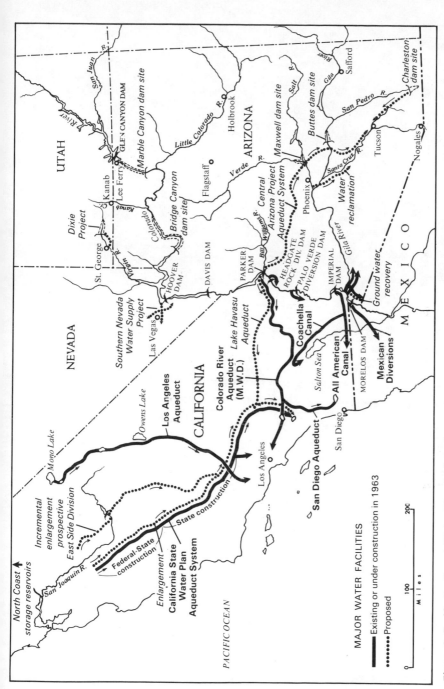

Figure 2. *Pacific Southwest Water Plan.* (Adapted from location map in USDI, *Pacific Southwest Water Plan Report, August 1963.*)

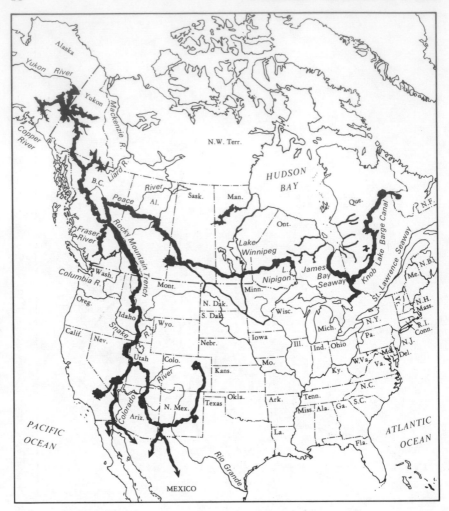

Figure 3. North American Water and Power Alliance System.

The Pacific Southwest Water Plan submitted by the Secretary of Interior[16] failed to gain sufficient political support and was succeeded by the Lower Colorado River Basin Project (H.R. 4671, 89 Cong.), which called for studies of importations into the Colorado of up to 8.5 million acre-feet annually. This project, like the Pacific Southwest Plan and earlier studies, included the Central Arizona Project for diverting 1.2 million acre-feet from the Colorado at Lake Havasu into Central and Southern Arizona.[17]

[16] U.S. Department of the Interior, *Pacific Southwest Water Plan*, Report prepared by Departmental Task Force (1963).

[17] A modification of this bill was passed by the 90th Congress, expressly forbidding any study of importations.

Another project that has been receiving increasing publicity is the West Texas and Eastern New Mexico Import Project. Now included in the Texas State Water Plan,[18] this project provides for importation of 12 million to 13 million acre-feet per year by the year 2020, at least 7.5 million acre-feet of which would go to the High Plains, a region devoted to irrigation agriculture and dependent upon a rapidly falling groundwater table. Nine routes are being studied by the Bureau of Reclamation, all diverting water from the Mississippi or its tributaries. The routes range from 913 to 1,312 miles in length and have total pumping heads of 3,869 feet to 4,208 feet.[19]

Plans for diverting Canadian water for use by both Canada and the United States include the Grand Replenishment and Northern Development (GRAND) Canal,[20] a concept involving the collection and diversion of runoff from the James Bay watershed into the Great Lakes for purposes of water level and quality control and power production. The proposed first stage would involve transfer of about 17 million acre-feet per year.

The largest plan of all is the proposed North American Water and Power Alliance (see figure 3). This proposal would involve a series of projects staged over a twenty-year period, having the following features: (1) provision of water to seven provinces of Canada, thirty-three states in the United States, and three northern states of Mexico; (2) 110 million acre-feet initially, with provision for expansion to 250 million; (3) 70 million kilowatts of power; (4) 40 million acre-feet annually to the Great Lakes; (5) an investment estimated to be about $100 billion.[21]

All of the plans mentioned above are of such a scale—physical, economic, and financial—that their construction and operation would mark a distinct departure from past projects in the field of regional water resource planning.

[18] Texas Water Development Board, *The Texas Water Plan*, Austin, Texas (1968).
[19] U.S. Department of the Interior, Bureau of Reclamation, *Progress Report on West Texas and Eastern New Mexico Import Project Investigations* (1968).
[20] Thomas W. Kierans, Consulting Engineer, Sudbury, Ontario, brochure (1964).
[21] The Ralph M. Parsons Company, *NAWAPA: North American Water and Power Alliance*, Brochure 606-2934-19, Los Angeles (no date).

2

The Economic Evaluation of Interbasin Transfers of Water: Conceptual Framework

The usual planning approach to answering the question, "How much water should be provided in region X?" is to apply a coefficient of water use to an extrapolated value of some index of economic activity to arrive at an aggregate "requirement" for water. The coefficient applied is usually derived from historical data. For example, in *Water Resources Activities in the United States*,[1] which has formed the basis of most current recommendations for water development, the procedure was to estimate total and urban population in each water resource region for 1980 and 2000, the quantity of water used per capita and per unit of product, total national output of water-related goods and services, and the regional distribution of production, and from these estimates to construct regional totals of water for withdrawal uses, on-site uses, and flow uses.

The potential shortcomings of the requirements approach are obvious, because the method in practice frequently incorporates the following unlikely assumptions: supplies of water will continue to be available at current prices; there will be no technological change; and current inefficiencies in the use of water will persist. This method can lead to quite erroneous results, for under the stimulus of water shortage and increasing prices for water, the relationship of water use to population and production will change substantially.[2] The most basic difficulty with the

[1] U.S. Senate Select Committee on National Water Resources, Committee Print 32 (1960b).

[2] In 1954, when actual water withdrawals by the pulp and paper industry amounted to 1,607 billion gallons, the Business and Defense Services Administration and Resources for the Future, Inc., independently estimated that withdrawals would be 2,140 billion gallons in 1959. Actual withdrawals in that year, according to a Census survey, were only 1,744 billion gallons, an increase of $8\frac{1}{2}$ percent. Production increased 30 percent, and pollution loads declined. Studies of the beet sugar and petro-

18

requirements approach is that it makes no attempt to measure water-related benefits, a quantity necessary for rational water development decisions.

In contrast to "requirements," "economic demand" refers to the quantities of water withdrawals demanded by direct users as a function of the price of water, the rate of technological change, income and locational changes, and other relevant variables; and the schedule of related direct and indirect benefits that would be generated by the application of the different quantities. If all benefits were to accrue to direct users and if water were generally purchased in competitive markets, these two steps could be merged into one by estimating the usual demand curve of economic theory, which shows not only the quantity demanded but the willingness of users to pay. When market imperfections or physical interdependencies cause benefits or costs to accrue to parties other than direct users, the amount that direct users are willing to pay must be supplemented by the amounts of benefits or costs accruing to other parties. Such indirect benefits and costs will be labelled "secondary."

Usually neither the benefits nor the costs of water transfers can be measured at just one point or in terms of the activities of just the initial user. Two complicating factors are involved: water use generally results in a return flow that affects other parties, beneficially or otherwise; and all direct users of water are related through markets to other activities that buy from or sell to the direct water user. The relative importance of return flows depends upon the geological and hydrological setting and the institutional framework through which such dependencies are handled when water supply conditions are changed. The possible existence of costs and benefits in market-related industries is not peculiar to water transfers; such secondary effects always depend upon how smoothly the economic system reallocates its resources and upon how fully employed it keeps those resources. However, there are conditions relating to water transfers which increase the likelihood of such indirect benefits and costs.

Because changes in water supply conditions usually involve parties other than those who receive new supplies and those who may be called upon to give up supplies—either through physical water relations or market relations—the extent to which total benefits and costs get incorporated in the benefit-cost analysis of a project will depend upon the effectiveness of the methods of analysis employed in tracing benefits and costs to indirectly affected parties and geographical areas. For example,

leum refining industries at Resources for the Future indicate that new plants are using far less water per unit of product and discharging far less waterborne waste than older plants.

most of the benefits generated by a Bureau of Reclamation irrigation project located in Idaho may be in the form of increased incomes within the state, while costs will be more widely spread because of tax-financed federal subsidies to irrigation and the displacement of agriculture (through a lowering of product prices) in other parts of the country. The benefit-cost ratio would then be considerably higher from a state point of view than from a national one. Obviously, what is good for a city or state is not necessarily good for the nation.

Even when all direct and secondary benefits occur within a particular region, the *incidence of the costs* of the project will still affect its evaluation from a regional point of view. A project that exhibits a benefit-cost ratio of less than 1 from the nation's viewpoint may appear quite attractive to the region in which the project is to be built because most of the benefits will accrue to residents of the region while a large part of the cost will be borne by the country at large. It is possible that a project having a national benefit-cost ratio that is greater than 1 could be unattractive to the region in which it is to be built because such a large part of the costs will have to be borne by the region itself. Such projects are rare in United States history.

Since the federal government represents all of the people of the United States it seems reasonable to have the benefits and costs of federal projects computed on a national basis. This need not and should not preclude other analyses of the geographical and social incidence of measurable project benefits and costs, and ecological, esthetic, or other impacts.[3]

<h2 style="text-align:center">NECESSARY CONDITIONS FOR ECONOMICALLY EFFICIENT INTERBASIN TRANSFERS</h2>

The economic demand for new water has been defined in terms of the schedule of national direct and secondary benefits per acre-foot that would be generated by the application of various quantities. Let the benefits from the actual use of water be called direct benefits (DB), and the costs of giving up the direct use of water (i.e., benefits forgone) be called direct costs (DC). Benefits and costs in market-related activities as seen from a national viewpoint will be referred to as secondary (SB, SC). TC represents the costs of the physical transfer system, and T_A the cost of the best alternative. Subscript X's refer to parties in regions exporting

---

[3] For work on the extension of public investment analysis to dimensions other than economic efficiency see Marglin (1962 and 1967), Maass (1966), and the U.S. Water Resources Council (1969). Much consideration is currently being given to the possible implementation of multi-objective evaluation.

water, M's to those in regions importing water, T's to affected parties in regions through which the transferred water will pass, and C's to parties in regions whose outputs are competitive with those of the water-importing region. It is now possible to state the set of conditions that must be fulfilled by any proposed interbasin transfer project if it is to be justified on grounds of economic efficiency.[4]

$$(DB_M + SB_M) + (DB_T + SB_T) > (DC_X + SC_X) + SC_C + TC \qquad (2.1)$$

$$TC + [(DC_X + SC_X) - (DB_T + SB_T)] < TC_A \qquad (2.2)$$

The first condition states that the increment to net incomes in the importing and transit regions must exceed the loss of incomes in the exporting region and in other regions where activities are displaced by the expansion of water-related activities in the importing region plus the costs of the physical transfer system, all properly capitalized on the basis of a consistent time period. The second condition states that the cost of the physical water transfer scheme (including the net opportunity cost of the water) must be less than the cost of the best alternative for supplying the same amount of water to the importing regions. This comparison presupposes the prior optimum sizing of the projects.

'I'hree questions are immediately raised by these conditions: (1) How do we measure direct benefits to the (initial) individual water user? (2) How do we trace and value the direct benefits from return flows generated by the initial users? (3) Under what conditions will there be secondary benefits and costs from a national point of view and how do we measure them?

THE MEASUREMENT OF DIRECT BENEFITS

There are several ways in which direct benefits from water can be measured. The first utilizes the demand function for water of some water-using entity, the level of aggregation depending upon the particular problem. A second method uses a budget approach to determine willingness to pay by computing a residual "leftover" to water. (The equivalence of these two approaches is made clear in the appendix to this chapter.) Other methods using data on farm sales, water sales, and water rentals are illustrated in chapter 3.

The demand function can be derived from historical water use statistics if there has been sufficient variation in the relevant variables, or it can be simulated from analyses of optimum water use patterns using

---

[4] These conditions represent a variant of conditions first suggested by Emery N. Castle in correspondence with Howe.

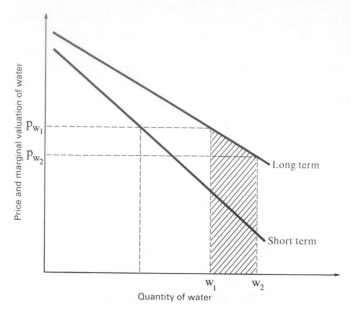

Figure 4. Demand functions for irrigation water.

linear or nonlinear programming methods to determine the schedule of increments of net income accruing from additions to the available supply of water. The level of aggregation can range from a particular or "typical" farm to an entire irrigation district. The demand function appears as in figure 4, with variables other than the water price generally causing the demand function to shift over time.

The demand for one input depends upon the degree of variability of the other inputs. Additional water may be worth very little to the farmer unless he can combine it with additional fertilizer, seeds, and more intensive cultivation. Thus the demand function for water will not be the same in the long run as it will in a short-term period when other inputs are fixed in supply. Logically, the longer-term demand function could lie either above the short-term function (as in figure 4) or below it.[5] The long-term function is clearly the relevant one for evaluating long-lived projects.

[5] This can be seen by looking at the marginal product functions of the generalized production function

$$y = a\left(\sum_{i=1}^{n}\alpha_i x_i{}^{\beta_i}\right)^{\gamma}.$$

The cross-partial derivatives can be positive or negative, depending on γ.

It is useful to note the nature of the producer's demand function for water in greater detail. Let us represent the production process by a production function,

$$y = f(x_1, x_2, \ldots, w),$$ (2.3)

in which y represents output, the x's various inputs, and w the water input. If it is assumed that competitive conditions hold, it can easily be shown that the producer, in attempting to maximize the profits from his operations, will select amounts of the various inputs $(x_1^*, \ldots, w^*)$, such that the following conditions hold simultaneously (p's represent prices as labeled):

$$p_y \cdot f_{x_1}(x_1^*, x_2^*, \ldots, w^*) = p_{x_1}$$ (2.4)
$$p_y \cdot f_{x_2}(x_1^*, x_2^*, \ldots, w^*) = p_{x_2}$$

.

.

.

$$p_y \cdot f_w(x_1^*, x_2^*, \ldots, w^*) = p_w.$$

The functions f_{x_i} represent the marginal products of the various inputs, i.e., the marginal contribution of each input toward additional output. The conditions simply state that the input volume is increased until an increment is reached for which the value of the additional output just equals the cost of the added input. If, for example, p_w is varied and the other prices are held constant, the amounts of water, w, and other inputs that will be demanded at different prices can be deduced from (2.4). Thus, the long-term demand curve of figure 4 is a plot of $p_y \cdot f_w(x_1^*, x_2^*, \ldots, w)$ versus corresponding values of w.

Not only does the demand curve give us a quantitative estimate of the amount demanded, but the area under the curve for a specified increment of water must represent the maximum amount the producer would be willing to pay to obtain that water. Since any particular small increment of water corresponds to some price indicated by the demand curve, this price must represent the value of output the producer can obtain by using this water minus the costs of other inputs which he finds it advantageous to adjust in the presence of the increased water supply.[6] In a competitive economy in which the prices of outputs represent marginal social values and the prices of inputs represent real (opportunity) costs, this willingness to pay is precisely a measure of the net contribution of the water to economic welfare. Thus, the direct benefits from an incre-

---

[6] That the area under the demand curve in fact equals the most the profit-maximizing producer could pay for an increment of an input is proved in the chapter appendix for the case of a Cobb-Douglas production function.

ment of water can be measured by the corresponding area under the demand curve.

In the absence of knowledge of the entire demand function, the *price* of water in an area may, under appropriate conditions, be used as an upper bound on the willingness to pay for more water (and thus on the direct benefits from water). Figure 4 indicates the way in which the water user adjusts to price *when he is free to purchase the desired quantity* of water and is aiming at maximum profit. When this adjustment has taken place, *price* indicates the net direct benefits to the water user at the *margin* of application (e.g., at w_2 in figure 4). Since the demand functions will always be downward sloping, the *existing price* can be taken as an *upper bound* on the direct benefits per unit of any *additional water* that might be made available.

It must be remembered, however, that price will have this characteristic only where supply conditions are such that users are free to adjust the quantity applied to the current price. Where irrigation districts or irrigation companies permit the seasonal rental or sale of water, markets arise that permit short-term transfers of water among users. As the prices of these transfers are competitively determined, they represent the water user's marginal willingness to pay. Similarly, in areas where water is provided by pumping, the pumping costs represent the effective price of water and can be assumed to be equated by management action to the actual maximum willingness to pay.[7]

When a new supply of water is diverted from some source by a user, only part of that water is actually evaporated or absorbed in crops or products. The rest is returned on or through the ground to some watercourse or aquifer where, if its quality permits, it may be used again. When a second diversion of the water is made, the same situation is repeated with the diminished quantity (and quality) of water.

If these possibilities of reuse all occur within the legal control of the initial buyer of the water (e.g., on his property), his willingness to pay would reflect the net values generated through reuse. However, when the return flow escapes the initial buyer by passing over (or under) his property line, his willingness to pay will omit the net values generated by the return flows.

When water is transferred out of an area through its sale by one party, there will, in similar manner, be downstream losses to those who had been using the related return flows. Naturally, the net value of these losses should be counted as a cost of the transfer.

The problem of valuing return flows, in a simplified situation, has

[7] See Hartman and Seastone (1970).

been nicely formalized by Hartman and Seastone (1965) as follows: Let the sequence of water users located along a watercourse be numbered 1, 2, . . ., n. Let

$db_i \equiv$ the direct benefits per unit of water to user i (i.e., the related net income). Assumed constant.

$r_i \equiv$ the proportion of water withdrawn by user $(i-1)$ which is returned to the supply system, $0 \le r_i < 1$.

Abstracting from the different priorities which different users may have by virtue of water law, assume that a unit (acre-foot) of water diverted would have been used first by user 1, his return flow being used by user 2, etc. Thus in a river basin, the total direct benefits, DB, would be

$$DB = db_1 + r_2 \cdot db_2 + r_2 \cdot r_3 \cdot db_3 + \ldots + r_2 \cdot r_3 \cdot \ldots \cdot r_n \cdot db_n. \quad (2.5)$$

If, because of similarities in the uses of water and the hydrologic properties of the terrain, the db_i's and r_i's tended to be the same, this would simplify to

$$DB = db\left(\frac{1-r^n}{1-r}\right). \quad (2.6)$$

Further, if n were large, this would be approximately

$$DB = db\left(\frac{1}{1-r}\right). \quad (2.7)$$

For example, if db were \$15 per acre-foot throughout a fairly large basin and $r = 0.4$, then $DB = \$15 \times 1\frac{2}{3} = \$25$ per acre-foot.

One water system characteristic that remains undetermined in many regions of the country and that is omitted from the above model is the *timing* of return flows. This aspect is less important when water applications are continuous, than when they are concentrated within a limited growing season. If return flows become available only after the period of useful application, their effective productivity may be zero. The methods of irrigation used will affect the timing of return flows. If runoff is captured in tailing canals and immediately redirected to a surface source or an aquifer from which pumping is currently taking place, the period of return flow will be shorter than if the water is left to percolate through the soil. Bittinger (1964, figure 2) indicates that in a relatively narrow, highly permeable aquifer, about 50 percent of the nonconsumptive application will return to the stream within one month after reaching the water table, 80 percent within two months, and practically all within four months. In other cases, the return flows may be much slower.

The above model ignores many other complicated facets of water-use patterns, including legal claims to water, but it serves to point out that allowance must be made for the values generated by water through the entire cycle until it evaporates or exits to the sea.

SECONDARY BENEFITS AND COSTS

The logical framework (or model) most frequently utilized in analyzing the economic desirability of new public projects contains the following three assumed conditions, which simplify analysis. The first is that productive resources of the economy are "fully employed," i.e., all labor desiring to work at existing wage and salary rates can find work and all industrial, commercial, and agricultural capacity that is not technologically obsolete is being utilized at rates close to "economic capacity."[8] The second assumed condition is that these resources are highly mobile and would be able to move quickly and without cost to other employments. The third assumed condition is the absence of economies of large-scale production. These assumptions imply that a new investment project yields no net benefits beyond its own net income; that any expansion of complementary activities is offset by a fall in activity and profits elsewhere; and that any alternative investment project could be expected to have similar indirect effects.

The full employment-mobility assumptions may not hold in some real situations and may be more relevant to some projects than others. Also, scale economies might be present in the expanding activities but not in the contracting activities. The appropriateness of including secondary benefits and costs in the analysis must then be carefully considered for each project.

The following definitions should clarify the meaning and suggest methods of measuring secondary benefits and costs:

Secondary Benefits: increases in net incomes of factors of production (land, labor, capital) engaged in activities related to the project through the market either as suppliers of inputs or as processors of project output. These income increases must be ones that would not have occurred in the absence of the project.

Secondary Costs: decreases in net incomes of factors of production engaged in activities on which expenditures are reduced because of the financing of the project (i.e., mainly because of taxes) or in activities that are displaced by the project through the market. Such income losses must be ones that would not have occurred in the absence of the project.

A breakdown in any one of the three assumptions previously discussed

[8] That is, at rates of output close to the design rate or the rate beyond which marginal production costs would turn up sharply.

would be sufficient to generate some secondary benefits and costs. If the labor hired indirectly as a result of the project would otherwise have remained unemployed, the secondary benefits equal the wages of this labor. If labor and capital cannot move quickly out of industries forced to contract by the project, then the decreases in their incomes *over the period of their immobility* constitute secondary costs. If industries that are expanding because of the project are able to experience decreasing unit costs and the industries that are forced to give up labor and capital experience constant unit production costs, the cost savings on the volume of activity that would have taken place without the project would constitute a secondary benefit. Contrariwise, if the expanding industry experiences constant unit costs and the contracting industries lose economies of scale, then secondary *costs* occur.

These observations illustrate the major condition circumscribing the existence of secondary benefits and costs: *that secondary benefits and costs can arise only through the existence of failures of the market mechanism,* the latter represented in particular by a departure of actual conditions from the three assumed conditions mentioned above.[9] Furthermore, the only type of unemployment that leads to legitimate secondary benefits is long-term, structural unemployment; the planning period, the construction period, and the useful life of public projects all will exceed the duration of cyclical unemployment.

Clearly, it will be difficult to determine which of the resources employed directly and indirectly by a project will be drawn from the unemployed during the project's construction period and operating life.[10] It usually will be even more difficult to determine what would have happened to those resources in the absence of the project. There are some situations, however, in which assumptions of unemployment and immobility can be justified because of the geographical isolation or high degree of specialization of the area involved. One of these is discussed below.

Rescue Operations: A Case of Secondary Benefits

The periods over which labor and capital will be withdrawn from declining areas or activities and injected into expanding ones differ sub-

[9] Increasing returns to scale in an expanding industry does not, in itself, represent market failure. However, scale economies frequently lead to such concentration of production in one or a few firms that competition is reduced or eliminated.

[10] Haveman and Krutilla (1968) have developed a model for tracing the labor and interindustry demand of a project during its construction phase. The model permits recomputation of the social cost of the project as a function of rates of unemployment among different labor skills. It does not include tertiary or "multiplier" effects.

stantially among types of activities, among inputs, and among locations. If steel production in city A contracts while construction activity expands, some types of labor will easily move into the construction industry, but others, possibly those with specialized skills, will be reluctant or unable to shift, and when their jobs disappear they will join the unemployed. There should be no problem in transferring certain types of capital such as trucks, for example, but it may be difficult or impossible to shift more specialized types of capital to a different location or to maintain a level of gross profitability high enough to permit full payout of the investment.

Labor and capital in irrigation areas may be immobile over substantial periods of time once the areas have been developed. Land improvement investments are sunk and capital equipment (pumps, piping, motors, etc.) may have only low salvage values. Agricultural labor may not have the skills required to make moving attractive. The opportunity cost of these factors is zero over the periods of their immobility—the life of capital equipment now in place and perhaps as much as a generation in the life of labor.[11] The benefits from providing water to areas that would otherwise be gradually closed down must include the incomes that the new water supply permits these immobile factors to earn over the period of immobility. Naturally, this item may be shown as either an added benefit or a reduction in production costs.

The situation envisioned here is a fairly large region that is almost wholly dependent on irrigated agriculture and agricultural processing industries. The physical capital structures of agriculture, related businesses, and social overhead have been established. The region is faced with the loss of some or all of its irrigation water, either because groundwater tables are falling or because of water right adjudications. Possible examples are the lower Rio Grande Valley of Texas and the Texas High Plains.[12] Making new supplies available to such regions may be termed a "rescue operation." How should this "new" water be evaluated and what time horizon should be used in planning for new water supplies?[13]

Under the extreme circumstances of complete labor and capital immobility, the entire value added by irrigated agriculture and related

[11] The extent and the duration of these factor immobilities depend upon the rate at which agriculture is being phased out relative to the size of the area. If agriculture is gradually phased out, it will be much easier for displaced labor and capital to be absorbed in the normal expansion of other types of activity.

[12] See chapter 3 for estimates of numerical values of secondary benefits in the Texas High Plains.

[13] The values that might be imputed to water in this situation are discussed in chapter 5 in a slightly different context, namely, the costs of transferring water out of agriculture. Measurement of such values is discussed at length in chapter 4.

businesses can be counted as benefits attributable to water for the period of immobility, provided there is no dry farming alternative. If there is such an alternative, then only the *difference* between value added in agriculture and related industries before and after water is made available can be attributed to water over the period of immobility or the lifetime of the new water project (whichever is less). The difference between the value added in consumer industries and services with and without the water can also be attributed to water if the same immobilities apply to those industries. Thus the *average benefits* to be attributed to the "rescue" water supply may be quite high. Even for farming operations that are currently yielding little or no net returns to capital and management, the value added per unit of water applied (and thus the short-run secondary benefits) may be fairly high under conditions of extreme immobility. Once reinvestment or job opportunities open up and factors regain mobility (positive opportunity costs), water must again be valued on the basis of the differential in net income generated directly in agriculture.

The question of the time horizon over which the higher values are applicable is relevant not only to the measuring of benefits but to the planning of capital reinvestment. Capital equipment currently in place does not have a uniform remaining economic life and, if replacement water is made available for a limited period, some equipment is likely to be replaced as it wears out. At the end of the period when it may have been planned to turn the replacement water to other uses, the same situation of factor immobility may once again exist.

This replacement cycle problem may be aggravated by the fact that short-run values attributable to water may be high while the ability of farm enterprises to pay for water may be low. In a rescue operation, water thus will probably have to be priced low, making capital replacement privately overly profitable. If it is determined that the provision of replacement water is economically justified over the short-run period of factor immobility but not beyond, it should be clearly stated that after a specified date, water will be provided, if at all, only at its full long-run marginal cost.

In planning how to rescue a region, consideration should be given not only to large-scale water transfers but to a wide range of alternatives, including ones that lie quite outside the traditional water resources area. Since the physical life of a transfer project is much longer than the period of immobility of the capital and labor it is supposed to rescue, it might be more advantageous to use public funds to encourage labor mobility through retraining programs and partial payment of moving expenses.

The Displacement of Agriculture in Other Regions:
A Case of Secondary Costs

If full employment and mobility of resources really characterized all parts of our economy, the displacement of agricultural activity in other parts of the country by expanded irrigation agriculture in the water-importing region would be of no consequence. Displaced factors would quickly move into new locations or occupations and, with the exception of land, be as well off as before. However, people are often slow or unable to move; capital is only partially mobile; and land is fixed. Thus, there will always be some who stay in the declining area.

The framework presented here is a very simplified general equilibrium analysis which will clarify the nature of the displacement process and the costs associated with it. The framework is a supply-response model built upon two important characteristics of agriculture: (1) the various agricultural regions of the United States are in competition with one another in a common market characterized by very inelastic demands; (2) though producing crops in common as well as substitute crops, the various regions differ in comparative advantage due to differences in soil and climate.

The way in which increased production due to federal irrigation projects affects other agricultural regions is illustrated by a simplified supply-response model of two crops and three regions (see figure 5). Each region has a supply function for each crop produced, the national supply being the sum of the supplies in each of the regions. The West and North are assumed to produce potatoes while the North and South produce corn. The supply curves are constructed assuming constant input prices, while the national demand curves are, for simplicity, drawn assuming corn and potatoes are not to be substitutes or complements in consumption.

The starting point is a general equilibrium among regions and between crops. There are no excess profits or losses to encourage farms to enter or leave the industry. The situation changes when there is an increase in potato production due to a sizable federal irrigation project in the West. The supply curve for the western region and for the United States shifts to the right and down, from S_1 to S_2. The increased production will cause potato prices to drop. Northern potato farmers who find they can no longer cover variable costs of production at the new price P_2 will cut back production. Prices will then move back towards a new equilibrium level where all firms are able to cover costs and marginal firms earn no excess profits. The supply curve in the North shifts to the

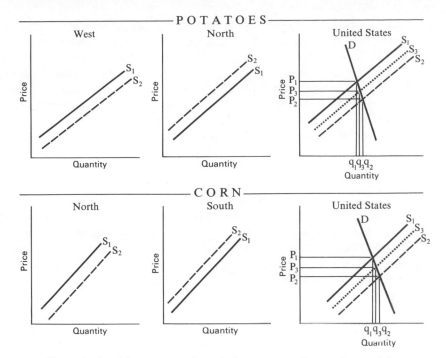

Figure 5. Graphic representation of the two-crop, three-region model.

left and up from S_1 to S_2 while the nation's total supply curve shifts up to S_3.

As northern farmers reduce potato production they increase production of the next-best alternative crop which, in this example, is assumed to be corn. The supply curve for corn in the North and the United States shifts to the right and down from S_1 to S_2. The increased corn production pushes the corn price down and affects all corn producers in the North and South. (For simplicity, corn is assumed not to be produced in the West.) The marginal producers, who are assumed to be in the South, are unable to cover variable costs and are forced to drop out of production. Since the marginal producer has no other production alternatives in agriculture, his resources must be used elsewhere or be removed from active production. Only under conditions of completely mobile resources, perfect knowledge of other opportunities, and full employment will these resources be assured of finding alternative employment.

An additional complication can be added by introducing substitution in consumption. This will not affect the direction of the shifts but will modify the shifts in production and resources use. If potatoes and corn are assumed to be substitutes in consumption (positive cross-elasticities of demand), consumers will buy more potatoes at the reduced price and less corn. The shift in the demand for corn will cause a further drop in corn prices, and more marginal producers in the South will be forced out of production.

The agricultural economy thus works towards a new general equilibrium after the shock of increased production from the new irrigation project. But as it does so, losses of at least a temporary nature are experienced in the regions where agricultural production is displaced.

The social costs associated with agricultural displacement in the South due to an irrigation project in the West depend upon the types of immobilities among the south's resources and the types of government support programs that are in effect.[14] Three cases are considered here.

In the first case, the displaced land moves into the next best alternative use. If labor and capital are perfectly mobile, the only loss in national income from the South will be the decline in the economic rent to the land. If labor and capital are not perfectly mobile, there will be additional secondary costs unless the new crop calls for much the same types and quantities of capital and labor. If it calls for less, the loss of income of the displaced factors over the periods of their immobility will constitute additional secondary costs.

In the second case, the federal government pays landowners in non-irrigation areas to retire a quantity of land equal in productivity to that irrigated by the new federal project. (Present programs either prohibit or restrict the use of the diverted land.) If labor and capital are perfectly mobile, the secondary loss in national income will be equal to the federal diversion payments. These payments will be equivalent to the return (rent) the land and permanent improvements would have earned if the land retirement program is operated in the most efficient manner. If the capital and labor are not mobile, all of the formerly utilized capital and labor will be left idle for some time. The national secondary costs will then include the loss of income to capital and labor over the periods of their immobility.

In the third case, the federal government maintains prices through a straight commodity loan program. Here, the secondary costs are the costs of perpetuating unneeded production. If excess production is a permanent feature of the agricultural scene, the real costs of the price support program will be the costs of producing the excess output and

_____

[14] An empirical investigation of agricultural displacement is reported on in chapter 6.

storing or otherwise disposing of it. Since there is no displacement of production, labor and capital mobility have no bearing on costs in this case.

Whether these losses in returns to land, labor, and capital in other regions will be offset by the project net benefits in the project region is the objective of the benefit-cost analysis. To leave these costs out of the analysis would be a gross error. Project evaluation procedures should allow for research to evaluate such effects.

Appendix to Chapter 2: The Equivalence of Direct Water Benefits and the Area under the Demand Curve: The Cobb-Douglas Case

The issue is to show that, given increment of water such as $(w_2 - w_1)$ in figure 4, the area under the demand function between w_1 and w_2 equals the value of the added output, less the cost of the other input increments optimally adjusted (least-cost combinations) to the new water supply.[15]

Let the production function be of the Cobb-Douglas form with k (all nonwater inputs) and w (water) as inputs:

$$f(k, w) = \alpha_o k^\alpha w^\beta. \qquad (2.8)$$

The price of k is taken as fixed, p_k, as is the price of output, p. Given the price of water, profit maximization requires that

$$p \cdot f_k(k^*, w^*) = p_k \qquad (2.9)$$
$$p \cdot f_w(k^*, w^*) = p_w.$$

Substituting the partial derivatives of (2.8) into (2.9) and taking the ratio of p_k to p_w one gets

$$\frac{p_k}{p_w} = \frac{\alpha w^*}{\beta k^*}, \qquad (2.10)$$

or

$$k^* = \frac{p_w \alpha w^*}{p_k \beta}. \qquad (2.11)$$

[15] The example in this appendix was provided by Clifford S. Russell of Resources for the Future, Inc.

That is, the profit maximizing value of k can be expressed as a function of the profit maximizing value of w.

Using the second condition in (2.9) above, then substituting for k as in (2.11):

$$p_w = p\beta\alpha_o k^\alpha w^{\beta-1} = p\beta\alpha_o \left(\frac{p_w \alpha w}{p_k \beta}\right)^\alpha w^{\beta-1}. \tag{2.12}$$

Simplifying

$$p_w = \left[p\beta\alpha_o \left(\frac{\alpha}{\beta p_k}\right)^\alpha\right]^{\frac{1}{1-\alpha}} w^{\frac{\alpha+\beta-1}{1-\alpha}}. \tag{2.13}$$

This expression represents the inverse of the demand function, i.e., the unit price that the producer would pay for the quantity w. Integrating the expression between w_1 and w_2 and simplifying yields

$$\int_{w_1}^{w_2} p_w(w)\,dw = (1-\alpha)(p\alpha_o)^{\frac{1}{1-\alpha}} \left(\frac{\alpha}{p_k}\right)^{\frac{\alpha}{1-\alpha}} \left[w_2^{\frac{\beta}{1-\alpha}} - w_1^{\frac{\beta}{1-\alpha}}\right]. \tag{2.14}$$

We have arrived at an expression (albeit rather messy) for the area under the demand curve.

We now turn to deriving an expression for the gross economic benefits attributable to the increment of water $(w_2 - w_1)$.
Let

$$y_1 = \alpha_o(k_1^*)^\alpha w_1^\beta \tag{2.15}$$

represent the output forthcoming when w_1 of water is utilized and k_1 is adjusted optimally (profit maximization) to k_1^* for the given w_1. Let

$$y_2 = \alpha_o(k_2^*)^\alpha w_2^\beta \tag{2.16}$$

represent the output when w_2 of water is utilized and k adapted optimally to k_2^*. The gross benefits attributable to the additional water $(w_2 - w_1)$ can be expressed as

$$p(y_2 - y_1) - p_k(k_2^* - k_1^*). \tag{2.17}$$

Substituting from (2.15) and (2.16) into the first expression of (2.17):

$$p(y_2 - y_1) = p\alpha_o[(k_2^*)^\alpha w_2^\beta - (k_1^*)^\alpha w_1^\beta], \tag{2.18}$$

and substituting for k^* from (2.11)

$$p(y_2 - y_1) = p\alpha_o \left(\frac{\alpha}{\beta p_k}\right)^\alpha [p_{w_2}^\alpha w_2^{\alpha+\beta} - p_{w_1}^\alpha w_1^{\alpha+\beta}]. \tag{2.19}$$

Substituting for p_{w_1} and p_{w_2} as shown in (2.13), we get

$$p(y_2 - y_1) = (p\alpha_o)^{\frac{1}{1-\alpha}}\left(\frac{\alpha}{p_k}\right)^{\frac{\alpha}{1-\alpha}}\left[w_2^{\frac{\beta}{1-\alpha}} - w_1^{\frac{\beta}{1-\alpha}}\right]. \qquad (2.20)$$

Similarly for the second expression in (2.17)

$$p_k(k_2^* - k_1^*) = p_k\left(\frac{p_{w_2}\alpha w_2}{p_k\beta} - \frac{p_{w_1}\alpha w_1}{p_k\beta}\right) = \frac{\alpha}{\beta}(p_{w_2}w_2 - p_{w_1}w_1). \qquad (2.21)$$

Substituting the appropriate values of p_{w_2} and p_{w_1} from (2.12), the above reduces to:

$$p_k(k_2^* - k_1^*) = \alpha(p\alpha_o)^{\frac{1}{1-\alpha}}\left(\frac{\alpha}{p_k}\right)^{\frac{\alpha}{1-\alpha}}\left[w_2^{\frac{\beta}{1-\alpha}} - w_1^{\frac{\beta}{1-\alpha}}\right]. \qquad (2.22)$$

Combining (2.20) and (2.22) we get a final expression for the gross benefits originally defined in (2.17):

$$p(y_2 - y_1) - p_k(k_2^* - k_1^*) = (1 - \alpha)(p\alpha_o)^{\frac{1}{1-\alpha}}\left(\frac{\alpha}{p_k}\right)^{\frac{\alpha}{1-\alpha}}\left[w_2^{\frac{\beta}{1-\alpha}} - w_1^{\frac{\beta}{1-\alpha}}\right]. \qquad (2.23)$$

It will be noted that (2.23) is identical with (2.14), proving that, for the case of the Cobb-Douglas production function, the area under the demand function is identical with the measure of direct benefits to water.

3

Direct and Secondary Water Benefits:
Studies of the Benefits from Water in Agriculture

The studies surveyed in this chapter provide estimates of direct and total benefits that may be expected to accrue from the use of water for agricultural purposes in various western states. Some of the studies measured only the direct benefits; others extended the analysis to include secondary benefits to market-related activities. While any program or project analysis should attempt to encompass total benefits, the conditions under which economically legitimate secondary benefits will exist are sufficiently complex and ill-understood that it seemed desirable to report separately on the more straightforward analyses of direct benefit estimates before getting involved in the measurement of secondary benefits.

None of the studies summarized here deal specifically with large-scale interbasin transfers of water. Their relevance stems from the fact that they measure benefits from agricultural applications of water, and it is just such applications that would have to absorb most of the water provided by the proposed large-scale transfers. Agriculture currently accounts for almost 90 per cent of consumptive water use in the West and constitutes the only potential demand that is large enough to absorb the supplies of proposed transfers (from 2.4 to 110 million acre-feet per year). Further, the water supply problems of agriculture are less susceptible to solution through technological change and innovation than are the water supply problems of municipal and industrial users whose basic consumptive requirements are much lower.[1]

[1] Also see Howe (1968). It is well documented that, when locational factors dictate, water-intensive industries can and do locate in arid areas. In the Four Corners area, the Arizona Public Service Co. has had a thermal electric plant for several years. WEST Associates are constructing an initial-stage plant of 1,500-megawatt capacity using air-

DIRECT WATER BENEFITS IN AGRICULTURE

Benefits in Groundwater Areas

The price charged for water can be taken as an upper bound on direct benefits to the immediate user when supplies are sufficient to permit the full adjustment of the quantity applied so that it results in maximum profits to the water-using activity. This adjustment can almost always take place in irrigation areas supplied primarily by groundwater. Since most state laws in no way restrict pumping, the usual "common pool" rationale (if I don't get it, my neighbor will) leads pumpers to apply water until the net value of its marginal product equals the unit cost of pumping.

Evidence on the value of water at the margin of application is thus provided by data on pumping costs. Taylor (1964) quotes pumping costs in the Madera Irrigation District (California) in 1961–62 averaging $5 per acre-foot with a variable component of $1.96. Young and Martin (1967, p. 13, table 3 footnote) state that variable pumping costs in Central Arizona range from $7 per acre-foot with a 315-foot lift to $12 with a 540-foot lift. In the Texas High Plains, Grubb (January 1966) shows pumping and delivery costs of $8.74 per acre-foot.[2] The evidence from these major potential importing regions points to water-use values having been pushed fairly low at the margin in terms of direct benefits.[3]

California

Brown and McGuire (1967) studied the problem of optimizing the distribution of surface water among the constituent districts of the Kern County Water Agency (KCWA) and simultaneously optimizing the pumping of groundwater. KCWA had contracted with the State of California for ultimate delivery of 1.1 million acre-feet, and the problem was how to price the water to guarantee that it would be fully utilized by the districts and that the allocation among districts would be economically efficient. A major component of the study was the estimation of the

---

fin cooling. Kaiser Steel, at Fontana, California, uses well water and purchases some water from the local utility; the intake rate of this plant is about 1,500 gallons per ton of product, contrasted to an average of 20,000 to 30,000 gallons for the industry.

[2] See table 8.

[3] Low values at the *margin of application* do not imply low values in *all* applications. In some types of agriculture the average value of product per acre-foot of water and the average value added per acre-foot are quite high. Some of these agricultural uses could compete successfully for water with industrial and commercial uses even in the absence of differential pricing of water.

water demand function for each district, i.e., the marginal value of water in each district as a function of the total amount applied.

Functions were fitted to two sets of data, one from the California Department of Water Resources and the other from a farm budget study for the districts in KCWA. The subsequent optimization analysis led to two optimum prices to be charged by KCWA to its constituent districts, depending upon which demand function was accepted as the more accurate. The cost of delivering water from KCWA to the district and the average delivery cost within each district were added to the optimum prices to arrive at the delivered prices (prospective marginal values of water) shown in table 3.

The figures in table 3 indicate that, when the districts served by KCWA begin receiving the water supplies already contracted for from the State Water Project, the averaged marginal value of water in that large area will be approximately $19 per acre-foot (Case 1) or $15 (Case 2), depending on which demand function is assumed. Additional water would yield direct benefits no higher than those figures.

Moore and Hedges (1963), whose detailed farm budget studies formed the basis for the Case 1 demand function mentioned above, derived demand functions for different sizes of farms representing a cross section of sizes found in Tulare County, California. In doing so, they also took account of differences in soil types, and in the acreages that could be used for high-value crops (cantaloupes, sugarbeets, and cotton). Table 4 gives their results for the case representing the least constraints on cropping patterns and illustrates the phenomenon of diminishing re-

Table 3. Prospective Marginal Values of Water in the Irrigation Districts of KCWA under Optimum Allocation

District	Annual delivery	Delivered price (= marginal value) per acre-foot	
		Case 1	Case 2
	1,000 acre-feet		
Belridge W.S.D.	206	$18.25	$14.60
Lost Hills W.D.	168	14.50	10.85
Rosedale–Rio Bravo W.S.D.	70	19.20	15.55
Semitropic W.S.D.	127	17.70	14.05
West Kern County W.D.	3	22.50	18.85
Antelope Plain W.D.	59	23.20	19.55
Wheeler Ridge–Maricopa W.S.D.			
No. 1	142	23.30	19.65
No. 2	29	28.75	25.10
Kern River Delta and others	309	18.00	14.35

Source: Brown and McGuire (1967), table 1, p. 39.

Table 4. *Marginal Value of Water as a Function of Water Applied, by Farm Size, Tulare County, California*

80 Acres		160 Acres		320 Acres		640 Acres		1,280 Acres	
Acre-feet	Net returns per additional acre-foot	Acre-feet	Net returns per additional acre-foot	Acre-feet	Net returns per additional acre-foot	Acre-feet	Net returns per additional acre-foot	Acre-feet	Net returns per additional acre-foot
0	$ –	0	$ –	0	$ –	0	$ –	0	$ –
28	77	56	77	115	80	229	83	459	82
32	54	280	50	505	53	1,009	56	2,019	56
144	43	289	48	562	52	1,125	51	2,250	51
176	36	351	40	580	49	1,160	50	2,320	50
181	24	369	17	703	38	1,408	42	2,817	38
187	21	609	13	720	27	1,443	29	2,886	27
309	14	636	10	759	19	1,517	19	3,337	22
320	12	637	9	963	14	1,926	17	3,853	19
347	9	694	8	1,210	13	1,950	14	4,866	18
348	8	728	2	1,330	10	2,457	13	5,180	17
351	3			1,377	10	2,650	9	5,615	16
380	2			1,400	9	2,807	8	6,017	8
				1,465	2			6,100	7
				1,519	1				

Source: Moore and Hedges (June 1963).

turns to water applications in this important farming area of California. The initial application, marking the transition from dry farming to some irrigated acreage, produces a rather high value per acre-foot, ranging from $77 to $82 per acre-foot, depending on farm size. Thereafter, the marginal value falls off steadily with increasing applications. It is precisely this phenomenon of diminishing returns plus downward pressure on market prices which limits the amount of water that can be used efficiently in agriculture.

Colorado

Hartman and Anderson (1962) studied the value of supplemental irrigation water in Northeastern Colorado through an analysis of farm sales data from the North Poudre Irrigation Company over the period from 1954 to 1960. This company started taking delivery of Colorado–Big Thompson (C-BT) water through the Northern Colorado Water Conservancy District in 1957. The company has issued shares which entitle the holder to a specified percentage of the total supply available in a given year. When farms are sold, the shares of stock are generally transferred with the farm, although there is an established market for these shares within the company.

The analysis, consisting of a regression of farm sales price on assessed value of buildings, acres of farmland, and shares of irrigation company stock transferred, indicated that a share was worth $105 in 1954–56 (before C-BT deliveries) and $198 in 1960 (after C-BT deliveries had begun). These figures are in general agreement with some independent sales of shares at about $70 in the early 1950s and at about $200 in the early 1960s. Water deliveries per share averaged 3.3 acre-feet in 1954–56 and 6.4 acre-feet for the 1957–60 period. Thus the average capitalized value per acre-foot of annual delivery for the increment of C-BT water was about $30 ([$198–$105]/[6.4–3.3]). The *annual value* for the incremental water is approximately $3 per acre-foot if a 10 percent capitalization rate is assumed, or $1.50 if a 5 percent rate is assumed.

Anderson (1961) studied the irrigation water *rental* market in the South Platte Basin. Rental prices for water on an interim basis are particularly suitable measures of the marginal value of water in a region such as the South Platte Basin where water rights are owned by irrigation companies and are readily transferable on a temporary basis within and between companies. Since there are many potential buyers of temporary rights to excess water, competition is likely to force the rental price up to the marginal value in the most productive use. There may, however, be exceptions to this stemming from community pressures to maintain a customary price (see Anderson, p. 57).

Table 5 below indicates rental prices charged by representative irrigation companies in 1959.

Table 5. *Rental Prices of Water, South Platte Basin, 1959*

Company	Rental price per acre-foot	
	Early season	Late season
North Poudre Irrigation Company	$2.50	$4.20
New Cache La Poudre Company	3.25	3.25
Greeley and Loveland Company	3.00	5.00
Water Supply and Storage Company	5.00	8.00
Farmers' Reservoir and Irrigation Company	4.60	6.00
Larimer and Weld Irrigation Company and Windsor Reservoir Company	2.70	2.70

Source: Anderson (1961).

Arizona

Crop irrigation accounts for more than 90 percent of the water *consumed* annually in Arizona. Of the water consumptively used on crop irrigation, about 60 percent is used to irrigate extensive crops such as alfalfa hay, sorghum, and barley and 40 percent is devoted to high-value intensive crops such as cotton, vegetables, and fruits.[4]

Young and Martin (1967) studied the value of water in Arizona agriculture by constructing budget studies for a farm typical of Central Arizona. The characteristics of the farm were synthesized from surveys of over 600 farms.[5] Table 6 indicates what they found in terms of the "average short-run ability to pay" for water for each of four crops, i.e., the excess of total revenue over variable costs. These figures indicate the *maximum* amount that such a farm could pay for water from any source for use on particular crops, covering only variable costs, and leaving no return for coverage of taxes, insurance, depreciation, interest on investment, or management. At water costs in excess of $34 per acre-foot (the highest "short-run ability to pay" figure for cotton), it would no longer pay this typical farm to produce cotton even if other crops were sufficiently profitable to pay all the farm's overhead. If water costs exceeded

[4] See Martin and Bower (1966), table 1, p. 2.
[5] Composition of the farm: 700 cropland acres, 39 percent in cotton, 16 percent in alfalfa, 25 percent in barley, and 20 percent in grain sorghum. Different pumping depths were assumed as shown in table 6.

Table 6. Typical Water Use and Average Short-Run "Ability to Pay" for Delivered
Surface Water in Arizona

	Pumping lift		
Crop and item	315 feet	460 feet	540 feet
Upland cotton:			
Water use per acre (acre-feet)	6.0	5.0	5.0
Income over variable costs per acre ($)	134	117	110
Income over variable costs per acre-foot ($)	22	23	22
Variable pumping costs per acre-foot ($)	7	10	12
Average short-run ability to pay per acre-foot ($)	29	33	34
Barley:			
Water use per acre (acre-feet)	3.0	2.5	2.0
Income over variable costs per acre ($)	32	22	18
Income over variable costs per acre-foot ($)	11	9	9
Variable pumping costs per acre-foot ($)	7	10	12
Average short-run ability to pay per acre-foot ($)	18	19	21
Alfalfa hay:			
Water use per acre (acre-feet)	6.1	6.1	6.1
Income over variable costs per acre ($)	33	13	5
Income over variable costs per acre-foot ($)	5	2	1
Variable pumping costs per acre-foot ($)	7	10	12
Average short-run ability to pay per acre-foot ($)	12	12	13
Grain sorghum:			
Water use per acre-foot (acre-feet)	3.3	2.75	2.2
Income over variable costs per acre ($)	33	23	18
Income over variable costs per acre-foot ($)	10	8	8
Variable pumping costs per acre-foot ($)	7	10	12
Average short-run ability to pay per acre-foot ($)	17	18	20

Source: Adapted from Young and Martin (1967), table 3, p. 13.

Note: Variable pumping costs are added to "income over variable costs" to arrive at "ability to pay" because the availability of delivered surface water would eliminate the need to pump.

$13, alfalfa hay would be dropped. At $20, grain sorghum would be dropped; and, at $21, barley would be dropped. In the longer term, the ability to pay for water would be reduced by an additional overhead cost of at least $8 per acre-foot that would have to be covered if this typical farm is to remain in business. It seems safe to conclude that the marginal value of water lies below $21 per acre-foot for the production of barley, alfalfa, and grain sorghum—the types of agriculture which account for more than 50 percent of total consumption in Arizona.[6]

Goss and Young (1967) compiled data on the pricing policies of the major water distributing agencies in Central Arizona (see table 7). The usual caveat applies to using prices as a surrogate for marginal values

[6] Some have contended that many of the low-value crops listed above are necessary links in programs of crop rotation. It appears, however, that the soil-conditioning effects of these rotations can be attained even more profitably through additional fertilization with natural manures and chemicals.

Table 7. Prices Charged for Irrigation Water by Major Water-Distributing Organizations in Central Arizona

Company	Water source	Average use per cropped acre (acre-feet)	Basic assessment per acre	Water entitlement per acre under basic assessment (acre-feet)	Price per acre-foot for water beyond basic entitlement
Yuma County Water Users' Association	Colorado R.	5.4	$12.50	5 (8)[a]	$1.50
Unit B: Yuma Auxiliary Project	Colorado R.	12.0	15.11	5	1.50
Yuma Mesa Irrig. and Drainage District	Colorado R.	14.0	12.15	9	1.60 for 4 acre-feet; 2.25 all over 4 acre-feet
North Gila Irrig. District	Colorado R.	6.7	8.50	all demanded	0
Wellton-Mohawk Irrig. and Drainage District	Colorado R.	6.2	12.60	4	3.40; 1.85 for 3 acre-feet[a]; 2.45 over 3 acre-feet[a]
Colo. R. Indian Reservation Project	Colorado R.	5.8	9.00	5 (8)[a]	2.00
Buckeye Irrig. Co.	Gila R. and Agua Fria R., wells	5.6	2.00	0	3.50 April–Oct.[b]; 3.00 Oct.–April[b]; 1.00 flood water when available[b]
Roosevelt Irrig. District	Wells	3.3	4.88	4	5.00 if salt < 2500 ppm[b]; 3.50 if salt > 2500 ppm[b]
Maricopa County Mun. Water Conservation District #1	Wells, local runoff	1.7	9.00	n.a.	10.00[b]
Salt River Water Users' Association	Salt R. and Verde R.	4.5[c]	4.00	0	3.00 surface deliveries[b]; 7.50 pumped water[b]
Roosevelt Water Conservation District	Wells, surface	3.0	7.0	2.5	8.50[b, d]
San Carlos Irrig. District	Gila R., wells	1.5	0.25	n.a.	9.00[b]
Cortaro Water Users' Association	Wells	2.2	12.00	1.5	8.00
Safford Valley Irrig. District	Gila R.	2.8	10.00[e]; 20.25	2.3; 2.7	n.a.

Source: Goss and Young (1967).

n.a.—Not available.

[a] Allotment for sandy or mesa soils.

[b] Charges per acre-foot on all water.

[c] Includes some residential and industrial use.

[d] Private sales frequently take place at prices from $2.50 to $10.00 above the District's charge of $8.50.

[e] Range of values among companies served.

(i.e., direct benefits). However, since most of the companies pump and supply groundwater without limit, it seems safe to assume that marginal values of water will not differ greatly from the prices charged for the water provided *beyond the basic allotment*. These prices range from zero to $10 per acre-foot.

Stults (1966) studied the impact on agriculture of the falling groundwater table in Pinal County in south-central Arizona. This county accounts for 25 percent of the state's cropped area, and includes 38 percent of the cotton planting. The study analyzed the changes that are likely to take place between 1966 and 2006 as a result of the falling water table (increased pumping costs), on the assumptions that optimum adaptation of cropping patterns took place, that the margin of returns over nonpumping variable costs remained the same, and that technology and government programs (including cotton allotments) remained as in 1966. The results were as follows: (1) a 50 percent drop in total acreage was projected—from 259,000 acres to 129,000 acres; (2) a 42 percent decline in water use amounting to 415,000 acre-feet; and (3) a 20 percent drop in net farm income amounting to $5.4 million per year. These results imply a value in terms of income forgone averaging $13 per acre-foot by the year 2006.

Texas

Grubb (January 1966 and October 1966) studied the value of irrigation water to the Texas High Plains. Since the late 1940s, there has been a shift from dry farming to irrigated agriculture based on groundwater pumping, and the irrigation of more than 5 million acres is causing the water table to fall by 3 to 4 feet per year. Concern over the groundwater situation has led to consideration of the West Texas and Eastern New Mexico project mentioned in chapter 1.

The direct benefits per acre-foot for a delivered surface supply replacing an exhausted groundwater supply consist of the difference between irrigated and dry farming incomes plus the pumping costs avoided. For a "composite acre" representative of the entire High Plains agriculture, Grubb projects direct benefits to 2020 under the following assumptions: (1) the composite acre, consisting of 32 percent cotton, 38 percent grain sorghum, and 21 percent wheat, remains constant; (2) crop yields per irrigated acre remain constant, but irrigation efficiency improves so that application per acre declines from 13 inches to 9 inches between 1970 and 1990; (3) prices of products and inputs remain constant; and (4) in the absence of irrigation, dry farming would be practiced with the same percentage distribution of crops.

Table 8 gives the value of projected irrigation benefits per acre-foot of water applied, the estimated pumping costs per acre-foot of groundwater, and the resultant average benefits attributable to delivered surface water. The average benefit figures provide an upper limit on the marginal direct benefits of water. Thus it appears that marginal direct benefits for the High Plains are currently no more than $27, with this limit increasing gradually to about $36 in the future as irrigation efficiency increases.

More detailed evidence is provided by Grubb (October 1966) on returns to irrigation in the Southern High Plains by crop and soil type. From those data, estimates of marginal benefits have been derived for different levels of water application (see table 9).

If cropping patterns are similar to those used by Grubb in his "composite acre" and if a preplant application plus 3 postplant applications is the general practice, the estimates found in the last row of table 9 are generally in agreement with the $27 to $36 average benefit figure of table 8.

Table 8. Projected Benefits from a Delivered Surface Water Supply, Texas High Plains

Year	Direct irrigation benefits per acre-foot[a]	Groundwater pumping costs per acre-foot[b]	Average surface water benefits per acre-foot
1959	$18.20	$8.74	$26.94
1970	18.20	8.74	26.94
1980	26.59	8.74	35.33
1990–2020	26.80	8.74	35.54

[a] Calculated from Grubb (January 1966), Report No. 11, table 4, using the assumption of 1.1 feet per acre through 1970 and 0.75 feet per acre thereafter.

[b] It has been assumed that the fuel and irrigation equipment items of Grubb's table 3 represent present and prospective costs of pumping and delivering groundwater. Part of these costs could not be escaped even if the water source were other than groundwater.

Table 9. Estimated Direct Benefits per Acre-Foot, Southern High Plains of Texas

Total application* (feet per acre)	Marginal net returns (per acre-foot)					
	Hardland soils			Mixed soils		
	Cotton	Grain sorghum	Wheat	Cotton	Grain sorghum	Wheat
0.52 (preplant only)	$75.48	$ 9.50	$ –	$ –	$ 3.00	$ 1.21
0.94 (preplant + 1 postplant)	99.28	18.97	14.51	2.52	14.11	18.77
1.35 (preplant + 2 postplants)	55.19	73.08	20.79	98.63	29.01	16.44
1.77 (preplant + 3 postplants)	10.17	19.71	20.05	45.36	24.13	16.90

* Preplant = 6.25 acre-inches; each postplant = 5 inches pumped.

Utah

Richard L. Johnson (1966) has made a study of the marginal value of irrigation water in the 9,000-acre Milford, Utah, area. The methods used were to estimate a Cobb-Douglas production function[7] for agriculture in that area and to construct a linear programming model of the area's agriculture. Both of these methods produce direct estimates of marginal water benefits. Part of the intent of the study was to compare the estimates produced by the two methods. The main results are displayed in table 10 below.

Table 10.   Estimates of the Marginal Value of Water in the Milford, Utah, Area, Derived from Three Production Models

Acre-feet of water used per acre	Marginal value		
	Cobb-Douglas model	Linear program I	Linear program II
1	$22	$14	$42
2	14	14	15
3	11	14	15
4	9	14	14
5	8	0	6
6	8		

Source: Richard L. Johnson (1966).

Most farms in the area applied between 3 and 5 feet of water per acre, and for these rates of application, the marginal value of water implied by the analysis ranged from zero to $15 per acre-foot, depending upon the production model used.

Fullerton (1965) and Gardner and Fullerton (1968) studied the water rental market in the Delta area of Utah, an area of about 180 square miles in the west-central part of the state. The total cultivated area varies from 35 to 60 percent of the total in different years, and 80 to 90 percent of this is in alfalfa. Four irrigation companies serve the area, diverting and storing water from the Sevier River. Prior to 1948, only *intracompany* temporary transfers among water users were permitted. Since 1950, exchanges on an intercompany basis among all companies have also been permitted. Naturally, it would be expected that the efficiency of water use would be improved by the greater flexibility of transfer. In the 1965 study it was found that the mean rental price was $3.21 per acre-foot up to 1948 and $9.60 after intercompany transfers began. Corrected for changes in price levels and for changes in the efficiency of water delivery, the latter price becomes $8.75, a measure of the marginal value of water under the more efficient water marketing arrangements. In the 1968 study

[7] The Cobb-Douglas production function has the form: $y = \alpha_o x_1^{\alpha_1} x_2^{\alpha_2}$.

the average price from 1955 to 1964 was reported to be approximately $12 per acre-foot.

Summary of Direct Benefits and Return Flow Data

The studies surveyed above indicate that the value of direct benefits to the agricultural user of water at the margin of application varies from place to place but is generally low. The figures revealed by the studies are listed in table 11 to indicate the range of values, but it should be kept in mind that some of these figures are *upper bounds* on direct benefits and may overstate actual direct benefits.

The figures in table 11 revealed only a range of benefits to direct water users and do not include an allowance for values generated through return flows. Return flows from agriculture are generally no more than 40 percent of withdrawals, but for illustration, let us assume 50 percent consumption and 50 percent return flow. If time lags are not important (as in a region of year-round irrigation), the value of the return-flow multiplier might be as high as 2. At the other extreme is the case where return flows have no effective value because they move into aquifers from which they cannot be recovered—a condition that apparently holds for Central Arizona where percolation rates are less than the rate of fall of the water table. However, if the growing season is less than a year, time lags in return flows can be quite important. For example, suppose that return flows are one-half of withdrawal and that 50 percent of the

Table 11. Summary of Direct Benefits per Acre-Foot at the Margin of Application: Western United States

State	Benefits per acre-foot
California: KCWA (after State Water Plan)	$ 19
Colorado:	
N. Poudre Irrigation Co. (rental)	3
S. Platte Basin	3–8
Arizona:	
Central Arizona, short-run	21
Central Arizona, long-run	13
Major distributing agencies, Central Arizona	0–10
Pinal County	9
Texas:	
High Plains, average, now	27
High Plains, 1990	36
Southern High Plains, hardland soils	10
Southern High Plains, mixed soils	45
Utah:	
Milford area	0–15
Delta	12

return takes place within one month, 80 percent within two months, and 100 percent within three months. If a four-month irrigating season is assumed, the actual multiplier value would be 1.34 rather than the limiting value of 2, largely because late irrigations contribute only to off-season return flows. However, as off-season return flows could be of value to other water users (e.g., for electric generation or navigation) and could be stored and used for irrigation in a later season, a reasonable upper bound on the return flow multiplier for most regions might lie in the neighborhood of 1.5.

For areas other than the groundwater dependent areas of Texas and Central Arizona, an assumed return flow multiplier value of 1.5 would raise the direct benefits as high as $30 per acre-foot in the surveyed parts of California. For the groundwater dependent areas of Texas and Central Arizona where values to the initial user are highest, a return flow multiplier much in excess of 1.0 would seem questionable. One can therefore conclude that benefits per acre-foot at the margin of application to direct water users in agriculture, including the value of return flows, generally lie below $30 per acre-foot in the major water-using areas covered by this survey.

EMPIRICAL STUDIES OF TOTAL BENEFITS PER ACRE-FOOT: THE SECONDARY BENEFITS ISSUE

To arrive at an estimate of total benefits, it is necessary to consider secondary benefits as well as direct benefits to water users. The direct users of water are tied to other sectors of the regional and national economy; and, as their activities expand or contract, so will the activities of those they supply or from whom they buy. The extent of these induced secondary changes and their relevance to an assessment of national benefits and costs depend very much on the circumstances of the industries and regions involved, as well as on national economic conditions. The basic issues in determining the presence and magnitude of any legitimate secondary benefits are:

(1) Which industries will contract as well as expand, and where are they located?

(2) Over what period do labor and capital immobilities exist and how are they finally resolved?

(3) What happens in the long run to the productivity of displaced factors?

(4) What economies of scale exist in expanding and contracting industries?

(5) What economies and diseconomies of scale are involved in providing public overhead services and housing for labor which migrates as a result of project construction and operation?

Without answers to these questions, one cannot know whether there are legitimate secondary benefits, let alone what their magnitudes might be. This is a much neglected field in economics and in public policy formulation. However, there have been several attempts to measure total benefits per acre-foot used in agriculture, and some of these are reported below.

Colorado

Hartman and Seastone (1966) analyzed the income losses stemming from the diversion of water from agriculture to municipal and industrial uses in northeastern Colorado. The gross value of products produced per acre-foot of water applied was found to be $27. Because there is a significant return flow to surface sources, the authors used a return-flow multiplier of 2, making their estimate of the total value of agricultural output $54 per acre-foot. The direct profit and rent components in agriculture and in its supplying industries were estimated to be $14.50 per acre-foot, of which $12.90 was directly in agriculture.[8] Thus, if there were no problems of labor immobility (no loss of labor income), the income losses would be somewhere in the range of $12.90 to $14.50 per acre-foot, the exact value depending upon the opportunities for the suppliers to pick up equally profitable business. This is what water would be worth to farms over the life of their present equipment and land improvements.

The total wage and salary income related to gross production of $54 was estimated at $17.20 ($10.25 for agriculture and $6.95 for related industries). If labor were immobile in both agriculture and the related sectors, $17.20 would have to be added to the opportunity cost of transferred water over the period of immobility. Thus, the benefits forgone from water transferred from agriculture to municipal and industrial uses would range from $14.50 to $31.70, depending upon the degree of labor mobility. The periods of labor immobility applicable to the various sectors are not known.[9]

[8] The method of analysis was a multi-county input-output model for northeastern Colorado.

[9] Hartman and Seastone emphasize that free market transactions in water rights are likely to reflect only the capitalized value of profits and rents accruing to the agricultural seller. If there are immobilities in related sectors, the consequent costs would not be considered in the decision to sell.

California

Hartman and Seastone (1970) also considered potential income losses stemming from the loss of agricultural water rights in the Imperial Valley. Their analysis utilized a California input-output model of Martin and Carter (1962) and resource requirements matrices of Zusman and Hoch (1965) to trace the indirect effects of the reductions in Imperial Valley production. Not only were the usual "backward linkages" of input-output analysis taken into account, but possible impacts on "forward linked" industries supplied by Imperial Valley agriculture were also analyzed. Such forward linkages can be important only when no close substitute commodities are available at comparable costs to sustain the dependent industry.

Hartman and Seastone concentrated on the particular forward linkage of food and feed grains to cattle feeding and meat processing. Their analysis showed total direct and indirect income losses of $32 per acre-foot of water used in the feed grain sector, but a total of $106 per acre-foot if a strict forward linkage to cattle feeding and meat processing is assumed. The authors conclude that $18 of the $106 represents income completely unrecoverable because of long-term immobilities. Thus, for a short period and assuming a rigid forward linkage, income losses might be as high as $106 per acre-foot. In the longer term this would drop to $18 as capital is recovered and as labor mobility increases.

Texas

Grubb (January 1966) studied the incomes generated directly and indirectly by irrigated agriculture in the Texas High Plains. As reported earlier in this chapter, he found direct benefits in agriculture to range from $18 per acre-foot presently to $27 per acre-foot after 1980. In addition, he estimated value added in the processing and marketing of irrigation output, in the provision of agricultural inputs, and in the satisfying of consumer demands stemming from those additions to income.

To interpret Grubb's figures, one must relate the notion of value added in related industries to the appropriately defined measure of secondary benefits. Value added equals the total income payments made to capital, land, and labor as the result of some productive process.

Grubb found direct benefits plus value added in the related industries to range from $81 per acre-foot to $119 per acre-foot after 1980. These figures substantially overstate *national* economic benefits per acre-foot of water supplied, because of the implicit assumption that all indirect inputs would be unemployed in the absence of irrigated agriculture. More realistically, when importation of replacement water is considered in order to sustain irrigated agriculture, at least some of the inputs would have alternative employments outside of agriculture, so that only part of the indirect value added can legitimately be counted as secondary benefits and only over the period when the inputs would have remained unemployed. The proportion of value added and the period would have to be determined by a much more thorough investigation of the local economy.

Furthermore, as pointed out by Professor Kelso (personal correspondence dated 19 July 1968), Grubb's indirect values added were not reduced by the amount of capital and operating inputs imported into the region. Thus the above figures would overstate benefits even under conditions of complete immobility of resources.

New Mexico

Wollman et al. (1962) studied the value of water in alternative uses in the San Juan and Rio Grande basins in connection with the diversion of water from the San Juan River (a Colorado tributary lying mostly in New Mexico) into the Rio Grande Basin via Rio Chama. This area serves as a microcosm for the entire semiarid, rapidly growing Southwest because of its urban-oriented growth and the signs of a growing disparity between the supply of and demand for water. Mining, agriculture, and industry are the major water users in descending order of total value of output in the region, but agriculture accounts for about 99 percent of total consumptive use.

New Mexico was awarded 838,000 acre-feet per year from the San Juan River under the Upper Colorado Interstate Compact. Wollman's objective was to determine the effects on the state's economy of different patterns of use by agriculture, industry, mining, and recreation of the 638,000 acre-feet then remaining unappropriated. Eight possible patterns of use were evaluated—four patterns of allocation under each of two schemes which called for the diversion of 110,000 acre-feet and 235,000 acre-feet per year. Total value added, total employment generated, and total water-related costs were estimated for each of the eight patterns of water use.

An additional comment on the use of value added as a measure of benefits is required before proceeding. It was argued in chapter 2 that value added directly and indirectly represents *an upper bound to short-term benefits* accruing to water provided in rescue operations. The New Mexico case, however, is one of a region expanding on the basis of a new water supply. What relation does value added bear to national benefits in such a situation?

A growing region that wants to stimulate economic activity and attract labor and capital from the rest of the economy might use the total value added (direct and indirect) in the region per acre-foot of water as a criterion for the selection of water uses *provided* the inputs used in expansion are not simply bid away from other activities in the same region. Even under these circumstances, the total value added per acre-foot is not necessarily correlated with an industry's ability to expand profitably. For example, assume that a region has 100 units of water to allocate between two industries and that the value added per unit of water consumed has been $100 for industry A and $1,000 for industry B. Making the 100 units available to industry B may seem to imply a potential regional income ten times that which would result from allocating all of the water to industry A. However, this does not of necessity follow from the conditions stated. An industry can be high in value added without being a high profit industry, and it is profitability that is the signal for expansion. Limited markets and high costs for inputs and transport may severely limit the ability of industry B to expand. Thus, value added is of limited usefulness as a valid regional criterion for the allocation of new water supplies to expanding activities without studies of product markets and input availabilities.

The relationship of value added in an expanding activity to national economic benefits is not, in general, at all clear except that value added per acre-foot constitutes an upper bound on national benefits. Wollman et al. (1962, table 13, p. 31) found that value added directly and through purchases ranged from $28 to $51 per acre-foot in agriculture, from $212 to $307 per acre-foot in recreational use, and to much higher figures in municipal and industrial uses. This again establishes a fairly low upper bound on benefits per acre-foot in agriculture in the San Juan and Rio Grande Valleys of New Mexico.

Arizona

Estimates of the value added directly and indirectly per acre-foot of water intake for different agricultural sectors of the Arizona economy are shown in table 12. These estimates were derived by adding water costs to the data on personal income (wages, rents, profits, and interest) derived by Young and Martin. So long as water is used for the production of food and feed grain, no new supplies can be credited with benefits in excess of $28 because the benefits of a proposed project cannot exceed the cost of providing the same service by the best alternative means. Imported water cannot be assigned benefits in excess of the incomes that would be lost if an equivalent amount of water were removed from existing agriculture.

Table 12. *Personal Income and Value Added, Directly and Indirectly, per Acre-Foot of Agricultural Water Intake in Arizona, 1958*

| Sector | Personal income per acre-foot[a] | | Estimated pumping cost per acre-foot[b] | Value added per acre-foot |
	Direct	Total		
Food and feed grain	$14	$17	$11	$28
Forage crops	18	19	11	30
High-value intensive crops	80	93	11	104

[a] Young and Martin (1967), table 1, p. 10 and related text.

[b] Representing a pumping depth of 315 feet and a cost of 3.5 cents per acre-foot of water per foot of lift.

Total Benefits: Summary

Under the conditions found in rescue operations, short-term total benefits may somewhat exceed $100 per acre-foot on the basis of evidence gathered in this chapter. These high values would obtain for only short periods after the introduction of new surface supplies, however, and would diminish to values not exceeding $30 to $50 per acre-foot. In situations characterized by the expansion of new areas, as in the New Mexico and Arizona cases, the upper bound on total benefits ranges from about $30 to $50. The relevant figures are summarized in table 13.

To illustrate the importance of the period of immobility of resources, let us consider a hypothetical situation using the Texas High Plains figures. It is assumed for illustrative purposes that complete capital and labor immobility in agriculture and related industries obtains from the time water is withdrawn or exhausted until year T, at which time all inputs except those still engaged directly and indirectly in dry farming would be able to move into new activities. The benefits from replacement water will be taken to be $119 per acre-foot from year zero to year T

Table 13. *Total Benefits per Acre-Foot in Agriculture*

State or region	Direct benefits	Total benefits
Northeastern Colorado	$12.90	$14.50–31.70
California, Imperial Valley (rescue operation)	–	106 very short term
		18 long term
Texas High Plains (rescue operation)	18.20–45.00	81–119 short term only
New Mexico	–	28–51
Arizona	9–21	28

Note: These figures are from the regional studies reported in this chapter; they are based on differing assumptions and should not be compared with one another without an understanding of these assumptions. See text, this chapter, and the original sources.

and then $27 per acre-foot from year T until year 50 (the assumed life
of a water transfer project). For different periods of immobility, the average annual value per acre-foot of water computed at 5 percent interest
over the 50-year life of a water import project would be as follows: $36
($T = 2$); $49 ($T = 5$); $66 ($T = 10$); and $90 ($T = 20$).[10] This simple
analysis makes it clear that the period of factor immobility is a crucial
factor in the determination of benefits from rescue-type water transfers.

A caveat should be added before concluding this discussion. Even
though total benefit figures can under certain circumstances be rather
large for short periods, the ability of the direct users *to pay* for water
will generally be much smaller because nearly all of the components of
value added that were counted in total short-run benefits under factor
immobility represent out-of-pocket costs to the farmer. Thus the financing of rescue operations will probably have to involve not only charges
to direct users for water delivered but also taxes on the wider set of
community economic values sustained by the water importation.

The Future Demand for Output from Irrigated Areas

The preceding sections have indicated ways of assessing the direct
and total benefits from irrigation water at the margin of application.
Such benefits are, of course, ultimately derived from the demand for the
crops produced in irrigated areas, and a growth in demand for irrigation
output could change the benefits picture. Future demands will depend on
the world food situation and on the federal government's future policies
with regard to the role of the United States as a supplier of world food.

Only a few years ago, it was universally true that rates of population
growth exceeded the growth of agricultural production in the underdeveloped areas. World grain stocks had decreased sharply from 1960
through 1966. In 1966, nearly one-fourth of the U.S. wheat crop was
shipped to India alone.

By 1967 signs of change were being perceived. A detailed projection
study by Abel and Rojko (1967) indicated that by 1970, world grain
production and consumption would likely be in balance. The study
further indicated that if the underdeveloped countries continued to make
moderate improvements in productivity and if the 1967 acreage of 165
million or more were to remain under crops in the United States, the
world would continue to have excess production capacity through the
1980s.

---

10 For the period of immobility, the computations used the present value of an
annuity of $119 for T years. To this was added the value of an annuity of $27 for
($50 - T$) years, discounted T years to time zero. This present value total was then
transformed to an equivalent annual value for 50 years.

The improvements in agricultural productivity which have taken place in the less developed countries, particularly in Southeast Asia, have exceeded all the expectations of 1967. The exciting story of the "green revolution" and its implications for world grain production has been told by Lester R. Brown (1970). If the underdeveloped nations are able to handle the tremendous social and economic changes imposed by the startling spread of highly productive grain culture, and if the aid-giving nations continue to assist in building up the infrastructure necessary to gain full advantage from the production breakthrough, Brown predicts not only self-sufficiency in grains for a large part of the underdeveloped world but possibly a reversal of export flows toward some of the more developed countries.

The United States has excess agricultural capacity that can be utilized on relatively short notice. About 56 million acres has been withdrawn under various government programs. Upchurch[11] stated in 1966 that in a period of a few years, a large part of this idle acreage could be brought back into production at about present levels of prices. If limitations on the acreage in cotton are continued and, at the same time, restraints on production of food and feed grains are relaxed, the United States could supply an additional 60 million tons of grain. Under present conditions, there seems to be no indication that anywhere near this much will be needed for food aid in the near future.

The Conservation Needs Survey of a few years ago showed that the United States had 638 million acres of land in the three classes best suited for cropping and that this land was available without further drainage or irrigation. In recent years only about 200 million acres have actually been used.

This land availability plus continuing innovation in plant breeding and food technology indicate a vast, untapped potential for increased production within the confines of presently croppable lands in the United States. Any likely demands of the next several decades, including the U.S. share of world food aid, appear quite capable of being met without opening up new lands.

[11] M. L. Upchurch, Administrator, Economic Research Service, United States Department of Agriculture (1966).

4

Long-Term Regional Impacts and National Benefits of an Interbasin Transfer

The interbasin transfers frequently mentioned as possibilities for the western United States, involving from 2.5 million to 100 million acre-feet per year, are so large that the changes in the volumes and locations of production stemming from them are certain to affect the rest of the regional economy and possibly the national economy in significant ways. The purposes of this chapter are to illustrate methods for analyzing such large projects and to establish ranges of national benefits per acre-foot that are likely to be generated under various circumstances. This type of sensitivity analysis leads to recommendations on data gathering and further research.

The proposed interbasin transfers in almost all cases are intended to provide water both for the replacement of water supplies that are being exhausted or degraded in quality and for the expansion of irrigated agriculture. While some of the transfer proposals mentioned in chapter 1 did not explicitly involve bringing water to new irrigated acreage, it is quite likely that the states of origin and the states through which the canals or aqueducts pass will have to be compensated and given permission to tap some water.

The analysis of the impacts of "replacement" water must, for several reasons, be somewhat different from the analysis of water to open new irrigated land. A region receiving replacement water will have an established economic structure that can be measured and analyzed in a fairly reliable manner. Predicting the success of a new area is a much more speculative matter. Other basic differences lie in the degree of fixity or immobility of the resources involved. Expanding areas are less likely to have unemployment and excess capacity in the project sector and market-related sectors than are established areas that are forced to contract for lack of water. In contracting areas, outward mobility from agriculture and related industries is likely to be limited, implying at least temporary unemployment and excess capacity.

The effects of these differences on the methods of analysis are illustrated in the case studies presented in this chapter. The studies exhibit impact analyses and project benefit-cost evaluations in the context of a hypothetical transfer from the Columbia and Colorado rivers that would open up new irrigated land in Oregon and prevent agricultural contraction in the Imperial Valley of California.

It was argued in chapter 2 that a very large part of the water delivered by interbasin transfer projects will be devoted to agriculture because of the amounts of water involved. This definitely does not imply, however, that other sectors of the regional and national economies will be unaffected by the importation of water. On the contrary, agriculture can have strong supply and demand tie-ins with other industries, both within and outside the region, and its expansion (or avoided contraction) can have an important effect on those industries. Whether such an effect is experienced or not depends upon several crucial factors, which are illustrated in this chapter.

The following simple examples illustrate the forward or "supply-push" linkages and the backward or "demand-pull" linkages between agriculture and other industries. Suppose that the expansion of a regional livestock industry (dairy and/or beef) has been held back by a shortage of local forage and feed grains and a lack of comparably priced substitutes. The expansion of forage and feed grains through new irrigation would then permit an expansion of the regional livestock industry. The livestock industry would, in turn, contribute to the expansion of the regional "food and related products" and "wholesale and retail trade" industries. Since the latter two industries deliver most of their output to final consumption demand, they would exert "backward" demands for needed inputs other than livestock—the effects analyzed in traditional input-output analysis.

It might well be, however, that the livestock industry and other heavy users of agricultural inputs have been limited by the markets for their products rather than by bottlenecks in supplies. The expansion of agricultural output would then not trigger expansion of these industries but would result in expanded deliveries to final demand, mostly to markets outside the region. The linkage to the rest of the regional economy would then be purely a backward or demand-pull linkage and could be traced through the usual type of input-output analysis.[1]

[1] In both of these cases, there might be additional effects of the Keynesian multiplier type, i.e., the generation of additional incomes when the original increments to

The ideal tool for analyzing interbasin transfer impacts would be a multiregional closed input-output model which would permit the tracing of impacts not only in the project region, but in all other regions. If locational factors could be included, one could trace not only the positive expansionary effects of the project but also the detrimental effects on regions that lose activity as a result of the project. Presently available models are limited to state or regional input-output models, which can handle locational decisions for economic activities only in an ad hoc manner. The basic models used in this chapter are *state* input-output models, but it is felt that their wise use can lead to substantial insights into the range of impacts that transfer projects can have and the benefits they may generate. The models employed will permit the tracing of impacts on all state industries in terms of increases in gross output and value added. However, the use of state input-output models precludes any industry-by-industry analysis of impacts outside the states directly affected by the transfer project, so impacts external to the region must be analyzed in ad hoc ways. Later in this book the displacement of agriculture in nonproject states is analyzed.

The usual caveats regarding state or regional input-output models must be observed. The coefficients are not necessarily the technical coefficients of the national input-output model; they reflect the existing trade patterns of the region with the rest of the country, and trade patterns may be less stable than technology. See Tiebout (1957) and Leven (1961).

The national input-output coefficients can be straightforwardly interpreted as technical production coefficients since imports are small relative to domestic production. As long as technology is stable and as long as relative prices do not change so as to induce significant input substitutions within the confines of existing technology, these coefficients can be expected to remain stable.

When a state input-output table is constructed, it is more nearly a representation of trade flows than of technical requirements, for the proportion of inputs provided by industry i for the output of industry j is

income are spent. Since the household sector is not included as an endogenous sector in most input-output models, such effects have to be analyzed separately. However, there will be no short-term Keynesian multiplier effects unless there is local unemployment and underutilization of capacity.

When the analysis is concerned with long-term impacts, multiplier effects may induce migration. The long-term potential expansion of working population would include the increased demands by project-linked industries for labor inputs and some (non-imported) portion of the increased consumption (Keynesian multiplier) demands by households. The possible importance of immigration and its relation to endogenous treatment of the household sector were pointed out by Irving Hoch.

as much a matter of the competitiveness of the local i industry with import substitutes as it is a matter of technological requirements. Thus, the state input-output coefficient may be less stable, since any change in the comparative advantage of the state vis-à-vis the rest of the country may cause the origins of inputs to change substantially.

THE INTERBASIN WATER TRANSFER SELECTED FOR ANALYSIS

No one plan could be chosen as a typical interbasin transfer project, and the one used for illustrative purposes in this chapter and its appendix is a hypothetical one calling for a diversion of 7.5 million acre-feet per year from the Columbia to the Colorado. The rationale for the size of the project is roughly outlined in the Colorado River water budget given below in table 14.[2] In terms of the potential markets for imported water in the Lower Colorado Basin, it seemed that 7.5 million acre-feet per year was as large a diversion as was consistent with anticipated markets for agricultural output.

The route for the project and its general features have been taken from Pirkey's Western Water Project, which has been publicly presented in greater detail than the other proposals listed in table 2, chapter 1.[3] The Western Water Project (see figure 1, chapter 1) contemplates diverting 15 million acre-feet per year from the Columbia River above The Dallas Dam. The water is then to be pumped up the Deschutes and Crooked rivers for storage in various reservoirs and lakes along the Oregon-Nevada route to Lake Mead. Since diversions are to take place only during flood season, the first segment of the system, involving a pumping life of 4,500 feet, is designed for a pumping rate of 36,000 cubic feet per second (cfs), compared with an initial main canal capacity of 21,000 cfs. At other times of the year the first segment is to be used as a pumped-storage operation for the generation of peaking power for the Columbia Basin.

Project items that do not relate directly to the delivery of water to Southern California and Arizona are not included in table 15, which indicates the components of the project considered here and the costs by type of expenditure. The parenthetical numbers in the last row of the table are the "scaled-down" cost components for a system designed to divert 7.5 maf/yr. rather than the Western Water Project's design capa-

[2] This water budget was constructed by the authors from various sources, with the full realization that substantial uncertainty surrounds the actual frequency distribution of Colorado River flows.

[3] The authors wish to acknowledge Mr. Pirkey's help in securing data on the project and permission to quote from his report on the Project, "Water for All."

Table 14.   Colorado River Basin Water Budget with a Large Transfer

Item		Million acre-feet per year
Flow at Lee Ferry (95% probability level)		12.8
Less flow required by Colorado River Compact		7.5
Available for Upper Basin uses		5.3
Less Ultimate Upper Basin use[a]		4.0
Excess available for Lower Basin		1.3
Plus Compact allowance (above)		7.5
Long-term availability for Lower Basin		8.8
Uses (maf/yr.):		
California (current)	5.2	
Arizona (Colorado River allotment plus remaining deficit of 2.3 maf/yr.)	5.1	
Nevada	0.3	
Mexico	1.5	
Evaporation	1.0	
Less uses listed above		13.1
Ultimate deficit in Lower Basin		4.3
Uses along interbasin transfer route		2.0
Total deliveries required of transfer		6.3
Plus losses en route (16 percent of total diversion)		1.2
Total amount to be diverted		7.5

[a] Author's estimates. No allowance made for development of oil shale production.

Table 15.   Western Water Project Cost Components

million dollars

Item	Dams and reservoirs	Conduit	Pump-turbine plants	Pumping plants	Power plants	Total
Right-of-way purchases						225
Relocation cost						100
Western Aqueduct	1,015	1,573	2,900	1,297	4,128	10,913
Arizona Conduit		200		240		440
Total, 15 maf/yr.	1,015	1,773	2,900	1,537	4,128	11,678
Est. total, 7.5 maf/yr.	(508)	(887)	(1,450)	(769)	(2,064)	

Source: Pirkey, 1963, table 5, p. 12.
Note: Figures in parentheses are "scaled-down" cost components. See text discussion.

city of 15 maf/yr. Insofar as there are substantial economies of scale in the construction of the different types of structure (dams, powerplants, etc.), the proportional reduction of costs used here will result in an understatement of costs.[4] The particular numbers used for this hypothetical project have been selected to be realistic but should not be taken as adequate for actual policy decisions.

The following Oregon and Southern California cases start with assumptions concerning the cropping pattern of the agriculture that will be phased out (or brought in) as regional water supplies for agriculture are diminished (or developed). These assumptions are based on analyses of the present cropping patterns or of cropping patterns of nearby projects in the case of new areas. Given the pattern of agricultural output, alternative assumptions are made regarding forward linkages to other local industries. The implications of such linkages for increased deliveries by those industries to final demand are traced. Finally, the increments in deliveries to final demand by agriculture and the industries it supplies are analyzed in terms of their "backward" linkages to other industries to determine their impact on all related supplying industries. The increments to gross output are then translated into increments of project-related value added, price adjustments are estimated, and the resultant value-added figures are further analyzed in terms of national economic benefits under alternative sets of conditions.

POTENTIAL REGIONAL IMPACTS AND NATIONAL BENEFITS GENERATED IN NEWLY EXPANDING REGIONS: OREGON

The Colorado River water budget constructed earlier in this chapter allowed for the use of 2 million acre-feet along the route of the diversion. Because of the availability of an input-output model for Oregon and the absence of one for Nevada, it has been assumed that the 2 million acre-feet would be diverted for irrigation in Oregon. The applicability of a state input-output table to the particular parts of the state through which the diversion project would pass depends in part upon the similarities between the present structure of the area vis-à-vis the whole state. Table 16 gives some data on personal income by industry of origin for the counties that rough judgment indicates would most likely be involved in an expansion of irrigation. The income patterns for the counties show no radical deviations from the state pattern.

---

[4] Taylor (1967, p. 28), indicates that scale economies in canal construction are virtually exhausted at a capacity of 7,000 cfs compared with 10,500 cfs of the present project. Evidence is not available on other components of the project.

Table 16. Income Structures of Oregon and Oregon Counties, 1965

County	Personal income		Per cent of personal income from:*			
	Thousand dollars	Percent of state total	Farm income	Manufacturing income	Wholesale and retail trade	Services
Crook	24,050	0.4	3.1	29.2	7.7	4.9
Deschutes	67,200	1.3	0.5	19.1	10.8	6.7
Harney	19,580	0.4	4.6	24.7	6.6	4.4
Jefferson	21,090	0.4	5.7	15.3	10.3	3.1
Klamath	120,350	2.2	1.9	18.3	11.0	5.7
Lake	17,810	0.3	4.5	17.2	7.0	4.1
Malheur	53,950	1.0	6.8	13.4	10.5	4.4
Waco	52,280	1.0	3.2	13.7	11.3	5.7
Entire state	5,350,000	100.0	1.1	19.0	12.4	6.4

Source: Data provided by the Bureau of Business and Economic Research, University of Oregon.

* Other sources include mining, construction, finance, transportation, communications and public utilities, and governments.

The Assumed Cropping Pattern

In Oregon the 2 million acre-feet of water would be used for *new* irrigation, as contrasted with the situations in Southern California and Arizona where the water might be used to prevent phasing out of existing agriculture. Cropping patterns, water use, crop values, and yields must therefore be estimated for the time when this land would be irrigated. The estimates used in this study are shown in table 17.

The crop distribution figures were derived from: the 1964–66 crop distribution on three sizable Bureau of Reclamation irrigation projects (Klamath, Deschutes, and Rogue River) that are fairly close to the transfer route; the total state crop distribution of irrigated land as shown in the 1964 Agricultural Census; and the projected crop distribution for the Columbia River Basin reclamation project area, which is not unlike parts of Southeastern Oregon.

It was estimated that an average of 4 acre-feet of water would have to be diverted from the main canal for each acre irrigated. This allows for losses in the laterals and in the farm application. Therefore approximately 500,000 acres would be irrigated by this 2 million acre-feet with a crop distribution as shown in table 17.

Table 17.   Assumed Crop Distribution and Value of Production on New Acreage Irrigated in Oregon by the Interbasin Water Transfer

	Acreage		Gross crop value*	
Crops	Percent of total	Thousand acres	Per acre	Total (thousands)
Wheat	5	25	$ 165	$ 4,125
Feed grains	25	125	125	15,625
Total grains	30	150		
Alfalfa hay	20	100	121	12,100
Other hay	5	25	72	1,800
Pasture	20	100	90	9,000
Total forage crops	45	225		
Vegetables	10	50	500	25,000
Fruits	10	50	1,108	55,400
Seed and misc. crops	5	25	230	5,750
Total	100	500		$128,800

Sources: U.S. Department of Commerce, *Census of Agriculture, 1964*, vol. 1, part 47 (Oregon), p. 367; A. L. Walker and others, *The Economic Significance of Columbia Basin Project Development*, Washington State University, Bulletin 669, 1966, p. 62; U.S. Department of the Interior, *Federal Reclamation Projects Statistical Appendix to Crop Report and Related Data, 1964, 1965*, and *1966*.

* Based on yields and prices projected for around 1980.

The gross value of the increased agricultural crop production in
Oregon would be $128.8 million, based on yields and prices projected for
around 1980.[5] Any change in the acreage planted to the high-value crops
such as fruits and vegetables could have a significant effect on the estimated gross value of production, as almost half the total gross value of
production is accounted for by fruits and about one-fifth by vegetables.
Shifts in the other crops would probably be less critical.

The Analysis

The input-output table for Oregon (Allen and Watson 1965) indicates that the output of the agricultural sector is distributed as follows:
livestock and products, 24 percent; agriculture, 8 percent; food and kindred products, 22 percent; lumber and wood products, 19 percent; finance-
insurance-real estate, 4 percent; government enterprises, 5 percent; and
final demand, 16 percent.[6] The cropping pattern developed in the preceding section indicates quite clearly that, as far as any forward linkages
are concerned, the only sectors that are likely to expand in direct response
to increased supplies of agricultural output are "food and kindred products" (which is supplied with wheat, vegetables, and fruits) and "livestock and products" (which is supplied with feedgrains, alfalfa, other
hay, and pasture).

The food and livestock sectors may experience sizable expansions
when agricultural production is increased. However, it should be kept in
mind that the increased crop production may simply displace some agricultural production elsewhere in Oregon or substitute for imports from
other states unless there are further opportunities for the profitable expansion of the food and livestock industries. The impact of increased
agricultural production on those sectors may thus range from insignificant
to large. Two cases which differ substantially in this regard are examined
below.

*Case I: Project agriculture strongly forward-linked to food and live-
stock sectors.* For this case, it has been assumed that the pattern of utilization of the new project output will be as shown in table 18.

Allocating the *total* possible increase in agricultural output to forward-linked industries and final demand leaves no "slack" to provide for

[5] Ideally, the input-output table should be adjusted to represent the likely technology and prices of 1980 but this was not done. Projected 1980 crop prices have about
the same relationships to each other as the prices used in the input-output table.

[6] Donald Watson, who graciously provided the input-output study and related data,
has cautioned that the model was hurriedly assembled and that great reliance should
not be placed on it for quantitative conclusions.

Table 18. *First-Stage Allocation of Project Output, Oregon, Case I*

Item	Thousand dollars
Inputs into "food and kindred products":	
Wheat	4,125
Vegetables	20,000
Fruits	27,700
Total	51,825
Inputs into "livestock and products":	
Feed grain	15,625
Alfalfa	12,100
Other hay	1,800
Pasture	9,000
Total	38,525
Output going to final demand:	
Fruits	27,700
Vegetables	5,000
Total	32,700
Seeds and miscellaneous inputs into agriculture	5,750
Total project output	128,800

the indirect requirements of other expanding sectors. However, the indirect requirements on the agricultural sector cannot be known until the expansion of all sectors is determined. A two-step analysis must be adopted which will permit the initial estimates of increases in gross outputs to be reduced so that the total requirements on agriculture, both direct and indirect, equal the additional output available.

The relevant columns of the 1963 Oregon input-output transactions, coefficient, and inverse tables are given in table 19, and the detailed final demand account is found in table 20. It is seen that the input from Oregon agriculture per dollar of "food and kindred products" output is $0.0782. If locally provided agricultural inputs had really been the bottleneck to further expansion of the "food and kindred products" industry, i.e., if no competitive inputs had been available from elsewhere, the availability of $51,825,000 of new agricultural produce would permit $662.7 million ($51,825,000/0.0782) of new output from "food and kindred products," provided there were no other bottlenecks and that a market existed for such output.

The "food and kindred products" industry provides certain of its own inputs, and an expansion of its gross output to $662.7 million would

Table 19. Input-Output Data for Oregon, 1963

Sector	Livestock and products			Agriculture, n.e.c.			Food and kindred products		
	Transactions (thous.)	Requirements per dollar of output		Transactions (thous.)	Requirements per dollar of output		Transactions (thous.)	Requirements per dollar of output	
		Direct	Total		Direct	Total		Direct	Total
Livestock and products	$47,590	$0.15863	$1.27277	$24,960	$0.07451	$0.10814	$211,510	$0.22991	$0.36134
Agriculture, n.e.c.	80,420	.26806	.38975	27,270	.08140	1.12691	71,940	.07820	.21559
Mining	80	.00027	.01228	1,320	.00394	.02153	750	.00082	.01576
Maintenance and repair construction	2,690	.00897	.02930	5,230	.01561	.03226	3,370	.00366	.02312
Food and kindred products	34,030	.11343	.17626	280	.00084	.02089	149,350	.16234	1.24751
Textiles and apparel	160	.00053	.00869	1,090	.00325	.01425	2,120	.00230	.01249
Lumber and wood products	20	.00007	.00610	1,410	.00421	.01045	1,470	.00160	.01020
Furniture	0	.00000	.00013	0	.00000	.00016	0	.00000	.00020
Paper and allied products	160	.00053	.01804	210	.00063	.01805	18,060	.01963	.05444
Printing and publishing	60	.00020	.01493	100	.00030	.02119	1,780	.00193	.02688
Stone, clay, and glass products	50	.00017	.00649	350	.00104	.00679	8,760	.00952	.01867
Nonmetal manufacturing	1,530	.00510	.08084	29,910	.08928	.16429	12,690	.01379	.08232
Primary nonferrous metal manufacturing	10	.00003	.00497	10	.00003	.00609	520	.00057	.00919
Metal manufacturing	650	.00217	.02468	770	.00230	.02351	25,730	.02797	.06565
Machinery	80	.00027	.00961	2,750	.00821	.01834	230	.00025	.01153
Electrical machinery	90	.00030	.00413	300	.00090	.00504	490	.00053	.00559
Manufacturing, n.e.c.	290	.00097	.00980	720	.00215	.01119	440	.00049	.01298
Transportation	5,930	.01977	.04948	3,820	.01140	.03076	36,980	.04020	.07976
Communications	610	.00203	.01010	1,050	.00313	.01216	2,290	.00249	.01294
Electricity, water, gas, and sanitary services	1,050	.00350	.01699	2,390	.00713	.01918	5,120	.00557	.02163
Wholesale and retail trade	10,460	.03487	.08212	13,970	.04170	.07083	32,700	.03554	.08673
Finance, insurance, and real estate	5,520	.01840	.08532	29,450	.08791	.13437	9,070	.00986	.06694
Hotels and repair services	0	.00000	.00136	0	.00000	.00166	540	.00059	.00243
Business services	530	.00177	.03301	11,900	.03552	.05645	23,090	.02510	.05478
Automotive services	690	.00230	.00719	700	.00209	.00518	4,060	.00441	.01049
Medical and educational services	1,730	.00577	.00851	180	.00054	.00213	1,050	.00114	.00448
Services, n.e.c.	0	.00000	.00084	0	.00000	.00102	90	.00010	.00113
Government enterprise	50	.00010	.00813	70	.00021	.00922	860	.00093	.01118
Activities, n.e.c.	210	.00070	.00899	420	.00125	.00985	5,370	.00584	.01717
Value added	105,310	–	–	174,370	–	–	289,570	–	–
Gross output	300,000	–	–	335,000	–	–	920,000	–	–
Total requirements	–	–	$2.38081	–	–	$1.96189	–	–	$2.54312

Source: Allen and Watson (1965).

millions

Table 20. Total Demands in Oregon State Output, 1963

Sector	Intermediate domestic demand (1)	Domestic final demand				Net external trade balance (6)	Net final demand met by state (7)	Total domestic output (8)
		Personal consumption (2)	Investment (3)	Government (4)	Total (5)			
Livestock and products	$ 295	$ 30	$ 0	$ 0	$ 30	$ −25	$ 5	$ 300
Agriculture, n.e.c.	280	40	0	−35	5	+50	55	335
Mining	120	5	0	0	5	−85	−80	40
Maintenance and repair construction	170	60	0	40	100	+30	130	300
Food and kindred products	220	680	0	30	710	−10	700	920
Textiles and apparel	110	190	0	0	190	−150	40	150
Lumber and wood products	225	15	55	10	80	+220	300	525
Furniture	5	40	20	10	70	−15	55	60
Paper and allied products	350	25	0	5	30	+340	370	720
Printing and publishing	160	40	0	10	50	−40	10	170
Stone, clay, and glass products	75	5	50	0	55	+10	65	140
Nonmetal manufacturing	390	200	25	15	240	−330	−90	300
Primary nonferrous metal manufacturing	190	0	10	20	30	+150	180	370
Metal manufacturing	315	10	120	10	140	−155	−15	300
Machinery	120	15	150	20	185	−30	155	275
Electrical machinery	115	65	50	30	145	+25	170	285
Manufacturing, n.e.c.	220	180	75	150	405	−125	280	500
Transportation	255	250	40	20	310	−45	265	520
Communications	75	70	5	5	80	−5	75	150
Electricity, water, gas, and sanitary services	165	120	10	10	140	−5	135	300
Wholesale and retail trade	315	830	80	10	920	+15	935	1,250
Finance, insurance, and real estate	295	640	30	10	680	−255	425	820
Hotels and repair services	25	150	0	5	155	+20	175	200
Business services	220	25	35	15	75	−15	60	280
Automotive services	45	60	10	5	65	+10	75	120
Medical and educational services	25	290	0	10	300	+25	325	350
Services, n.e.c.	30	45	0	65	110	+10	120	150
Government enterprise	110	75	20	50	145	+10	155	265
Activities, n.e.c.	120	5	0	5	10	−15	−5	115
Value added	30	90	375	525	990	−60	930	
Total	5,070	$4,250	$1,150	$1,050	$6,450	$−450	$6,000	6,000

67

require $107.6 million ($0.1623 per dollar of output) to be used as its own intermediate input. The remaining $555.1 million would go to final demand.

The inputs from agriculture to "livestock and products" are somewhat more difficult to trace because large quantities of "livestock and products" go to both final demand and "food and kindred product."[7] The direct input coefficient from agriculture to livestock being 0.26806, the allocation of $38,525,000 additional output of feed grains and forage to livestock would permit an increase of $143.7 million in livestock output, other supplies and the market permitting. Since livestock provides $0.15863 of its own input per dollar of output, a total of $22.8 million of the $143.7 million would be required for intermediate inputs, leaving $120.9 million output to go to "food and kindred products" and final demand. It has been assumed that the distribution is 15 percent ($18.1 million) to final demand and 85 percent ($102.8 million) to "food and kindred products." Since the livestock input to "food and kindred" is $0.2299 per dollar of output, the additional "food and kindred" output would be $447.1 million ($102.8 million/0.2299). The "food and kindred" industry would need $72.6 million (0.16234 per dollar of output) for its own intermediate output, and $374.5 million would go to final demand.

Thus, under the assumptions that agriculture is the bottleneck to expansion, that market prices of outputs do not fall, and that market prices of inputs do not increase enough to make the implied expansions unprofitable, the first-round estimate of the gross value of increased outputs is as follows:

	Deliveries to final demand (million dollars)	First-round estimate of increases in gross output (million dollars)
Livestock and products	18.1	143.7
Agriculture	32.7	128.8
Food and kindred products	929.6	1,109.8

However, an inconsistency has been introduced into the analysis by failing to account for the indirect demands that will be made upon agriculture as the industries supplying other inputs expand. If the three increments of deliveries to final demand given above are multiplied (in the vector sense) by the direct and indirect requirements matrix $(I - A)^{-1}$, it

[7] Agriculture and livestock sell small amounts to many other industries, but forward linkages would probably not be important because imports can be more easily substituted for these inputs.

is found that they imply the following gross outputs: livestock and products, $362.4 million; agriculture, $244.3 million; and food and kindred products, $1,163.6 million. The agricultural requirements figure is much higher than the originally assumed feasible increment of agricultural output of $128.8 million. What was needed initially was to "reserve" some of the added agricultural capacity to provide for the indirect demands that will be made on that sector. If only 53 percent (128.8/244.3) of the possible output of $128.8 million is initially allocated to "forward linkages" and final demand, the result is, as shown below, a set of deliveries to final demand that is consistent with an increase of $128.8 million in gross agricultural output and the required intermediate inputs.

	Deliveries to final demand (million dollars)
Livestock and products	9.5
Agriculture	17.2
Food and kindred products	489.3

These values, multiplied by the direct and indirect requirements matrix $(I - A)^{-1}$, imply the gross outputs recorded in table 21.

The preceding values of deliveries to final demand as well as the results of table 20 assume stable price levels in the face of expanding deliveries to final demand for the livestock, agriculture, and food and kindred products sectors. In terms of figure 6 (which might represent any sector expanding its deliveries to final demand), the increment of output $(Q_2 - Q_1)$ has been valued at price p_1. In fact, the analysis should allow for some *depression* of price for most commodities. The proper measure of gross national benefits would be the shaded area of figure 6. Rather than attempting the conceptually correct but deceptively refined procedure of calculating the area under the demand curve, the authors have chosen a simple downward adjustment of price to p_2.

The impact of the new supplies on price can be calculated if the relevant price elasticities of demand and market sizes are known.[8] Determining how one should define the relevant market (national, regional, state) for the project's output and the outputs of linked industries is neither a simple nor a well-settled matter. The price elasticities of demand applicable to the project will not be the same in each market area

[8] This begs the question of how soon the newly irrigable lands would be brought into production. A sudden flooding of the market with the output of half a million acres could have disastrous effects on prices. Restricting the activation of new land to the rate of growth of the market might prevent the depression of prices but, by deferring output to later periods, would reduce the present value of that output.

Table 21.   Project-Related Gross Output and Value Added, Oregon, Case I

millions

Sector	Gross output	Value added[a]
Livestock and products	$ 190.7	$ 66.9
	(143.0)[b]	(19.2)[b]
Agriculture, n.e.c.	128.8	67.0
	(95.8)[b]	(34.0)[b]
Mining	8.2	4.8
Maintenance and repair construction	12.2	7.4
Food and kindred products	612.4	192.9
Textiles and apparel	6.4	2.2
Lumber and wood products	5.2	1.8
Furniture	0.1	0.05
Paper and allied products	27.1	10.3
Printing and publishing	13.7	6.5
Stone, clay, and glass products	9.3	4.5
Nonmetal manufacturing	43.9	17.1
Primary nonferrous metal manufacturing	4.6	1.6
Metal manufacturing	32.7	13.2
Machinery	6.1	2.8
Electrical machinery	2.8	1.4
Manufacturing, n.e.c.	6.6	2.7
Transportation	40.0	24.8
Communications	6.6	5.4
Electricity, water, gas, and sanitary services	11.1	5.3
Wholesale and retail trade	44.4	32.1
Finance, insurance, and real estate	35.9	24.4
Hotels and repair services	1.2	0.7
Business services	28.1	13.2
Automotive services	5.3	2.6
Medical and educational services	2.3	1.6
Services, n.e.c.	0.6	0.2
Government enterprise	5.7	2.8
Activities, n.e.c.	8.6	–
Totals	$1,300.4	$516.3
	(1,219.7)[b]	(435.6)[b]

[a] Value-added coefficients were taken from the direct requirements table of Allen and Watson (1965).

[b] Figures in parentheses are values corrected for anticipated price changes as explained in text.

because of differing substitution possibilities. In fact, the only elasticity estimates available are national elasticities. For highly processed food and kindred products, the national market is probably the relevant one, but for livestock and some parts of agriculture, the state or regional market may be more relevant because transport costs tend to isolate these markets. Since a high degree of isolation was assumed for agriculture and livestock in Case I, price impacts are calculated for those sectors. The procedure is illustrated in Table 21.

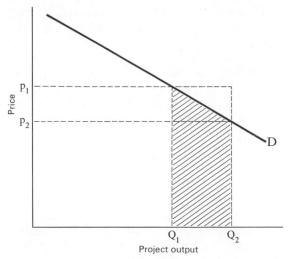

Figure 6. Gross national benefits from additional water.

Let the price elasticity of demand be defined as

$$E = \frac{\Delta Q/Q}{\Delta p/p}, \qquad (4.1)$$

where Q stands for the total preproject output in the relevant market area and ΔQ represents the project's addition to total output. Since the above analyses were carried out in terms of unchanged prices (as is necessary in using input-output analysis), we may use the change in value of output, V, as a surrogate for the change in quantity, i.e.,

$$\Delta V = (Q_2 - Q_1)p_1 \equiv \Delta Q \cdot p_1, \qquad (4.2)$$

where Q_1 and Q_2 are indices of physical output. From equation (2) it follows that

$$\frac{\Delta V}{V_1} = \frac{\Delta Q \cdot p_1}{Q_1 \cdot p_1} = \frac{\Delta Q}{Q_1}. \qquad (4.3)$$

This may be substituted back into equation (4.1), which, with minor manipulation, yields

$$\frac{\Delta p}{p} = \left(\frac{1}{E}\right)\left(\frac{\Delta V}{V}\right), \qquad (4.4)$$

which permits the calculation of percentage price changes from available data.

Under case I, an elasticity of -0.5 is assumed for agricultural commodities as a whole.[9] Assume that the total output in the relevant re-

[9] See Brandow (1961), table 12, p. 59.

gional market at the time of completion of the proposed new irrigation project will be \$1 billion *without* the project. (The 1963 level of gross output in Oregon was \$335 million.)

$$\frac{\Delta V}{V} = \frac{\$129 \times 10^6}{\$1 \times 10^9} = 0.13. \tag{4.5}$$

From this it would follow that the likely price impact of the project on agriculture in the regional market would be

$$\frac{\Delta p}{p} = \left(-\frac{1}{0.5}\right)(0.13) = -0.26. \tag{4.6}$$

A fall in the value of gross output of 26 percent (\$33 million) reduces value added in agriculture from \$67 million to \$34 million (shown in parentheses in table 21).

Similar calculations may be made for the livestock sector. Again assuming a market size of \$1 billion without the project (gross Oregon output in Oregon was \$335 million.)

$$\frac{\Delta V}{V} = \frac{\$191 \times 10^6}{\$1 \times 10^9} = 0.19. \tag{4.7}$$

Elasticity of farm-level demand for cattle is about -0.68 and that for calves about -1.08.[10] An overall elasticity is therefore taken to be -0.75, from which it follows that

$$\frac{\Delta p}{p} = \left(-\frac{1}{0.75}\right)(0.19) = -0.25. \tag{4.8}$$

Applying this price reduction to livestock output and value added reduces them by \$47.7 million, as shown in table 21. Total project-related value added is reduced to \$435.6 million.

Case I is intended to illustrate the *maximum* possible impact of the project. How much of the total value added might represent a net addition to Oregon's income depends upon how much the project displaces other Oregon activity. The interpretation of the results of the analysis to date from the national point of view will be deferred until case II has been presented.

Case II: Project agriculture not forward-linked to food and livestock. Under this set of assumptions the increase in agricultural production affects the rest of the economy through the usual input-output (backward) linkages. There are no forward linkages because imported agricultural commodities have been so plentiful that shortages of local agricultural outputs have not served to constrain other industries. The increase in

10 Brandow (1961), table 12.

agricultural output will be delivered to final demand, probably as regional exports. The following figures emerged from a two-step analysis like that in case I where the $128.8 million of agricultural output was first allocated to intermediate agricultural inputs and final demand; as

	million dollars
Increment of agricultural output	128.8
Required for agricultural sector intermediate inputs	10.5
Required for other sectors intermediate demands	4.0
Deliveries to final demand	114.3

The above allocation of the agricultural output implies the gross outputs and values added given in table 22. In keeping with the assumption that inputs from nonproject areas have been plentifully available, it is as-

Table 22. Project-Related Gross Output and Value Added, Oregon, Case II

millions

Sector	Gross output	Value added
Livestock and products	$ 12.4	$ 4.4
Agriculture, n.e.c.	128.8	67.0
Mining	2.5	1.5
Maintenance and repair construction	3.7	2.3
Food and kindred products	2.4	0.8
Textiles and apparel	1.6	0.5
Lumber and wood products	1.2	0.4
Furniture	–	–
Paper and allied products	2.1	0.8
Printing and publishing	2.1	1.0
Stone, clay, and glass products	0.8	0.4
Nonmetal manufacturing	18.8	7.3
Primary nonferrous metal manufacturing	0.7	0.2
Metal manufacturing	2.7	1.1
Machinery	2.1	1.0
Electrical machinery	0.6	0.3
Manufacturing, n.e.c.	1.3	0.5
Transportation	3.5	0.2
Communications	1.4	1.1
Electricity, water, gas, and sanitary services	2.2	1.1
Wholesale and retail trade	8.1	5.9
Finance, insurance, and real estate	15.4	10.5
Hotels and repair services	0.2	0.1
Business services	6.5	3.1
Automotive services	0.6	0.3
Medical and educational services	0.2	0.1
Services, n.e.c.	0.1	–
Government enterprise	1.1	0.6
Activities, n.e.c.	1.1	–
Total	$224.2	$112.5

sumed that this expanding agricultural output is competing in a national
market, so that no significant price impact will be felt.

The vast differences between the increments in project-related gross
output and value added in cases I and II demonstrate that a crucial question at this stage of evaluating the project is whether or not agricultural
output in the project area has constituted a bottleneck to the expansion
of other industries. Insofar as substitutes are available from other regions
(including other parts of Oregon), the total impact of the project on
Oregon's economy is likely to be closer to the results of case II than of
case I.

Interpretation of the Oregon Results in Terms of National Benefits

The figures for project-related gross output and value added (tables
21 and 22) can be of value to state planners concerned with providing
and financing overhead services to the affected area. However, they cannot be taken to measure net economic benefits either to the state or to
the nation. Thus it is now necessary to examine the relationship between
value added and national economic benefits.[11]

The value added by an industry or industrial sector is usually
broken down in national statistics into the following five categories:
employee compensation, net interest, capital consumption allowances,
indirect business taxes, and "profit-type" income.[12] What portion of each
of these types of income really represents net additions to the national
income?

Project-related employee compensation will constitute national benefits insofar as those employed directly or indirectly by the project have
stepped up from lower-paying, less productive jobs or have been drawn
from the long-term unemployed. In the present example, only guesses
can be made concerning the portion of employee compensation stemming
from one or the other of these conditions. We here postulate a lower
limit of 10 percent, representing stepped-up productivity under assumed
full employment. Haveman and Krutilla (1968, p. 72) make a "best estimate" of about 25 percent as the probability that a person hired by a
project will be taken from the ranks of the unemployed when the regional rate of unemployment is 10 percent. This leads us to take 35

---

[11] It is worth noting that total value added equals the value of all new deliveries
to final demand less any imports incorporated in the products.

[12] See the *Survey of Current Business*, U.S. Department of Commerce, Office of
Business Economics, the National Income Issue, issued annually in July. The data used
here were taken from table 1.22, Gross Product in Current Dollars by Industry, for the
year 1964, found in the July, 1968 issue. "Profit-type" income includes corporate (before
tax) profits, proprietor and rental incomes.

percent as an upper bound to the national benefits component of employee compensation.

Capital consumption allowance, net interest, and "profit-type" income represent the gross returns to project-related capital investment including land. What part of this gross return represents true national benefits can be seen more clearly if one considers the economic (as opposed to accounting) breakdown:

Gross return to capital including land = capital
consumption allowance + net return forgone in
best alternative investment + excess of return
in project-related uses over best alternative.

This breakdown makes it clear that in an expanding area, where the capital invested in the project could have been invested elsewhere, the only component of gross returns to capital and land that constitutes a net addition to the national income is the excess of return in project-related uses over returns in alternative investments (i.e., profit in the true economic sense), and the increase in land rents. How much of the overall category "profit-type income" is represented by land rents and premium returns on capital is not known. We pick 25 percent as the minimum part

Table 23. Composition of Value Added by Industry, United States, 1964

percent of total

	Employee compensation	Net interest	Capital consumption allowances	Indirect business taxes	Profit-type income
All industries	58	3	9	10	21
Agriculture, forestry, fisheries	16	8	21	7	49
Mining	35	–	23	8	35
Contract construction	74	1	5	3	18
Manufacturing					
Nondurable	61	–	8	14	16
Durable	71	–	7	5	17
Transport	68	2	14	8	9
Communications	44	3	13	13	27
Electricity, gas, and sanitary services	32	8	19	11	29
Trade	56	–	5	18	20
Finance, insurance, and real estate	20	10	16	18	35
Services	61	1	8	3	27
Government	98	–	–	–	2

Note: Percentages were computed by the authors from data in Survey of Current Business, National Income Issue, vol. 48, no. 7 (July 1968), table 1.22, p. 27. Totals may not equal 100 because of rounding.

Table 24. *Breakdown of Project-Related Value Added into Possible National Benefit Components, Oregon, Cases I and II*

Sector	Value added	Employee compensation			Profit-type income		
		Total	National benefits		Total	National benefits	
			Min. (10%)	Max. (35%)		Min. (25%)	Max. (50%)
				Case I			
Livestock and products	$ 19.2	$ 3.1	$ 0.3	$ 1.1	$ 9.4	$ 2.4	$ 4.7
Agriculture, n.e.c.	34.0	5.4	0.5	1.9	16.7	4.2	8.3
Food and kindred products	192.9	30.9	3.1	10.8	94.5	23.6	47.3
Paper and allied products	10.3	6.3	0.6	2.2	1.7	0.4	0.8
Transportation	24.8	16.9	1.7	5.9	2.2	0.6	1.1
Wholesale and retail trade	32.1	18.0	1.8	6.3	6.4	1.6	3.2
Finance, insurance, and real estate	24.4	4.9	0.5	1.7	8.5	2.1	4.3
All others	97.9	56.8	5.7	19.9	20.6	5.1	10.3
Total	$435.6		$14.2	$49.8		$40.0	$80.0
				Case II			
Livestock and products	$ 4.4	$ 0.7	$ 0.1	$ 0.2	$ 2.2	$ 0.5	$ 1.1
Agriculture, n.e.c.	67.0	10.7	1.1	3.8	32.8	8.2	16.4
Maintenance and repair construction	2.3	1.7	0.2	0.6	1.1	0.3	0.6
Nonmetal manufacturing	7.3	5.2	0.5	1.8	1.2	0.3	0.6
Wholesale and retail trade	5.9	3.3	0.3	1.2	1.2	0.3	0.6
Finance, insurance, and real estate	10.5	2.1	0.2	0.7	3.7	0.9	1.8
Business services	3.1	1.9	0.2	0.7	0.8	0.2	0.4
All others	12.0	7.0	0.7	2.4	2.5	0.6	1.3
Total	$112.5		$3.3	$11.4		$11.4	$22.7

Source: Tables 21 and 22.

Note: The correspondence between the sectors of the Oregon input-output model above and the gross sectors for which value-added breakdowns are available from the Office of Business Economics are as follows: livestock, agriculture, food and kindred products = agriculture, forestry and fisheries; paper and allied products = nondurable manufacturing; transportation = transportation, general; wholesale and retail trade, and finance, insurance, and real estate correspond to the same sectors; maintenance and repair construction correspond to contract construction; and nonmetal manufacturing corresponds to manufacturing (durable).

Table 25. *Summary of Oregon Project Benefits*

Annual project benefits	Case I		Case II	
	Min.	Max.	Min.	Max.
Total (million dollars)	54	130	15	34
Per acre-foot (dollars)	27	65	7	17

of "profit-type" incomes that constitutes an addition to national income and 50 percent as the maximum portion.[13]

Indirect business taxes, which constitute a set of sales and manufacturing taxes assessed against businesses, may be taken to represent the costs of services rendered by various government units and thus they give rise to no net benefits.

Table 23 shows the percentage composition of value added for gross *national* industry categories. There is no assurance that the value-added composition of an industry in a particular region will be the same as the national average.

The possible national benefits components of the project-related value added are listed in table 24. Detail is shown for the seven sectors that have the greatest additions to value added. The remaining twenty-two sectors are lumped in an "all other" category to which the "all industry" percentage breakdown (row 1, table 23) was applied.

Comparison of the annual project benefits as summarized in table 25 points up the critical nature of the unemployment assumption as exhibited in the variation between the minimum and maximum national benefit figures, and the critical importance of the assumption regarding forward linkages between agriculture and other sectors which is exhibited in the variation from case I to case II.

Under the conditions most favorable to the project, total benefits go as high as $65 per acre-foot. The coincidence of conditions of strong forward linkage in an expanding region with sustained high unemployment of capacity and labor (case I, maximum) is highly unlikely. It seems much more plausible that total benefits should fall in the lower end of the case I range or the upper end of the case II range.

POTENTIAL REGIONAL IMPACTS AND NATIONAL BENEFITS GENERATED IN
RESCUE OPERATIONS: SOUTHERN CALIFORNIA

The Colorado River water budget presented earlier allowed Southern California a total rate of withdrawal of 5.2 million acre-feet (maf)

[13] Haveman and Krutilla (1968, p. 73) indicate that if 10 percent of industrial capacity is idle, a maximum estimate of the probability that capacity needed to produce project-related inputs will be drawn from the unutilized pool is 25 percent.

per year. Assuming no augmentation of Lower Basin supplies, full use of Arizona's allotment, and ultimate Upper Basin use of 4.0 maf, Southern California would have to reduce its Colorado River withdrawals by 0.8 maf per year to meet the allocation decreed by the Supreme Court in 1964.[14] The impact postulated for Southern California is thus not one of opening up new territory for irrigated agriculture, but one of preventing the phasing out of some existing irrigated agriculture. The benefits will be a function not only of the degree of forward linkage of agriculture to other sectors but of the extent and direction of agricultural input immobilities.

The Assumed Cropping Pattern

In the cases that follow, it is assumed that diversions from the Colorado will be diminished by 0.8 maf/year and that farmers will adjust by cutting back on the crops with the lowest net value at the farm.

The Imperial Valley and Riverside County farmers receive irrigation water from the Colorado River through the Bureau of Reclamation's All-American Canal. In 1964, approximately 3.1 maf were diverted from the Colorado and 2.7 maf were delivered to farm headgates. The distribution of this water among principal crops (in terms of water diverted) is estimated in table 26, and estimates of the net value of the crops per acre-foot of water are shown in table 27. The figures in table 26 represent average values for each crop, and it may be that the net values at the margin differ in order from these. However, the values in table 27 are taken as an indication of which crops would likely be dropped in the face of water shortage. Forage crops, with an average net value of $16 per acre-foot of water, would probably be dropped first, and some grains might be phased out.

The water requirements of table 26 are stated in terms of amounts diverted. A reduction of 0.8 maf would thus imply a reduction of 127,000 acres from forage or more than the entire acreage of grains. Naturally the actual pattern of cutbacks would depend on how the total cut was distributed among farms. Some schemes might require a reduction in high-value crops.

A factor that should be taken into account at this point is the likelihood that irrigation efficiency would be increased in the face of reduced water availability. The efficiency of delivery from diversion point to farm

---

[14] The Supreme Court's decision helped to settle a long-standing conflict among the Lower Basin States over the use of water allocated to the Lower Basin by the Colorado River Compact of 1922.

Table 26. *Estimated Water Use by Principal Crops in Imperial and Riverside Counties*

Crop	1964 harvested acreage[a]	Water diverted per acre per year[b]	Estimated total water use
	1,000 acres	*acre-feet*	*1,000 acre-feet*
Forage crops	250	6.3	1,575
Grains	151	3.3	498
Sugarbeets	65	4.0	260
Cotton	77	6.3	485
Vegetables	91	3.4	309
Fruits	67	3.8	255
Total	701		3,382

[a] Data from: U.S. Department of Commerce, *Census of Agriculture, 1964*, vol. 1, part 48 (California); U.S. Department of the Interior, *Federal Reclamation Projects Statistical Appendix to Crop Report and Related Data, 1964, 1965* and *1966;* and Charles V. Moore and Trimble R. Hedges (1963), p. 79.

[b] Water use measured at the farm headgate was taken from Douglas M. Jones (1967) for crops in Yuma County, Arizona, where soil types and climate are similar to those of the Imperial Valley. Jones's rates of application were divided by the estimated efficiency of diverting from the Colorado River via the All-American Canal and delivering to the farms. In 1964, efficiency was estimated at 2.7 maf/3.1 maf.

Table 27. *Estimated Short-Term Net Value of Agricultural Water Use by Selected Crops in Imperial and Riverside Counties*

Crop	Gross crop value per acre	Variable cost per acre	Net value per acre	Net value per acre-foot of water used
Forage crops	$ 150	$ 50	$100	$ 16
Grains	85	25	60	18
Cotton	400	160	240	38
Sugar beets	300	125	175	44
Vegetables	1,000	600	400	118
Fruits	700	200	500	132

Sources: See table 26, footnotes.

headgate in 1964 appears to have been about 87 percent (2.7 maf/3.1 maf), and farm efficiency may be considerably lower than that, perhaps around 65 percent.[15] If the cost of saving water by such means as lining canals, grading fields, etc., is less than the loss of net income from acreage reduction, these opportunities would be exploited first and the decline in acreage would be less.[16] Since no estimates are available of the schedule of

[15] Blaney and Criddle (1962) show average farm efficiencies (water beneficially deposited in the root zone divided by water taken in at farm headgate) for twelve large reclamation projects to be 65 percent.

[16] It might be noted that a 10 percent increase in farm efficiency implies 270,000 acre-feet more available for irrigation. The required acreage reduction would be cut by one-third or over 42,333 acres.

costs versus amounts that might be saved, no further consideration is given to this possibility.

Five cases are discussed below. Cases I, II, and III refer to situations where the acreage in forage crops is cut back, with decreasing numbers of important forward linkages. Cases IV and V assume that the water loss is split between forage and grain crops; case IV introduces some new forward linkages from grain; and case V assumes no forward linkages. The analyses of these cases is made more interesting by the greater detail of the available Southern California input-output table.[17]

Case I: Reduction in forage with two-stage forward linkages. A withdrawal of 800,000 acre-feet of water from forage production (which uses 6.3 acre-feet per acre) is assumed to result in the withdrawal of 127,000 acres with a gross value of output of $19 million per year ($150 per acre).

The input-output table for Southern California indicates that no forage goes directly to final demand and none to its own intermediate demand. All forage output is absorbed by the meat animals sector (50.5 percent) and by the farm dairy products sector (49.5 percent). For present purposes, we assume a 50-50 split of $9.5 million to each of these sectors. Each of these sectors has, in turn, its own linkages to final demand.

The meat animals sector uses $0.17 of input from forage per dollar of output. Assuming that local forage inputs will be the bottleneck to the expansion of meat animal output, the induced contraction of meat animal output will be $55.9 million ($9.5 million/0.17). As the meat animals sector contracts, its supplies to "meat and poultry processing" shrink, causing a multiple contraction of approximately $284.2 million in "meat and poultry processing" deliveries to final demand.[18]

The farm dairy products sector uses approximately $0.13 of forage per dollar of output. This implies a decrease in farm dairy output of $73.1 million stemming from the reduced forage input. Allowing for a 3 percent reduction in its own intermediate use, "farm dairy products" reduces its deliveries to the "dairy products" sector by $70.9 million. Assuming that there is no substitute for Southern California farm dairy output, the resultant decrease in the value of the output of the dairy products sectors is $186.6 million ($70.9/0.38), all of which goes to final demand.

[17] Carter and Ireri (1967).
[18] $55.9 million/0.19 = $294.2 million. Deducting an intermediate use in "meat and poultry processing" of $10 million ($294.2 × 0.034) leaves deliveries to final demand of $284.2. The coefficient 0.19 was recomputed for this sector to reflect the fact that the only input being curtailed was beef and not poultry.

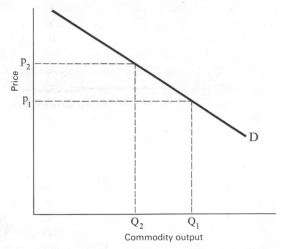

Figure 7. Upward price adjustment from water withdrawal.

Thus, in our first round of calculations, the total *decreases* in deliveries to final demand amount to:

	million dollars
Meat and poultry processing	284.2
Dairy products	186.6

When these decrements in deliveries to final demand are inserted in the input-output model, the total implied reduction in forage output is $19.2 million, slightly more than initially assumed but not enough to warrant a second round of computation. Using these two decrements of deliveries to final demand, it is possible to determine the related decreases in gross output and in value added.[19]

Price changes will be in an *upward* direction in areas where agricultural output is being reduced (see figure 7). The analysis of this section has generated a decrement of value for each crop which is represented by $p_1 (Q_1 - Q_2)$ and which understates the loss of gross value. While measuring the loss of gross value by $p_2 (Q_1 - Q_2)$ results in an overstatement, this simple upward adjustment in price is used here. For those commodities whose markets have been assumed to be isolated from national competition—namely, meat animals, farm dairy, and forage crops— elasticity estimates of −0.75, −0.25, and −0.20 have been used, and

---

[19] These operations require only the input-output inverse $(I - A)^{-1}$ and the value added coefficients for each sector.

the estimated price increases are 12 percent, 30 percent, and 50 percent.[20] The resulting figures are given in parentheses in table 28.

Case II: Reduction in forage with one-stage forward linkages. As before, all forage goes to the "meat animals" and "farm dairy products" sectors, but in this case the outputs are assumed to be exported rather than processed locally. As before, the decreases in outputs are $55.9 and $70.9 million respectively, but in this case these are decreases in deliveries to final (export) demand.[21] Applying the input-output inverse table and the value-added ratios yields the results shown in table 28. In this case, only the forage sector is presumed to be isolated from national markets, so the appropriate price increase (approximately 50 percent) has been made for that sector.

Case III: Reduction in forage with no forward linkages. In this case, it is assumed that California forage crops are in competition with forage from other areas to the extent that phasing out local forage causes no reduction in the output of California industries that have been using local forage as input. Thus, a reduction in forage production affects the rest of the local economy only through those sectors which supply inputs to the forage sector itself. There will be no significant price adjustment in this case because of the assumption of competition in large markets. These results are also shown in table 28.

Case IV: Reduction in forage and grain outputs with two-stage forward linkages. As in case I, it is assumed that there are no substitutes for either the major Southern California forage and grain inputs or for the outputs of the sectors directly supplied by them (meat animals, farm dairy products, food and feed grains, forage crops, and grain mill products). The initial computations assume that 400,000 acre-feet of water will be withdrawn from forage production (equivalent to 63,500 acres, or a gross value of $9.5 million) and that 400,000 acre-feet will be withdrawn from grain production (equivalent to 121,200 acres, or a gross value of $10.3 million). Once the indirect uses of these commodities are taken into account, it may not be possible to maintain the same allotments and still reduce water use by precisely the desired 800,000 acre-feet.

A reduction in forage output of $4.75 million is allocated to the meat animals industry, leading to a reduction of $27.9 million in meat animal production ($4.75 million/0.17). This meat animal output is, in

---

[20] The relevant total outputs in the absence of the project are taken to be $600 million, $1 billion, and $200 million.

[21] Again, no second-round computations seem warranted.

Table 28. *Project-Related Gross Output and Value Added Forgone, Southern California, Cases I to V*

millions

Sector	Case I Gross output	Case I Value added	Case II Gross output	Case II Value added	Case III Gross output	Case III Value added	Case IV Gross output	Case IV Value added	Case V Gross output	Case V Value added
Meat animals and products	$ 54.1 (61.0)	$ 5.2 (12.1)	$ 55.9	$ 5.6	$ —	$ —	$ 37.9 (41.1)	$ 3.6 (6.8)	$ —	$ —
Poultry and eggs	14.4	0.5	—	—	—	—	10.1	0.4	—	—
Farm dairy products	76.9 (100.0)	26.3 (49.4)	73.1	24.9	—	—	59.2 (73.4)	20.2 (34.4)	—	—
Food and feed grains	4.6	2.3	3.9	2.0	—	—	5.0a (5.5)	2.5 (3.0)	10.4	5.2
Cotton	—	—	—	—	—	—	—	—	—	—
Vegetables	—	—	—	—	—	—	—	—	—	—
Fruit (excluding citrus) and nuts	—	—	—	—	—	—	0.1	0.1	—	—
Citrus	—	—	—	—	—	—	—	—	—	—
Forage	19.2 (28.8)	14.2 (23.8)	19.0 (28.5)	14.1 (23.6)	19.0	14.1	14.2a (19.2)	10.4 (15.4)	9.5	7.0
Miscellaneous agriculture	2.5	2.0	2.0	1.6	0.8	0.6	2.0	1.6	0.9	0.7
Grain mill products	15.0	6.2	11.1	4.6	—	—	34.2 (35.9)	14.0 (15.7)	—	—
Meat and poultry processing	294.2	41.2	0.1	—	—	—	206.3	28.7	—	—
Dairy products	200.0	28.0	—	—	—	—	153.8	21.7	—	—
Canning, preserving, freezing	—	—	—	—	—	—	—	—	—	—
Misc. agricultural processing	11.9	4.6	0.6	0.2	—	—	10.2	3.9	—	—
Chemicals and fertilizers	9.9	3.8	1.8	0.7	0.7	0.3	8.4	3.2	1.0	0.4
Petroleum	7.1	2.1	2.0	0.6	0.9	0.3	5.6	1.7	1.4	0.4
Fabricated metals and machinery	11.8	4.7	4.8	1.9	1.3	0.5	9.3	3.8	1.9	0.8
Aircraft and parts	3.4	2.1	0.5	0.3	0.1	—	2.5	1.6	0.1	—
Primary metals	2.1	0.8	0.7	0.3	0.2	0.1	1.7	0.6	0.3	0.1
Other manufacturing	18.2	8.0	2.5	1.1	0.3	0.1	15.0	6.7	0.5	0.2
Mining	1.1	0.7	0.2	0.1	—	—	0.9	0.6	0.1	—
Utilities	6.8	2.9	1.7	0.7	0.2	0.1	5.2	2.2	0.2	0.1
Selected services	14.9	6.7	1.4	0.6	0.2	0.1	10.9	4.9	0.3	0.1
Trade and transportation	53.3	37.8	11.2	8.0	0.7	0.5	41.1	29.3	1.1	0.8
Unallocated	52.9	33.9	9.6	6.1	1.5	1.0	40.1	25.8	2.3	1.5
Totals	$874.3 (913.9)	$234.0 (273.6)	$202.1 (211.6)	$ 73.4 (83.3)	$ 25.9	$ 17.7	$673.7 (698.3)	$187.5 (212.1)	$ 30.0	$ 17.3

Note: Figures in parentheses have been corrected for price changes.
a Note difference from original acreage cut.

turn, withdrawn from the meat and poultry processing sector whose output must fall a total of $146.8 million ($27.9 million/0.19). After a reduction in own-sector intermediate use of $5.0 million, the reduction in
deliveries to final demand by the meat and poultry processing sector is
$141.8 million. In a similar manner, the reduction of $4.75 million in
forage inputs into the farm dairy sector leads to a reduction in deliveries
to final demand by the dairy products sector of $93.2 million.

The grain phase out of $10.3 million is distributed among four
sectors: meat animals, 17 percent, $1.75 million; farm dairy products,
11 percent, $1.13 million; poultry and eggs, 17 percent, $1.75 million;
and grain mill products, 55 percent, $5.7 million.

The consequent reduction in meat animals output might be con-
strued to lead to a reduction in deliveries to final demand by the meat
and poultry processing sector of $272.7 million if a purely mechanical
analysis of the sequence of impacts were followed: (1) a reduction of
$1.75 million in grain inputs into the meat animals sector leads to a
reduction in that sector's output of $53.4 million ($1.75 million/0.03),
which in turn reduces the output of the meat and poultry processing
sector by $272.7 million ($53.4 million/0.19). The first step of this *assumed*
linkage is too tenuous, however, to appear realistic. The extremely small
input of Southern California grains into the meat animals sector technically creates a large multiplier effect, but it also means that, because of
its relative unimportance, substitutes can be found. Thus, the only production loss is assumed to be the $1.75 million of grain output.

The reduction in grain inputs to the farm dairy sector leads to an
ultimate reduction in dairy product deliveries to final demand of $22.1
million ($1.13 million/0.13 = $8.4 million; $8.4 million/0.38 = $22.1
million).

The reduction of $1.75 million in grain inputs into the poultry and
egg sector technically could lead to a reduction in poultry and egg
deliveries to final demand of $41.3 million and a reduction of $272.6
million in meat and poultry deliveries to final demand. Again, however,
the input coefficients are so small as to make such a large impact entirely
implausible, so the only production loss was assumed to be the grain
output of $1.75 million.

The reduction of grain inputs of $5.7 million to the grain mill
products sector results in a reduction in grain mill products of $81.8 mil-
lion ($5.7 million/0.07), which not only seems somewhat implausible
because of the small technical coefficient but is difficult to trace because
the grain mill products output is, in turn, spread over four sectors. The
$81.8 million reduction in grain mill products would be divided roughly
8 percent to meat animals, 8 percent to farm dairy, 16 percent to miscellaneous agricultural processing, and 68 percent to final demand. Since

this case presumably represents the maximum impact, these effects are traced through to the following additional decrements of deliveries to final demand: meat and poultry processing, $331.8 million; dairy products, $226.3 million; grain mill products, $55.0 million.

The total of all decrements in deliveries to final demand as estimated in this first round of case IV is summarized below:

	million dollars
Meat and poultry processing	473.6
Dairy products	341.6
Grain mill products	55.0

When these decrements in deliveries to final demand are "run through" the input-output model to determine the total decrements (direct and indirect) to gross outputs of all sectors of the regional economy, the implied decrements in outputs for forage crops and grains are substantially larger than those originally specified: $33.9 million versus $9.5 million for forage and $11.9 million versus $10.3 million for grains. The total decrease in water use in these two sectors is 1.9 million acre-feet as opposed to the originally specified 0.8 million acre-feet. Since the objective is to measure the impact of withdrawing 0.8 million acre-feet of water and not to follow a particular program of crop reduction, we take the factor of overstatement of water use (0.8 maf/1.9 maf = 0.42) as the factor by which the above decrements to final demand must be diminished. This adjustment results in the following:

	million dollars
Meat and poultry processing	199.0
Dairy products	341.6
Grain mill products	55.0

When these are run through the input-output table, the decreases in sector gross outputs and in value added shown in table 28 are generated.

Price corrections were computed for those sectors which were assumed to be largely isolated from the competition of national markets: meat animals, farm dairy, food and feed grains, forage crops, and grain mill products. The results of these calculations are shown in parentheses in table 28. As in case I, the total impact is seen to be quite large as a result of the strong forward linkages assumed (absence of competitive inputs or alternative sources of supply).

Case V: Reduction in forage and grain outputs with no forward linkages. As in case III, it is assumed that, when local supplies of agricultural inputs fail because of water withdrawal, other sources of supply will permit the processing (forward-linked) industries to continue existing levels of production. This assumption seems plausible when the Southern California inputs are relatively unimportant, but it may also hold when those inputs are important because substitute commodities from nearby areas are available. The agricultural production patterns of adjacent areas, western Arizona and the Central Valley of California, are similar to the pattern in Southern California.

In this case, the decreases in forage and grain outputs will affect only those sectors directly or indirectly supplying inputs to forage and grain production. Again, the results are shown in table 28. No price adjustments are made because of the assumption of competition within large markets.

Summary and Interpretation of the Southern California
Results in Terms of National Benefits

Five illustrative cases have now been calculated to show the dependence of the impacts of a water withdrawal on the strength of forward linkages from agriculture to other sectors. This is mostly dependent upon the availability of substitutes for locally provided inputs. The vast differences among the cases were summarized in table 28. It is seen that cases I and IV and cases III and V are similar in result since similar forward linkages from agriculture were postulated.

We now must ask what the differing implications of these cases would be from a national benefits point of view. As in the Oregon analysis, the problem is to determine what part of the project-related value added constitutes a national benefit. Since the importation of water to Southern California represents a "rescue operation," we must determine what part of the value added would accrue to immobile factors of production and what their periods of immobility might be in the absence of the importation project.

The losses of income that would be averted by importation and that are countable as national benefits may be broken down into short-term and long-term income losses. In the short term, some labor will remain immobile and unemployed, as will certain types of capital equipment. As time passes, less and less labor will remain unemployed, and capital goods will be sold to other sectors of the economy or will deteriorate and become useless. Finally, the only remaining (and permanent) loss of income will be the rent to land and its permanent improvements as the land reverts to less productive uses or is abandoned (the latter is assumed here).

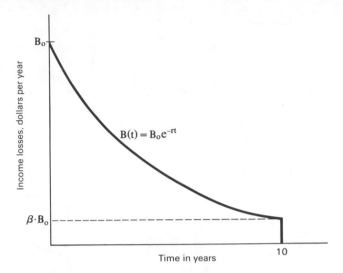

Figure 8. Assumed pattern of income losses to labor left unemployed by phase out of agricultural acreage.

Value added for cases I-V has been broken down into returns to labor and returns to capital as closely as available data will permit (see table 29). Returns to labor for a given sector are assumed to be determined by the percentage shown in table 23 for the relevant industry (e.g., for "meat animals and products" see "agriculture, forestry, and fisheries" in table 23). Returns to capital are taken to consist of interest, capital consumption allowances, and profit-type incomes (including land rent) as shown in table 23.[22] For each case, the five sectors experiencing the greatest impacts were treated separately, while all other sectors were treated as an aggregate having a breakdown of value added as shown in the "all industries" column of table 23. Employee compensation was determined on a sector-by-sector basis, as were the returns to capital.

The first question addressed was, "What might be the pattern of labor immobility in a particular sector (e.g., farm dairy products)?" No empirical evidence was gathered regarding potential immobilies, but three plausible alternative patterns of the extent and duration of immobilies of labor were postulated so that their implications might be investigated. The general pattern is shown in figure 8. An exponential decrease in the

[22] Indirect business taxes, the remaining category from table 23, are taken to represent the costs of services of government at all levels. Since there is no guarantee that the level of such services will be affected by the phasing out of acreage, this item is not considered as a possible source of income losses.

Table 29. *National Benefits Analysis for Southern California, Cases I-V*

Sector	Employee compensation						Returns to capital and land						
			Present value of lost labor income when				Total				Present values		
	Total value added^a	Percent of value added^b	Total	β = 20% (4.18)^c	β = 10% (3.35)^c	β = 5% (2.78)^c	Percent of value added^d	B_o	Rent as percent of value added^e	α	T_m = 5	T_m = 10	T_m = 15
	millions		. . . . . *millions*					*millions*			. . . . . *millions*		
Case I													
Meat animals and products	$ 12.1	16%	$ 1.9				78%	$ 6.6	30%	0.38	$ 69	$ 81	$ 91
Farm dairy products	49.4	16	7.9				78	40.9	30	.38	425	503	564
Meat and poultry proc.	41.2	61	25.1				24	9.9	10	.42	109	127	140
Dairy products	28.0	61	17.1				24	6.7	10	.42	74	86	94
Trade and transportation	37.8	68	25.7				25	9.1	10	.42	100	116	128
Other sectors	107.8	58	62.5				33	35.6	10	.30	331	406	459
Totals	273.6		140.2	$585.6	$469.3	$389.5					1,108	1,319	1,476
Case II													
Meat animals and products	5.6	16	0.9				78	4.4	30	.38	46	54	61
Farm dairy products	24.9	16	4.0				78	19.4	30	.38	202	239	268
Forage	23.6	16	3.8				78	20.7	30	.38	215	255	286
Grain mill products	4.6	61	2.8				24	1.1	10	.42	12	14	16
Trade and transportation	8.0	68	5.4				25	1.9	10	.42	21	24	27
Other sectors	16.6	58	9.6				33	5.5	10	.30	51	63	71
Totals	83.3		26.5	112.4	90.1	74.8					547	649	729
Case III													
Forage	14.1	16	2.3				78	11.0	30	.38	114	135	152
Misc. agriculture	0.6	16	0.1				78	0.5	30	.38	5	6	7
Fab. metals and machinery	0.5	71	0.4				24	0.1	10	.42	1	1	1
Trade and transportation	0.5	68	0.3				25	0.1	10	.42	1	1	1
Chemicals and fertilizer	0.3	61	0.2				24	0.1	10	.42	1	1	1
Other sectors	1.7	58	1.0				33	0.6	10	.30	6	7	8
Totals	17.7		4.3	18.0	14.4	12.0					128	151	170

Case IV

Farm dairy	34.4	16	5.5			78	27.8	30	.38	289	342	384
Forage	15.4	16	2.5			78	13.3	30	.38	138	164	184
Meat and poultry proc.	28.7	61	17.5			24	6.9	10	.42	76	88	97
Dairy products	21.7	61	13.2			24	5.2	10	.42	57	67	73
Trade and transportation	29.3	68	19.9			25	7.0	10	.42	77	90	99
Other sectors	81.0	58	47.0			33	26.7	10	.30	248	304	344
Totals	212.1		105.6	443.1	355.1		294.7			885	1,055	1,181

Case V

Food and feed grains	5.2	16	0.8			78	4.1	30	.38	43	50	57
Forage	7.0	16	1.1			78	5.5	30	.38	57	68	76
Misc. agriculture	0.7	16	0.1			78	0.5	30	.38	5	6	7
Fab. metal and machinery	0.8	71	0.6			24	0.2	10	.42	2	3	3
Trade and transportation	0.8	68	0.5			25	0.2	10	.42	2	3	3
Other sectors	2.8	58	1.6			33	0.9	10	.30	8	10	12
Totals	17.3		4.7	19.6	15.7		13.1			117	140	158

a Figures from table 28.

b Percentages from table 23.

c β = % of initial labor force still unemployed at end of 10 years. The figures in parentheses represent the present value of all wage and salary incomes lost over a ten-year period per dollar of wage and salary income at the time of project phase out.

d Sum of percentages for interest, capital consumption allowances, and profit-type income from table 23.

e Assumed values.

B_0 = initial returns to capital and land.

α = (returns to land) ÷ (returns to capital and land).

T_m is the number of years it takes after the project is phased out for one-half of the mobile capital resources to have moved to alternative uses.

incomes accruing to immobile labor was assumed, the alternative patterns being characterized by the percentage of the labor still unemployed at the end of 10 years: 20 percent, 10 percent, and 5 percent, corresponding to alternative values of β in figure 8.[23] All immobilities are assumed to be overcome beyond 10 years. The total present value of this income loss is given by

$$PV_L = \int_0^{10} [B_o e^{-rt}] e^{-\rho t} dt = B_o \left[\frac{1 - e^{-10(\rho+r)}}{\rho + r} \right] \tag{4.9}$$

where r is the rate of decrease implied by the assumed value of β, and ρ is the discount rate.[24] The value of the last bracketed expression in (4.9) was computed for each of the three assumed immobility patterns with $\rho = 0.05$.

The next question was, "for a given sector, what might be the pattern of income losses to land and capital over time?" The answer would depend on the composition of the capital goods and the relative importance of rents to land and its improvements in the sector being analyzed. Again, an exponential decay pattern was assumed, starting at a level of the full payments to capital and land just prior to acreage reduction and decreasing to the level of returns to land and its permanent improvements—the loss to the land and its improvements being a permanent income loss. The pattern is illustrated in figure 9.

The pattern of capital and land income losses is characterized by *two* parameters: α, the percentage of total returns to capital and land represented by returns to land and its permanent improvements; and T_m, the time (in years after the acreage phase-out) by which 50 percent of the stock of capital goods (excluding permanent land improvements) has either been sold to other users or has deteriorated beyond economic usefulness. That is, after T_m years, half of the potentially mobile capital resources have moved or been discarded. T_α represents the time at which all potentially mobile capital has been moved or has completely deteriorated. Each sector has its own values of α and T_m. We have assumed that rents to land and its permanent improvements amount to 30 percent of value added in the agricultural sectors and 10 percent for others. We have undertaken alternative computations for three assumed values of T_m, namely 5, 10, and 15 years.

[23] Actually, it is the percentage of initial payments accruing to labor still unemployed.

[24] Equation (4.9) utilizes continuous discounting rather than discrete period-by-period discounting.

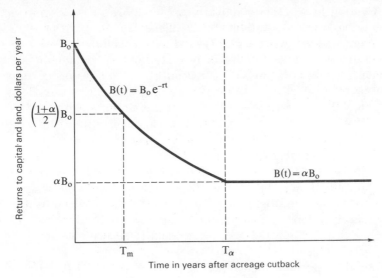

Figure 9. Assumed pattern of income losses to capital and land left unemployed by phase out of agricultural acreage.

The present value of these returns to capital and land for a particular sector is given by

$$PV_K = \int_0^{T_\alpha} [B_o e^{-rt}]e^{-\rho t}dt + \int_{T_\alpha}^{\infty} \alpha B_o e^{-\rho t}dt$$

$$= B_o\left[\frac{1 - e^{-T_\alpha(\rho+r)}}{\rho + r}\right] | B_o \frac{\alpha}{\rho} e^{-\rho T_\alpha}$$

(4.10)

Once we are given T_m and α, it is easy to infer the related values of r and T_α.[25]

Thus we have present value multipliers for labor payments as a function of the percentage remaining unemployed at the end of ten years [equation (4.9) and table 29] and, for each sector, present value multi-

[25] By definition of T_m,

$$B_o e^{-rT_m} = B_o\left(\frac{1 + \alpha}{2}\right).$$

This is solved for r. Then by definition of T_α,

$$B_o e^{-rT_\alpha} = \alpha B_o,$$

which is solved for T_α.

pliers for returns to capital and land as functions of α (proportion of returns to land) and T_m.[26] These multipliers, combined with the allocations of value added to labor and capital payments (table 29), permit the computation of the present value of incomes forgone by immobile factors after acreage is phased out as a function of: (1) the degree of forward linkage or the availability of substitutes as represented by cases I–V; (2) labor immobility characterized by percent remaining unemployed at the end of 10 years, β; and (3) the degree of capital mobility characterized by T_m. These present values and the corresponding equivalent annual values per acre-foot are given in table 30.[27]

It can be seen from table 28 that it is not the differing degrees of labor and capital immobility but the degree of forward linkage from agriculture to other sectors that is the crucial factor in determining the magnitude of national benefits from rescue operations. The assumption that no substitute inputs would be economically available must therefore be carefully analyzed.

The "multipliers" which result from small technical (input-output) coefficients are high. In case I, for example, the meat animals sector used only $0.17 of forage input per dollar of output. The withdrawal of $12.1 million worth of forage output thereby implied a reduction of $71.2 million in meat animal output. This reduction in meat animal output, in turn, was taken to imply a reduction of $358.8 million in meat and poultry processing because of a technical coefficient (adjusted) of $0.19. The final meat and poultry processing reduction was implied to be thirty times the direct reduction in forage output! While it seems quite likely that some marginal firms in the meat animals and meat and poultry processing sectors will be forced out of business by having to pay somewhat higher prices for imported forage substitutes and butcher animals, many firms will be able to survive such a transition, especially as their output prices rise in response to curtailed supply. A well-known economic theorem ("the importance of being unimportant") states that the smaller the proportion of total production costs represented by an input, the less elastic the demand for the input. Thus it is precisely when input-output coefficients are low and the implied output-to-input ratio is high that firms will seek substitutes even at higher prices.

Mobility of capital seems to rank next in importance, and mobility

[26] The labor payments multipliers are 4.18, 3.35, and 2.78 for β equal to 20, 10, and 5 percent. For values of α of 0.30, 0.38, and 0.42, the capital and land returns multipliers are as follows: for $T_m = 5$, 9.3, 10.4, and 11.0; for $T_m = 10$, 11.4, 12.3, and 12.8; and for $T_m = 15$, 12.9, 13.8, and 14.1.

[27] The annual equivalent value is simply $\rho PV_T = 0.05 PV_T$. When this is divided by 800,000 acre-feet, one gets a factor of 0.0625 for converting the present values of table 30 to annual values per acre-foot.

Table 30. Estimated Range of Present Values of National Benefits, Total and per Acre-Foot, for Southern California Replacement Water

	Reduction in forage						Reduction in grain and forage								
Present value	Case I: 2-stage forward linkage			Case II: 1-stage forward linkage			Case III: no forward linkage			Case IV: 2-stage forward linkage			Case V: 1-stage forward linkage		
	β=20%	β=10%	β=5%	β=20%	β=10%	β=5%	β=20%	β=10%	β=5%	β=20%	β=10%	β=5%	β=20%	β=10%	β=5%
							$T_m = 5$								
Total (million)*	$1,694	$1,577	$1,498	$659	$637	$622	$146	$142	$140	$1,328	$1,240	$1,180	$137	$133	$130
Per acre-foot†	106	99	94	41	40	39	9	9	9	83	76	74	9	8	8
							$T_m = 10$								
Total (million)*	1,905	1,788	1,709	761	739	724	169	165	163	1,498	1,410	1,350	160	156	153
Per acre-foot†	119	112	107	46	46	45	11	10	10	94	88	84	10	10	10
							$T_m = 15$								
Total (million)*	2,062	1,945	1,866	841	819	804	188	184	182	1,624	1,536	1,476	178	174	171
Per acre-foot†	129	122	117	53	51	50	12	12	11	102	96	92	11	11	11

* Present value of all incomes forgone.
† Present value reduced to an annual value per acre-foot.
T_m = the number of years required for half of the depreciable capital either to have moved to alternative activities or to have become economically useless.
β = the percent of labor still unemployed at the end of ten years from the date of phase out of agriculture.

of labor is last, although still of some significance. Naturally, these results depend upon the breakdown of value added that is used in the analysis and the particular trial values of α, β, and T_m, but there is no reason to expect the ordering of importance of the three factors to be different for other values of these parameters.

The one remaining factor that has not been taken into account is the temporal pattern of the acreage phase-out. We have posed it as a sudden phasing-out from the the immediate loss of 800,000 acre-feet per year, whereas the water would probably have to be given up only gradually. Improvements in water use efficiency through various forms of investment that are made profitable by the impending water shortage could mitigate the impacts. Then a gradual phasing-out would permit more effective utilization of capital goods until they are worn out, a more effective consolidation of abandoned acreages into larger farms, and a more leisurely period of search and retraining for displaced labor. Thus, the incomes likely to be lost in fact are smaller for each case than the figures of table 28.

The table does hold implications, nonetheless, for the evaluation of replacement water supplies and for further economic research. Much more must be learned about the degrees of forward linkage from agriculture, i.e., the conditions under which substitute supplies will and will not exist; the mobility of the capital resources of agriculture; and the mobility of labor.

*Comparisons of the Interbasin Transfer Benefits with Estimated
Income Losses Due to Decreased Acreage in Arizona*

The hypothetical transfer which has been the subject of this chapter is assumed to provide 3.5 million acre-feet annually for Arizona—the amount now being provided by groundwater mining. We did not analyze the potential benefits of this water ourselves; but the studies reported below indicate the likely benefits per acre-foot in Arizona and these figures serve as a basis of comparison for the figures we have derived for Southern California.

Stults (1966) estimated the phasing out of acreage in Pinal County which is likely to result from the falling water table, and predicted that the total water applied to crops in 2000 would be 415,000 acre-feet per year less than in 1966. He also estimated that returns over variable costs would fall by $5.4 million—a reduction in income at the farm of $13 per acre-foot of reduced water use. Clearly, the direct farm benefits of imported water cannot exceed this value.

Young and Martin (1967) indicate direct plus indirect personal income of $19 per acre-foot of water applied for forage crops and $17 for food and feed grains, computed on the basis of no forward linkages. Just what forward linkages may exist and what portions of these figures represent permanent and temporary income losses are not known. One could add about $10 to the above figures to cover the saving in (full) pumping costs to arrive at a measure of the benefits from replacement water that would occur during the period of labor and capital immobility under the assumption of few forward linkages. The study by Young and Martin also indicates that the Central Arizona Project (CAP) (intended to bring approximately 1.2 million acre-feet of water from the Colorado River into the Central Valley) would not find agricultural customers for its water at the proposed price of $10 per acre-foot and that if farmers were forced to shift to CAP water at that price to "preserve" existing groundwater sources, the rate of farm failure would be greater than with the present rate of decline of the water table. The study concludes that the only way to market the imported water would be to provide farms with water at prices below present pumping costs—an operation that would require a large and continuing subsidy.

Jacobs (1968) has calculated the direct and indirect income losses that are likely to occur as the city of Tucson diverts increasing amounts of water from agricultural to municipal uses. His schedule of costs includes losses of income to land, labor, and capital, as well as the pumping and delivery works costs. Deducting the pumping and delivery costs, increasing the interest rate from 3.5 percent (used by Jacobs) to 5 percent, and adding miscellaneous indirect costs of $5 per acre-foot yields a range of total incomes lost for the various available sources of water from $16 to $53 per acre-foot.

The above figures, considered in the light of the similarities between Arizona and Southern California, suggest that the more relevant of the cases considered for Southern California would be cases II, III, and V for which national benefits range from $8 to $53 per acre-foot.

Appendix to Chapter 4: The Measurement of Construction Period Impacts

This appendix illustrates a type of analysis that should be made of every large-scale investment program so that federal and state authorities and private industry will be aware of the specific demands that will be made on the economy during the construction period. Interbasin water transfer projects, because of their large total cost, the special composition of their labor and material inputs, and the likelihood that they will be located in isolated areas, particularly call for such analysis. Such analysis may also assist in rational project selection since the political attractiveness of so many projects is found in the prospects of a local boom during construction rather than in operating benefits.

Four types of economic impact are traced in this appendix for the reduced Western Water Project described in chapter 4: (1) on-site labor, materials, supplies, and equipment demands; (2) the gross outputs required of various industries to provide the on-site material and equipment requirements; (3) the distribution of total incomes generated by the construction of the project by labor skill category and other types of income; (4) breakdowns by region of items (2) and (3) above.

The ability to perform the analysis quickly is provided by an input-output-labor requirements model designed by Haveman and Krutilla (1968). Given the breakdown of project construction cost into (a) on-site labor requirements by occupation or skill, (b) expenditures for on-site materials, equipment, and supplies, and (c) contractors' profit, overhead, and other items not included in (a) and (b), the model permits the computation of items (1) to (4) above.

The structure of the model is as follows:

$$\text{Total project cost} = \text{on-site labor cost} + \text{materials cost} + \text{contractors' overhead and profit.} \tag{4.11}$$

$$g = (I - A)^{-1} \cdot f \tag{4.12}$$

where g is the vector of gross industry outputs (in value terms) required by the on-site bill of materials f, and $(I - A)^{-1}$ is matrix notation for the input-output inverse.

$$m = B \cdot g \tag{4.13}$$

where m is the vector of off-site labor man-year requirements by skill

96

category needed to produce gross industry outputs g, and B is the co-efficient matrix needed to make the translation.

$$i_1 = W \cdot m \qquad (4.14)$$

where i_1 is the vector of total off-site wage and salary payments by skill category and W is a diagonal matrix of annual income coefficients.

The model also permits the measurement of gross industry outputs and indirect wage and salary payments by region as a function of the region in which the project is undertaken through a sequence of steps

Table 31. *Regions of the Haveman-Krutilla Model*

Region	Designation	States
1	New England	Maine, Vermont, New Hampshire, Massachusetts, Connecticut, Rhode Island
2	Mid-Atlantic	New York, New Jersey, Pennsylvania
3	East North Central	Michigan, Ohio, Indiana, Illinois, Wisconsin
4	West North Central	Minnesota, South Dakota, North Dakota, Iowa, Missouri, Nebraska, Kansas
5	Southeast	Georgia, North Carolina, South Carolina, Florida, Alabama, Mississippi
6	Lower Atlantic	Virginia, West Virginia, Maryland, Delaware, District of Columbia
7	Tennessee-Kentucky	Tennessee, Kentucky
8	West South Central	Oklahoma, Louisiana, Arkansas, Texas
9	Mountain	Montana, Wyoming, Idaho, Colorado, New Mexico, Arizona, Nevada, Utah
10	West Coast	California, Oregon, Washington

Table 32. *Regional Distribution of Reduced Western Water Project Structures and Expenditures*

Region	Dams and reservoirs	Conduit (canal)	Pump-turbine plants, pumping plants, power plants
West Coast:			
Structures	11 reservoirs	265 miles	11 P-T plants 7 pump plants 3 power plants
Expenditures	$508 million	$204 million	$2,381 million
Mountain:			
Structures	0 reservoirs	900 miles	0 P-T plants 6 pump plants 9 power plants
Expenditures	$0	$683 million	$1,902 million

Table 33. *Regional Distribution of Reduced Western Water Project Expenditures in Terms of Haveman-Krutilla Project Types*

Project type	West Coast		Mountain		Total	
	Million dollars	Percent of total	Million dollars	Percent of total	Million dollars	Percent of total
Large earth dams	254	4	–	–	254	4
Medium concrete dams	356	6	341	6	697	12
Levees	102	2	342	6	444	8
Powerhouse construction	2,381	42	1,902	34	4,283	76
Totals	3,093	54	2,585	46	5,678	100

that classify industries as "local" (goods or services produced and sold only in the same region) or, to various degrees, "national" (goods sold in national markets regardless of the point of production). (For a definition of the ten regions, see table 31.)

Since the Western Water Project is located partially in the Mountain Region and partially in the West Coast Region, the first step was to determine the distribution of physical structures and costs between these regions. The results, based on project layout, are shown in table 32.

To apply the Haveman-Krutilla analysis one needs a detailed bill of goods and on-site labor for the portions of the project located in each region. Unfortunately, the design of the Western Water Project has not been carried out in sufficient detail to produce such breakdowns, i.e., the costing was carried out using rules of thumb that bypass detailed design work. To get around this difficulty the project expenditures were equated with project types for which Haveman and Krutilla had obtained detailed (82 industries, 154 labor-skill categories) breakdowns of the inputs required on-site. The assumed *equivalences* are stated below, the final bill of goods and labor inputs being expressed as a weighted average of the bills of goods of the Haveman-Krutilla projects per thousand dollars of project cost.

Pirkey expenditure class		Haveman-Krutilla project types
Dams and reservoirs	=	0.5 large earth fill dam / 0.5 medium concrete dam
Conduit (canal)	=	0.5 levee / 0.5 medium concrete dam
Pump-turbine / Pumping plant / Power plant	=	Powerhouse construction

Table 34. *Total Project Cost Allocated to Industry and Occupation per $1,000 Contract Cost and Total*

Sector and category	Per $1,000 contract cost	Project total
Production Sector		*thousands*
Agriculture, forestry, and fisheries	$ 0.30	$ 1,703
Mining, incl. crude petroleum	12.00	68,136
Nondurable goods manufacturing	19.15	108,734
Durable goods manufacturing:		
Lumber and wood products	10.10	57,348
Stone, clay, glass products	22.81	129,515
Primary metals	14.03	79,662
Fabricated metal products	44.40	252,103
Nonelectrical machinery (excl. construction)	198.74	1,128,446
Construction machinery	38.70	219,739
Electrical machinery	221.49	1,257,620
Transportation equipment	10.84	61,550
Miscellaneous	2.34	13,287
Total, durable goods	*563.45*	*3,199,269*
Transp. and warehousing	23.87	135,534
Wholesale and retail trade	87.72	498,074
Services	27.96	158,757
Total material, equipment, and supply cost	734.45	4,170,207
Occupational Category		
Professional, technical, managerial, clerical, and kindred	31.25	177,438
Craftsmen, foremen, and kindred:		
Carpenters	24.18	137,294
Cement finishers	2.13	12,094
Iron and metal workers	12.05	68,420
Construction equip. operators	19.40	110,153
Other building trades	27.05	153,590
Mechanics	3.51	19,930
Labor foremen	15.51	88,066
Others	19.80	112,424
Total, craftsmen and kindred	*123.63*	*701,971*
Operatives and kindred:		
Trucks and tractor drivers	10.40	59,051
Sailors and deckhands	1.41	8,006
Others	27.67	157,110
Total, operatives and kindred	*39.48*	*224,167*
Laborers	26.53	150,637
Total on-site labor	220.89	1,254,213
Total unallocated	44.66	253,579
Totals	$1,000.00	$5,678,000

These equivalences may well be far off the mark in terms of particular detailed industrial and labor inputs required, but the overall accuracy is likely to be greater because of the degree of aggregation used here to report industry outputs and labor requirements. The project equivalences permit a transformation of the regional project distribution of table 32 into a regional distribution of equivalent project types as shown in table 33.

The percentages in table 33 permit the results of the Haveman and Krutilla analysis to be translated into results for the reduced Western Water Project. The allocation of total project cost to purchased inputs and direct on-site labor is given in table 34.

Distribution of Impacts

Three things stand out in tables 33 and 34: the very large percentage of total project expenditure devoted to "power house construction" or "machinery" and "electrical machinery"; the rather small percentage of total expenditure on direct labor; the concentration of labor requirements in the professional and highly skilled categories.

Table 35. *Direct and Indirect Outputs Required to Meet Final On-Site Demands*

Production sector	Per $1,000 contract cost	Project total
		thousands
Agriculture, forestry, and fisheries	$ 11.83	$ 67,171
Mining (including petroleum)	49.32	280,039
Construction (maintenance)	10.63	60,357
Nondurable goods manufacturing	118.16	670,912
Durable goods manufacturing:		
Lumber and wood	19.88	112,879
Stone	37.85	214,912
Primary metals	167.08	948,680
Fabricated metals	78.77	447,256
Machinery (excl. C & E)	274.17	1,556,737
Const. machinery	50.55	287,023
Electrical machinery	274.27	1,557,305
Transportation equipment	41.00	232,798
Misc. manufacturing	11.68	66,319
Total, durable goods	*955.25*	*5,423,910*
Transportation and warehousing	63.98	363,278
Wholesale and retail	133.35	757,161
Services	193.46	1,098,466
Total gross output	$1,535.98	$8,721,294

Note: These figures are generated by running the figures of the upper half of table 34 through the national input-output model.

Table 36. Distribution of Gross Output Related to the Reduced Western Water Project, by Industry and Region

Industry	New England 1	Mid-Atlantic 2	East North Central 3	West North Central 4	South-east 5	Lower Atlantic 6	Kentucky-Tennessee 7	West South Central 8	Moun-tain 9	West Coast 10	All regions*
Agriculture, forestry, and fisheries	3.3	4.1	9.8	13.9	8.2	2.9	1.8	8.7	4.2	10.4	67.2
Mining (including petroleum)	0.9	19.6	21.0	25.4	7.3	14.1	7.0	61.0	82.4	41.0	280.0
Construction (maintenance)	2.3	9.0	13.0	2.1	1.5	1.4	0.6	2.5	12.6	17.3	60.4
Nondurable goods manufacturing	48.0	140.0	158.8	32.8	55.2	36.2	23.4	83.9	21.3	79.7	670.9
Durable goods manufacturing:											
Lumber and wood	4.2	6.2	10.4	3.3	11.8	3.6	2.7	6.1	7.7	56.8	112.9
Stone	9.9	42.3	52.0	15.6	15.0	11.1	6.0	13.7	11.3	40.8	214.9
Primary metals	52.6	272.2	346.9	28.5	31.2	55.0	8.5	30.4	73.4	67.2	948.7
Fabricated metals	34.8	97.5	157.4	20.7	14.8	11.1	9.8	15.2	8.8	85.4	447.3
Machinery (excl. C&E)	150.8	487.3	697.3	57.0	14.1	16.9	19.6	15.3	5.9	124.5	1,556.7
Const. machinery	3.2	21.8	143.1	19.7	4.3	3.2	1.9	46.8	11.7	34.9	287.0
Electrical machinery	126.1	443.3	613.3	74.9	32.5	30.5	11.7	13.8	10.5	235.9	1,557.3
Transportation equipment	9.4	32.4	126.9	10.9	8.5	9.1	1.9	6.8	1.2	28.3	232.8
Misc. manufacturing	9.9	29.2	14.4	3.4	1.7	0.6	0.7	1.1	0.9	5.6	66.3
Total durable goods	*400.9*	*1,432.1*	*2,161.7*	*233.9*	*137.0*	*141.0*	*16.7*	*149.3*	*131.5*	*679.4*	*5,423.9*
Transportation and warehousing	11.8	47.1	66.9	10.8	7.8	7.0	3.2	11.2	91.9	113.4	363.3
Wholesale and retail	16.7	58.5	86.0	11.2	7.9	7.3	3.6	9.4	243.3	328.3	757.2
Services	38.8	138.8	201.6	29.3	19.6	19.5	9.4	36.2	191.5	276.1	1,098.5
All industries	522.6	1,849.1	2,718.8	361.0	241.6	229.6	112.0	362.2	778.7	1,545.7	8,721.3
Percent of total	6.0	21.2	31.2	4.1	2.8	2.6	1.3	4.2	8.9	17.7	

* Totals may differ from those of table 35 because of rounding.

The direct and indirect (gross) outputs required to yield the final materials and equipment demands of the project are given in table 35. Again, the heavy concentration of demands on machinery and electrical machinery stand out. Heavy indirect demands are in evidence—contrast the materials *on-site* input of $734 per $1,000 of contract cost (table 19) with the total direct and indirect required output of $1,536 (table 35). The large indirect demands are felt primarily in nondurable goods, primary metals, transportation equipment, transport and warehousing, and

Table 37.   Total Direct and Indirect Labor Costs and Other Components of Value Added

Categories	Per $1,000 contract cost	Project total
		thousands
Professional, technical, and kindred	$ 78.09	$ 443,395
Managers, officials and proprietors	76.53	434,537
Clerical and kindred	67.95	385,820
Sales	13.87	78,754
Craftsmen, foremen, kindred:		
Carpenters	26.93	152,909
Cement finishers	2.16	12,264
Iron and metal workers	12.86	73,019
Construction equipment operators	19.34	109,813
Other building trades	33.68	191,235
Mechanics	12.74	72,338
Labor foremen	36.32	206,225
Other craftsmen	80.36	456,284
Total, craftsmen and kindred	*224.39*	*1,274,087*
Operatives and kindred workers:		
Truck and tractor drivers	23.23	131,900
Sailors and deckhands	1.68	9,539
Other operatives	130.66	741,887
Total, operatives and kindred	*155.57*	*883,326*
Service workers	9.86	55,985
Laborers, excl. farm	46.91	266,355
Farmers and farm workers	2.68	15,217
Total labor cost	675.85	3,837,476
Net interest	9.43	53,544
Depreciation	58.81	333,923
Indirect business taxes	60.64	344,314
Corporate profits	85.13	483,368
Proprietor and rental income	33.45	189,929
Net imports	26.91	152,795
Unallocated costs	49.78	282,651
Total cost	$1,000.00	$5,678,000

services, with the largest occurring in nondurable goods and primary metals.

Table 36 exhibits the likely distribution of industry gross outputs among the ten Haveman-Krutilla regions, although it has not been possible to establish, for purposes of comparison, the regional capacities of each industry in order to determine the present capabilities of meeting these demands.

The striking feature of table 36 is the concentration of project-related gross output in the Mid-Atlantic and East North Central regions, which together receive 52 percent of the gross output demands, while the Mountain and West Coast regions receive only 27 percent. Of course, the distribution of industrial capacity, an important factor in the Haveman-Krutilla regional model, may change in response to large projects of this type, and the project regions themselves would then produce a larger part of the total required input.

The final evidence on the likely construction period impact of a project like the reduced Western Water Project is presented in table 37 and represents the distribution of incomes (by type of income) generated directly and indirectly through input-output linkages.

Under the conditions prevailing in the early 1960s (from which the parameters for the Haveman-Krutilla model were estimated), the breakdown would be: wages and salaries (68 percent), interest (1 percent), depreciation and indirect business taxes (12 percent), corporate profits (9 percent), proprietor's and rental income (3 percent), and net imports and unallocated costs (7 percent). In terms of total labor requirements, one again observes a heavy concentration in the professional and highly skilled categories. The indirect demands were particularly high for "operatives and kindred workers," as well as being high for "managers, officials, and proprietors" and "clerical and kindred" who were not directly engaged on the project at all. The small demands on the unskilled categories again demonstrate that the project would be a skill-intensive undertaking.

Summary

In this appendix we have sought to supplement the long-term benefit analysis by estimating the construction period impacts of a reduced Western Water Project on the various industries, regions, and labor skill categories. While the figures used are not precise, it is felt that they constitute "ball-park" estimates and serve to illustrate a type of analysis that is feasible and desirable to carry out in advance of large expenditure programs.

The major findings could be summarized as follows: (1) there will certainly be a heavy concentration of gross industry demands in "machinery and electrical machinery"; (2) labor requirements will be concentrated in the professional and highly skilled categories; (3) indirect demands for manufactured inputs will have quite a different structure than on-site demands and will be particularly heavy for nondurable manufactures, primary metals, transportation and warehousing, and transport equipment; (4) there is likely to be a very heavy concentration of industrial demands in the East-Central industrial belt and surprisingly little in the construction regions themselves.

5

The Direct Costs of Interbasin Transfers and Their Alternatives

In this chapter we look at the costs associated with interbasin transfers in order to complete the picture of the net benefits that might be forthcoming from these projects. However, the demonstration of positive net benefits is not sufficient economic justification for the public undertaking of such projects. It is also necessary to find out whether or not the water-related alternatives to interbasin transfers would generate even higher net returns. For example, an interbasin transfer project might show benefits in excess of costs and a rate of return of 10 percent, but it would not be the economically-preferred project if an alternative—possibly a watershed management program for higher runoff right in the basin of use—could provide the same amount of water at a lower cost per acre-foot. The discussion of interbasin costs is therefore followed by information on the costs and potential yields of a variety of alternatives ranging from increased agricultural efficiency to precipitation modification schemes.

ESTIMATES OF PROJECTED INTERBASIN TRANSFER COSTS

Any interbasin transfer will have associated with it three classes of costs. These include not only the direct construction, operating, and maintenance costs but also the opportunity costs of both the land involved at the project site or sites and the water in the area of origin, and the external costs imposed on parties removed from the project site. External costs may stem from water quality degradation, or they may take the form of a loss of incomes to immobile resources in regions which "lose out" competitively to those receiving new water.

An extreme example of the relevance of the opportunity cost of water can be taken from the lower Colorado Basin. The construction, operating, and maintenance costs of the proposed Central Arizona Project are generally quoted at about $35 per acre-foot of water delivered at canal side. Because of the high degree of commitment of the Colorado River's waters at present, the diversion of 1.2 million acre-feet for this project would require cutbacks in water use elsewhere. It might mean a reduction in withdrawals by the Metropolitan Water District of California, or by the Imperial Valley Irrigation District which is served by the All-American Canal, or by other California users; or it might require calling a halt to further development in the Upper Basin, where the allotment of 7.5 million acre-feet per year has not been fully utilized. If California irrigators have to reduce water use, the established farm enterprises and the economies of related communities will be affected. If the irrigators try to offset the effects of reduced deliveries by increasing efficiency in application, the costs of lining canals, installing instrumented control systems, and so on, would represent a true opportunity cost. These opportunity costs are not shown in benefit-costs analyses of the Central Arizona Project, but they are true costs and should be included.

Generally, it has not been possible to determine what the opportunity costs of water exported from different regions actually are except for the values of hydroelectric power forgone. The methods of tracing forward and backward linkages of water-related activities exhibited in chapter 4 could be applied to the analysis of opportunity costs in the areas of origin if the forgone uses could be identified. This has not been done in this study.

With respect to land, all of the major western proposals for inter-basin diversions involve the inundation of valley land to create new channels and storage. Under present federal practice, if the lands transferred to this new use are federal lands, *no* opportunity costs would be counted in project costs unless the lands contained salable minerals or forest products. In some cases where reservoirs required land clearing that resulted in the permanent loss of timber growing areas, *net benefits* have been counted if the value of the cut timber exceeded the costs of cutting it! The full opportunity costs of land involved in the project must be counted as project costs. There are reasons to suspect that even the prices that would have to be paid in the market for the types of land involved would not reflect the wildlife and unique aesthetic values of these valley bottomlands.[1]

There may be externalities in the form of ecological impacts or side effects, both beneficial and detrimental, which should be counted in

[1] See Krutilla, 1968a and 1968b.

assessing project costs. For example, any diversion of water from the Columbia will likely speed the development of base-load thermal power in the Columbia Basin. This will be accompanied by increased use of hydropower for peaking, causing larger fluctuations in flows and creating problems for fish, recreation, navigation, and shoreline facilities.

Because of lack of information, the following estimates of interbasin transfer costs reflect only the traditional construction, operation, and maintenance costs, plus the opportunity costs of hydropower forgone. To facilitate comparing the costs of alternative proposals, acre-foot costs are recomputed where possible on the assumption of a 5 percent discount rate and a 50-year life. The discount rate is a minimum under current conditions, and the 50-year life can be defended on grounds of technological advance and general uncertainty beyond 50 years. A second 50-year period would make little difference in present values anyway. The present value of a payment of $1 per year at 5 percent is $18.26 over 50 years and only $19.85 over 100 years.

California

Los Angeles is constructing the Second Los Angeles Aqueduct to transport an additional 152,000 acre-feet of Inyo-Mono water to the San Fernando Valley area. Cost estimates range from $24 to $30 per acre-foot, depending upon whether or not it is found necessary to line the Owens Valley canal (Socha 1965). This development represents an expansion of a system, and only some of the components of the original system have to be expanded. Thus economies are available that would not be present in a completely new system.

The California State Water Project was planned to deliver 4.23 million acre-feet per year from Northern California to the San Joaquin Valley and the Southern Coastal Area. The total capital cost of presently authorized features, was originally estimated at $2.8 billion (*Engineering News Record,* 18 May 1967), which implies an average capital cost of about $35 per acre-foot, assuming a 5 percent interest rate and a 50-year life. The 2 million acre-feet scheduled for delivery to the Metropolitan Water District of Southern California will be more costly because of pumping over the Tehachapi Range. About $807 million of the original cost estimates was attributable to southern deliveries (Tehachapi Division, East Branch Division, and West Branch) and to enlarging the Feather River facilities, the Delta facilities, and the California aqueduct.[2]

[2] For cost figures on components of the system, see California Department of Water Resources, Bulletin No. 132-65. Also see Gardner M. Brown, Jr. (1964), especially appendix table 3A, p. 204.

The original estimates of total costs per acre-foot thus vary from about $18 for deliveries in the San Joaquin Valley to about $65 for water delivered to the Metropolitan Water District.[3,4] Recent informal reestimates indicate an increase of about 30 percent in these figures.

Western Interstate Proposals

The Pacific Southwest Water Plan was proposed by the U.S. Department of the Interior in August 1963 as a possible solution to water shortage in the Southwest (U.S. Department of the Interior, 1963). The plan, no longer under active consideration, called for the transmission from Northern California of 1.2 million acre-feet to Southern California and 1.2 million acre-feet to Lake Havasu on the Colorado. The average total cost of the water implied by the cost figures in the USDI report was about $44 per acre-foot, but substitution of a 5 percent interest rate and a 50-year life would increase this figure to $90.

Samuel B. Nelson, formerly General Manager and Chief Engineer of the Department of Water and Power, Los Angeles, presented an alternative to certain parts of the Southwest Water Plan, calling for the diversion of 2.4 million acre-feet from the Snake River close to Twin Falls, Idaho, into the Colorado at Lake Havasu (Nelson 1963). The water would be lifted 3,200 feet from an initial elevation of 3,000 feet and conveyed across the high plateau of eastern Nevada. A drop of 4,500 feet into Lake Mead would permit generation of approximately 10 percent more power than that consumed in pumping. The Colorado River Aqueduct of the Metropolitan Water District would be used to transport 1.2 million acre-feet to Southern California. Nelson's estimated average cost of the 2.4 million acre-feet is $32. The use of a 5 percent interest rate and a 50-year life increases this cost to $46 per acre-foot.

An enlarged Modified-Snake-Colorado Project was proposed by William G. Dunn (1965). This plan calls for an initial diversion of 5 million acre-feet per year from McNary Dam on the Columbia near Pasco, Washington, and an ultimate diversion of 15 million acre-feet. The water would be conveyed up the Snake River to Brownlee Reservoir (elevation 2,077 feet), pumped to an elevation of 5,150 feet, and carried

[3] California Department of Water Resources, Bulletin No. 132-65, table 4.4, p. 68.

[4] The earliest investigation of California diversion possibilities was reported on in the Interim Report on Reconnaissance of California Section, United Western Investigation, U.S. Department of the Interior, Bureau of Reclamation, 22 December 1950. The Northern California Diversion investigated therein was to deliver 6.7 million acre-feet per year, including 1.2 million acre-feet for replacement of Colorado River water. The average total cost was calculated to be $25 per acre-foot which would be about $50 at current cost levels.

by a conduit through eastern Oregon and western Nevada, 1,016 miles to Lake Mead. Branch aqueducts would carry water into Idaho, Oregon, and California. Dunn estimated the delivered cost at $38 per acre-foot of water; a 5 percent interest rate and a 50-year life would increase this cost to $54 per acre-foot.

Another proposed source of water for the Colorado is the Sierra-Cascade Project proposed by E. Frank Miller (ASCE 1967).[5] This proposal calls for an initial capacity of 7.5 million acre-feet and for increases in two stages—to 15 million and then to 30 million acre-feet. Water is to be pumped from Bonneville on the Columbia into Wickiup Reservoir, and then moved by aqueduct and pumping to storage in a 75-million-acre-feet reservoir in Warner Valley from which controlled releases would be made into Lake Mead. Miller assumed that 2-mill off-peak power would be available in the Columbia Basin for pumping 7.5 million acre-feet and that additional power would cost 4 mills. His calculations showed that power recovery between Warner Valley and Lake Mead would generate net benefits for this leg of the system of $10 per acre-foot released (overall power recovery of about 80 percent). According to Miller, total costs would average $9 per acre-foot for 7.5 million acre-feet, $15 per acre-foot for 15 million acre-feet, and $20 per acre-foot for 30 million acre-feet. The increase in incremental costs—$21 per acre-foot for the second 7.5 million acre-feet and $25 per acre-foot for the next 15 million acre-feet—appears to be caused by higher power costs offsetting the economies of scale in construction of later stages in a stepwise project. Lack of cost breakdown between capital and operating and maintenance costs precludes the adjustment of costs to a 5 percent interest rate and a 50-year life.

Colonel F. Z. Pirkey (1963) proposed the Western Water Project containing the initial diversion of 15 million acre-feet from the lower Columbia at The Dalles via an ascending series of twelve reservoirs up the Deschutes and Crooked rivers to an altitude of 4,600 feet. The Western Aqueduct portion of the project would carry the water through eastern Oregon, northern California, and western Nevada to Lake Mead and along the route of the Owens Valley aqueduct to southern California. Various additional features are included in the project. We have calculated that the average delivered cost, on the basis of Pirkey's data, would be roughly $58 per acre-foot, assuming a 5 percent interest rate and a 50-year life.

Lewis G. Smith (1968) proposed a Western States Water Augmenta-

---

[5] The information on this project is from the indicated reference and from personal conversation and correspondence with Miller.

tion Concept which would divert 38 million acre-feet annually from the Liard and Mackenzie River systems, through a channel in the Rocky Mountain Trench, and into the Columbia, Snake, Salmon, Colorado, Missouri, and other river systems via natural channels, canals, and tunnels. The estimated capital cost of the system, including the secondary distribution system, is estimated at $75 billion. Computed on the basis of a 5 percent interest rate and a 50-year life, the capital costs alone amount to $108 per acre-foot.

For the eastern half of the continent, Thomas W. Kierans (1964) designed the GRAND Canal, a system that would tap Canadian waters flowing into James Bay by reversing their flow through artificial and natural channels into the Great Lakes. This project is proposed to serve navigation, power, and water quality and supply objectives in the United States and Canada. About 17 million acre-feet per year are involved in the proposal. With the annual costs stated to be $110 million, the cost per acre-foot of water delivered into Lake Huron works out at $6 per acre-foot.

The largest of the interbasin transfer proposals is the North American Water and Power Alliance (NAWAPA), a concept developed by the Ralph M. Parsons Company "for utilizing the excess water of the Northwestern part of the North American continent and distributing it to the water deficient areas of Canada, the United States, and Mexico."[6] This proposal calls for reversing the flows of the Yukon and Tanana rivers, damming the Peace River and creating a 500-mile long reservoir in the Rocky Mountain Trench. The runoff in the drainage area of the project is estimated to be about 633 million acre-feet per year, of which 110-250 million acre-feet per year could be made available. Net electrical power capacity could range from 60 to 180 million kilowatts.

Cost estimates for the entire project are about $100 billion, but the project has not been engineered in sufficient detail to permit even "ball park" estimates of the delivered costs of water to different areas. Since the project contemplates deliveries to such diverse regions as Mexico, Colorado, Utah, and the Great Lakes, the incremental costs may differ widely.

Summary

It is difficult to generalize about interbasin transfer costs because of geographical diversity and because the current proposals do not go beyond the preliminary design stages. Estimates provided by the originators of the various plans for diversions into the Colorado ranged from $9 per

6 Brochure 606-2934-19 (no date). For engineering details, see Parsons (1964).

acre-foot for 7.5 million acre feet (Miller) to $44 per acre-foot (Pacific Southwest Water Plan) for 2.4 million acre feet. Adjusting these estimates to a 5 percent discount rate and a 50-year life span would boost the likely range to $30-$108. The escalation of construction and equipment costs would, by 1970, raise these estimates by 20 to 30 percent. Clearly, much closer cost studies are needed before interbasin transfers can be considered seriously in the context of western water problems.

Several general points gleaned from study of the preceding proposals are of great relevance to the planning process:

(1) The cost of power and the extent to which off-peak power can be utilized for project pumping is an important determinant of the cost of interbasin transfers.

(2) The extent to which power recovery is possible is of great importance. It is estimated for Columbia-Colorado diversions that 75-80 percent of the pumping power can be recovered—naturally at different locations. Diversions where recovery is not possible are clearly at a disadvantage, e.g., the Texas High Plains project.

(3) There are substantial economies of scale in construction. The extent to which these economies are offset by increasing power costs, rising marginal opportunity costs of water in the areas of origin, and falling marginal values of water at the point of delivery, is not clear, even for specific projects.

What Are the Alternatives to Interbasin Transfers?

Defining the range of alternatives to be considered in a planning process is probably the most important phase of the study. If the set of alternatives is too small, the finest optimizing of system design may still fall short of the social optimum. Yet, any planning process has limited time and budget and, even more to the point, any planning organization will have only limited expertise for the evaluation of alternatives.

This discussion of alternatives is confined to different sources of supply and different ways of economizing of the demand side and includes the following: increased efficiency in agriculture; transfers from agriculture to municipal and industrial uses; additional development of surface supplies; wastewater reclamation; desalting; groundwater development; vegetative management and soil treatment; weather forecasting and modification; and belt tightening for humid areas faced with infrequent but severe drought.

For each method, it is important to specify both the unit costs of producing or conserving water and the quantities that could be obtained, i.e., the supply function for each alternative. Water quality should also be considered. Further, the alternatives considered need not be mutually exclusive. For example, a desalting plant with a daily capacity of 50 million gallons (154 acre-feet) cannot be considered a substitute for an interbasin transfer of 2.4 million acre-feet per year (6,600 acre-feet per day), but it might be included in a comprehensive plan as a stop-gap means of providing water until other sources are developed. Later, if water *quality* is a problem, desalted water might be mixed with imported water to improve the quality of the supply.

Increased Efficiency in Agriculture

This alternative needs serious consideration if only because agriculture accounts for very high percentages of total water withdrawals and consumptive uses. In 1965, U.S. agriculture withdrew approximately 140 million acre-feet of which about 78 million acre-feet were consumed and 27 million acre-feet constituted conveyance losses. In the Western Region in 1965, fourteen times as much water was consumed in agriculture (55 million acre-feet per year) as in all mining, municipal, steam-electric generation, and manufacturing uses (4 million acre-feet). If these proportions still hold, a 7 percent reduction in U.S. agricultural consumptive uses would provide for a doubling of all other consumptive uses in the West (see table 1, chapter 1).

Bagley (March 1965) cites several instances illustrating the possibilities of increased efficiency. In the Milford Valley of Utah, the imposition of pumping restrictions resulted in average efficiency increasing from 48.5 percent in 1959 to 60.9 percent in 1961. In the Cache Valley's Porcupine Dam and Paradise Irrigation Project, farmers along a new canal could irrigate 1,675 acres of the rolling land with flood irrigation; with sprinkler irrigation they were able to irrigate an additional 1,175 acres using the same quantity of water.

A clearer picture of opportunities for increasing efficiency may come from figure 10 which depicts three concepts of efficiency: project efficiency, farm efficiency, and field efficiency. The general definition suggested here is

$$e = \frac{C}{G - \rho R}$$

where C is the amount of water usefully stored in the root zone during one application, G is the gross amount withdrawn from the source, R is the return flow of water finding its way back to some surface or ground watercourse, and ρ is the percentage of the return flow that is useful for the other applications, account being taken of the *quality* and *timing* of the return flow. If (G) is measured at the point of diversion (e.g., for a ditch company), the above measure is called project efficiency; if G is

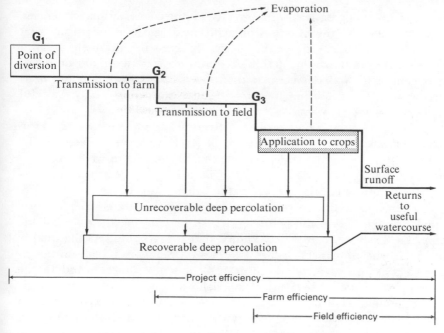

Figure 10. Concepts of physical efficiency of irrigation.

measured at the farm headgate, then e is the farm efficiency; and if G refers to the amount delivered to the field, e is called field efficiency.

Blaney and Criddle (1962) in their classic work on irrigation water requirements indicated average values for various losses and for field and farm efficiency, with no account taken of possible return flows (see table 38). It should be clear from their data and from figure 10 that there is plenty of room for increasing efficiency—at a cost, of course.

Phelan (1964) has stated that during the last ten years, research has yielded a great deal of knowledge about better use of irrigation water,

Table 38. Typical Water Losses and Irrigation Efficiencies, by Soil Type

	General soil type		
Item	Open, porous	Medium loam	Heavy clay
Farm lateral loss (unlined ditches)	15%	10%	5%
Surface runoff loss	5	10	25
Deep percolation loss	35	15	10
Field irrigation efficiency	60	75	65
Farm irrigation efficiency	45	65	60

Source: Blaney and Criddle (1962).

but that this apparently has not greatly improved irrigation efficiencies. Limited data and the opinions of many field researchers indicate that while delivery systems are getting better, progress in improving on-farm use of water is slow. One possible reason is reflected in the oft-heard statement that "water is cheaper than labor." It is clear that the practice of heavily subsidizing irrigation water stimulates socially wasteful water management practices.

Figure 11 summarizes project delivery efficiency and average farm irrigation efficiency on twelve Bureau of Reclammation projects for the years 1950 to 1960. Project delivery efficiencies are seen to have improved marginally from 62 to 65 percent, but farm irrigation efficiency appears to have deteriorated, the average value being about 52 percent in 1960.

There are indications that excessive irrigation water is frequently applied, judged from the point of view of maximizing the value of the crop. For example, it is widely known that irrigation lowers the quality of winter wheat (Musick, Grimes, and Herron, September 1963), although the yield is increased. Diminishing returns set in quickly, and in the experiments reported by Musick, the yields attained by the "dry" irrigation treatment (fall irrigation only) were significantly exceeded only in one year over the period 1954–59 by the "medium" (fall plus one irrigation at boot stage) and "wet" (fall plus three or four irrigations) treat-

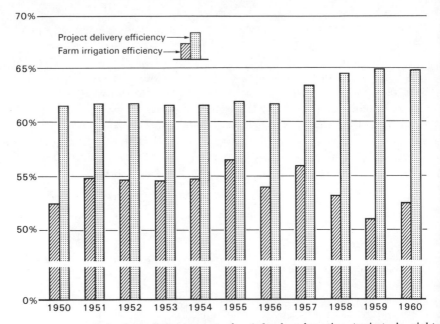

Figure 11. Farm irrigation efficiency on twelve federal reclamation projects in eight states from 1950 to 1960. (Source: Phelan, June 1964.)

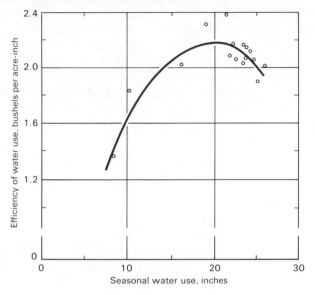

Figure 12. Relation between seasonal water use and efficiency of water use for grain production. (Source: Musick, Grimes, and Herron, 1963.)

ments, other inputs being held constant. More favorable straw/grain ratios and higher percentages of protein were found in the wheat that received fewer applications of water. The relationship found by Musick, Grimes, and Herron between water use and yield is shown in figure 12.

The increases of efficiency most commonly mentioned relate to the lining of canals to avoid seepage. Taylor (1964, p. 35) points out that measured project efficiencies run as low as 25 percent (and seldom exceed 80 percent), while approximately 25 percent of the water entering unlined canals and laterals in the West is lost by seepage before reaching the fields. A 1958 report of the Senate Committee on Interior and Insular Affairs[7] estimated annual conveyance losses in five western basins; these estimates are shown below with estimates for 1965 from table 1, chapter 1.

	Million acre-feet	
	1958	1965
Colorado River	2.5	3.4
Great Basin	2.9	1.5
Pacific Northwest	10.0	7.9
South Pacific	2.7	4.7
Missouri River	7.1	3.7

In some basins, the conveyance losses are of the same order of magnitude as some of the proposed interbasin diversions.

[7] Committee Print No. 1, April 14, 1958, table I, p. 12.

The costs of avoiding conveyance losses are affected by the types of soil, the slope of the canal, the quality characteristics of the water itself, and by whether a new canal is built or an old one is lined.[8] Testimony before the House Subcommittee on Irrigation and Reclamation[9] showed that the capital cost of lining 35.6 miles of the All-American Canal in southern California would be about $43 million (an annual capital cost of $2.4 million at 5 percent for 50 years) to save 52,000 acre-feet per year. Subtracting an estimated operating and maintenance cost saving per year of $200,000 (Howe estimate) yields a cost of $42 per acre-foot saved, a cost unlikely to be absorbed by agricultural users.

However, costs for various alternatives to an unlined canal for the proposed California aqueduct indicate that canal preparation beyond an unlined state can be an inexpensive way of avoiding loses (see table 39).

Various procedures other than canal lining have been used which appear to be worthy of expansion. The Coachella Valley Irrigation District has built terminal reservoir storage for water from the All-American Canal so that, when weather changes, growers can make last-minute adjustments in their applications. Neither the amount of water nor the cost per acre-foot saved are known.[10]

Irrigation return-water systems have been used in California to pump the water that collects at the lower end of fields (tailwater) back through the irrigation system. Costs of such recirculation have varied from $2 to $6.50 per acre-foot.[11] When return systems are used, gross withdrawals are reduced, and consumptive use may also be reduced because less water is lost by evaporation from tailwater disposal ponds.

Subirrigation systems have been coming into use, particularly in pumping areas where they not only yield evaporation savings but also permit continuous operation, thus requiring smaller wells than would be required by intermittent flooding operations. Capital costs have been reported to be about $200 per acre.[12] Savings have not been measured.

The irrigation of orchards has posed particularly difficult problems because of the difficulty in measuring the impact of moisture conditions on tree growth. Studies in Idaho show that orchardists are irrigating from two to three times too often each year.[13] Trunk growth has proven

[8] To some extent, seepage is recovered in return flows but this need not always be true. In Central Arizona where the primary source is groundwater, the rate of percolation is said to be slower than the rate of fall of the water table, so that seepage loss and excessive application will never be recovered if current conditions continue.

[9] U.S. House of Representatives, *Hearings*, March 13–17, 1967.

[10] Colorado River Association News Release dated 2/18/66.

[11] Houston and Shade (1966).

[12] *The Cross Section* (monthly publication of the High Plains Underground Water Conservation District No. 1) October 1966, p. 3.

[13] *Idaho Agricultural Science*, 2nd quarter, 1962, p. 3.

Table 39. Costs of Water Saved through Various Types of Canal Lining Compared with an Unlined Canal, California Aqueduct, San Luis Division

Lining type	Construction cost	Present value of O&M costs[a]	Annual cost[a]	Annual cost increment above "unlined"	Annual loss	Increment of water saved above "unlined"	Average cost per acre-foot saved
	. . . . thousand dollars				. . . thousand acre-feet . . .		dollars
Unlined	22,300	X	1,031 + x	–	483	–	–
Heavy compacted earth	30,700	X	1,419 + x	388	89	394	1.00
4" concrete lining	46,100	X − 7,100	1,803 + x	722	67	416	1.85
4" concrete, asphalt sublining	49,300	X − 7,428	1,936 + x	905	53	430	2.10
4" concrete, plastic sublining	52,700	X − 7,733	2,079 + x	1,048	40	443	2.35

Source: Data from Wineland and Lucas (1963).

[a] The present values stated in the source were computed at 3½ percent for 50 years. It was not possible to adjust to a 5 percent rate.

X indicates the unspecified value of O &M costs for an unlined canal and x the annual cost equivalent of X. When cost differences are taken, these amounts cancel.

a good indication of the water needs of apple, peach, and plum orchards, and dendrometers have been developed to measure daily tree growth. When tree growth drops below 80 percent of a test plot of frequently watered trees, irrigation is called for. Irrigation applications have been cut to one-half or one-third of former practice with negligible or no decrease in yields and better coloring of the fruit. Costs in commercial applications are not known.

Control of Evaporation Losses

Vast amounts of water are lost by evaporation each year, and the problem has been aggravated by the tremendous increase in reservoir capacity since World War II. In the western states, where the rates of evaporation are much higher than they are in the East, 4 to 8 acre-feet per year are evaporated from each acre of water surface.[14] Lake Mead behind Hoover Dam on the Colorado River evaporates an average of 700,000 acre-feet annually.

How much evaporation from water surfaces can be saved, given current technology? Control methods involving the spreading of hexadecanol or other retardants have proven effective for small ponds of several acres, but there is no practical economic way of controlling evaporation from large bodies of water at the present time (Lauritzen 1967).

A study of evaporation from water surfaces in the eleven western states found that a relatively small quantity (748,000 acre-feet per year) is lost from small ponds and reservoirs that are currently amenable to evaporation control while vast amounts (7.9 million acre-feet per year) are lost from the larger reservoir surfaces (see table 40). Retardation of evaporation from small ponds may, however, be a worthwhile endeavor in some areas, for costs of water saved appear to range from low to moderate in terms of alternative sources (see table 41).

Additional Surface Water Development

Surface water is generally the first source developed, and, if flows are sufficiently regular, it is likely to be the cheapest source. Where flows are irregular, either seasonally or cyclically over the years, more storage is required so that peak flows can be held over for use during periods of low flows. With no evaporation or seepage loss, it would be possible in theory to develop sufficient storage in a river system to guarantee a yield approaching the mean annual flow with a specified probability of short-

---

[14] U.S. Senate Committee on Interior and Insular Affairs (1958), p. 11.

Table 40. Evaporation from Water Surfaces in Eleven Western States, by Major Basin

thousand acre-feet

Basin	Average annual evaporation from:			
	Lakes and reservoirs over 500 acres	Streams and canals	Small ponds and reservoirs	Total
Upper Mississippi	3	0	0	3
Missouri River	1,301	300	150	1,751
Lower Mississippi	106	17	34	157
Western Gulf	159	51	38	248
Colorado River:				
Upper Basin	83	276	78	437
Lower Basin	1,231	518	81	1,830
Great Basin	1,748	48	74	1,870
South Pacific	998	216	120	1,384
Pacific Northwest	2,176	1,514	173	3,863
Total	7,855	2,940	748	11,543

Source: U.S. Senate Committee on Interior and Insular Affairs (1958), table II, p. 13.

Table 41. Estimated Cost of Water Saved from Evaporation from Small Ponds

Evaporation rate per year	Annual saving per surface acre	Cost per acre-foot
feet	acre-feet	
4	1.0	$24.50
6	1.5	15.00
8	2.0	12.15

Source: From U.S. Senate Committee on Interior and Insular Affairs (1958), table III, p. 23. Data originally from Commonwealth Scientific and Industrial Research Organization, "Saving Water in Dams," Leaflet No. 15, Melbourne, Australia, 1956.

age, but increasingly long periods of carryover plus evaporation and seepage make the approach to this theoretical maximum exceedingly expensive. Typical relationships between gross yields and net yields (less evaporation losses) and required storage are shown in figure 13. Note that a uniform rate of withdrawal is assumed.

Detailed analyses have recently been completed by Wollman and Bonem at the University of New Mexico giving the marginal costs of further surface water development for each water resource region. Their analyses utilized detailed inventories of existing and potential reservoir sites. Table 42 gives, for each water resource region, the marginal costs of developing additional net yields from surface sources through the provision of additional in-stream storage on the assumptions that the largest (and thus lowest cost) reservoir sites would be developed first and that the rate of water withdrawal would be uniform throughout the year. The

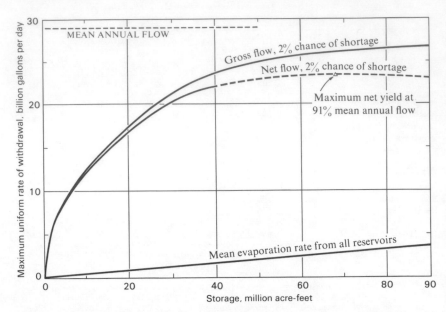

Figure 13. Storage required in Upper Missouri region to obtain specified yields with 2 percent chance of shortage. (Adapted from Löf and Hardison 1966, figure 4.)

costs represent only the storage costs and do not include distribution or treatment of the water. The net flows indicated and related storage represent a probability of 0.98 that the flows will be generated by the related storage, i.e., in two years out of 100 the indicated net flow would not be available. Not all of the Wollman and Bonem figures are given since marginal costs generally rise very rapidly after some point, and sources other than local surface water would then be developed.

Wastewater Reclamation

The reuse of treated sewage flows represents an almost untouched possibility for developing "new" water. Past experience indicates that domestic (as opposed to industrial) wastes can be reclaimed for many uses, up to and including human consumption, and that the reclaimed water is quite inexpensive in relation to its alternatives. The California projects described below give some idea of the costs and methods of reclaiming wastewater.

An extensive water reclamation program has been undertaken by the County Sanitation Districts of Los Angeles County, California. These districts discharge about 285 million gallons per day (mgd) of wastewater,

Table 42.   Marginal Storage Costs for Surface Water Development

Region	Cumulative developed net flow	Marginal storage cost per acre-foot[a]
	maf/year	
New England	25 (present)	–
	41	$ 0.8
	53	1.3
	63	3.3
	67	16.6
Delaware and Hudson	8 (present)	–
	30	4.9
	31	38.1
	32	88.7
Chesapeake	4 (present)	–
	30	0.6
	39	2.4
	47	6.8
	51	47.6
Ohio	22 (present)	–
	67	1.3
	89	3.9
	107	14.7
	108	302.2
Eastern Great Lakes	4 (present)	–
	22	1.1
	30	4.2
	34	8.8
	36	41.1
Western Great Lakes	10 (present)	–
	22	1.7
	28	4.6
	31	8.2
Upper Mississippi	17 (present)	–
	24	0.5
	29	1.1
	34	1.5
	41	3.7
	45	5.2
	48	8.8
Lower Missouri	6 (present)	–
	10	1.1
	12	2.3
	14	4.2
	16	6.5
Southeast	106 (present)	–
	124	0.8
	145	1.5
	187	3.3
	199	14.0
	205	19.9
Cumberland	13 (present)	–
	15	2.6
	16	9.8

Table 42.   Marginal Storage Costs for Surface Water Development—Continued

Region	Cumulative developed net flow	Marginal storage cost per acre-foot[a]
	maf/year	
Tennessee	27 (present)	–
	34	2.4
	39	5.9
	43	15.0
	44	99.8
Lower Mississippi	2 (present)	–
	17	0.5
	33	1.3
	37	2.5
	39	6.8
Lower Arkansas-White-Red	27 (present)	–
	30	1.4
	45	1.8
	55	3.8
	60	6.8
	62	9.5
Western Gulf	17 (present)	–
	20	2.6
	22	3.9
	25	6.8
	27	13.0
	28	19.2
Central Pacific	29 (present)	–
	42	2.9
	46	8.5
	48	17.9
	50	41.4
Pacific Northwest	70 (present)	–
	120	1.4
	145	5.2
	148	56.1
	149	139.9

Source: Wollman and Bonem (1971).

Note: It will be noted that there are no data for the Upper Missouri, Upper Arkansas-White-Red, Colorado, Great Basin, Rio Grande-Pecos, and Southern Pacific because the flows in these regions already are highly regulated relative to maximum yield.

[a] An annual cost factor of 0.0425 was used, equivalent to an assumed discount rate of 3½ per cent and a project life of 50 years. This discount rate is far too low for current circumstances.

at least one-third of which is considered suitable for reclamation and reuse.[15] The districts currently have three reclamation plants in operation with a combined capacity of 15.7 mgd; the largest plant is the Whittier Narrows Plant with capacity of 12 mgd. Cost experience has been very good, and water quality has remained high. The reclaimed water is re-

[15] See County Sanitation Districts of Los Angeles County, California (July 1963).

charged to groundwater through spreading basins. Water from Whittier Narrows is purchased at $15.25 per acre-foot by the Central and West Basin Water Replenishment District, which also purchases Colorado River water from the Metropolitan Water District for groundwater recharge. The reclaimed, Colorado River, and natural recharge waters percolate toward the coast. There they are pumped by municipal and industrial users who are metered and pay the Replenishment District.

The actual costs of product water at the existing plants and estimated costs for proposed plants are given in table 43. The total cost figure represents the cost of producing and recharging product water; it does not include the pumping costs of downstream users; nor does it include the cost of treating the solids that are removed from the wastewater and sent through sewers to standard treatment plants. The removal of water and the concentration of wastes upstream reduce the required capacity of the downstream sewer and waste disposal systems, and the net total cost reflects these savings.

Table 43. Actual and Estimated Reclaimed Water Costs, Los Angeles County, 1963

Plant	Actual or design capacity	Total cost per acre-foot	Net total costs per acre-foot[a]
	mgd		
Whittier Narrows			
Existing plant	12.0	$16.85	$11.05[b]
First expansion	12.0	15.61	9.81
Second expansion	26.0	16.49	10.76
Walnut Creek	10.0	21.08	12.50
Azusa			
Existing plant	0.7	–	–
Expansion	1.0	21.40	10.00
Arroyo	6.0	23.20	16.00
Eaton	1.5	27.18	17.75
Pomona			
Existing plant	3.0	–	–
Expansion	5.0	9.25	6.83
Alamitos	15.0	24.80	13.90
Inglewood	3.0	29.37	16.94
Dominguez	23.0	20.79	16.54
Total	118.2	–	–
Weighted average	–	19.10	12.60

Source: County Sanitation Districts of Los Angeles (1963), table 2, p. 4.

[a] Total cost less estimated savings to downstream sewer and waste disposal systems. See text.

[b] In a paper entitled "Water Re-Use in Los Angeles County—A Supplementary Supply," delivered to the American Society of Civil Engineers, New Orleans, 4 February 1969, John D. Parkhurst, Chief Engineer and General Manager, County Sanitation Districts of Los Angeles, stated that current operations are showing variable operating costs of $9 per acre-foot and total costs of $18 per acre-foot.

If the planned expansions take place, Los Angeles County will have a "new" source of water yielding over 100 mgd (112,000 acre-feet per year) at a cost of about \$12.60 per acre-foot (or \$19.10 if the downstream economies are not netted out). Clearly, this is low-cost water in relation to the alternatives.

Another California reclamation project that exhibits the total systems planning approach is that of the Santee County Water District (Stoyer 1967; FWPCA 1967), a public agency providing water and sewerage service for a community of about 14,500. The district faces rapid population expansion, increasing costs for imported water (\$39.25 per acre-foot as of 1 July 1967, increasing to \$74 per acre-foot by 1973), and increasing difficulty in waste disposal. Plans called for developing a reclamation system capable of producing water for irrigation and recreational purposes, and for a separate distribution system for delivery of reclaimed water for fire protection and other volume uses.

The system produces 1.5 mgd, and water is sold at \$40 per acre-foot. When completed, the system is to have a capacity of 16 mgd and operate as a nearly closed system. Tertiary inplant treatment will replace ground percolation as a means of producing potable water, and the reclaimed water supply will be supplemented by imported water and by desalted local brackish water.

The costs of this system have not been published, but a rough cost estimate is shown below.[16] These costs refer to the present development of the system beyond ordinary secondary treatment and do not include the ultimate developments involving desalting and the production of potable water.

	Capital costs	O&M costs
Oxidation pond	\$202,000	\$ 7,800
Pumping (combined costs)	–	3,550
Spreading basin	24,000	4,950
Lakes (land only)	250,000	–
	\$476,000	\$16,300

If the capital cost is spread uniformly over a 20-year period with a 5 percent discount rate, the total annual cost of the system appears to be in the neighborhood of \$55,000, representing the costs of producing the water used for golf course irrigation and for supplying the recreational

[16] These estimates were made by Richard Frankel from a description of the system. The investment in the lakes was taken from FWPCA (1967).

lakes. As the system currently produces about 1.5 mgd (about 1,700 acre-feet per year), the above figures would yield an average cost of about $32 per acre-foot.

Two other instances of water reclamation in California deserve notice. In the Coachella Valley, domestic wastes have been reclaimed for irrigation and recreation uses at a cost of about $17 per acre-foot.[17] At Oceanside, California, the wastewater is given primary treatment and then pumped into a lake for secondary oxidation. Some of the water is then used for irrigation of grains and forage, and the remainder is used for groundwater recharge in the San Luis Rey Basin to assist in repelling salt water. Current reuse averages 1.8 mgd.[18]

The potentialities of water reclamation have barely been tapped. This will undoubtedly become a major source of additional water within the next two decades.

Desalting

The desalting of brackish or ocean waters may provide certain areas with economically feasible incremental water supplies. The capacities of most plants today fall between 50,000 gallons and 15 million gallons per day; the larger ones using distillation techniques on sea water, and the smaller ones using electrodialysis or vapor compression processes on brackish water. Results to date indicate costs in the neighborhood of $1.00 per thousand gallons, but new plants may be able to produce water at much lower costs.

It was thought in the mid-sixties that a dual-purpose electrical generating and desalting plant planned for Southern California[19] would be able to produce water at a cost of 22 cents per thousand gallons ($72 per acre-foot). In 1968, when it was found that costs would be much higher than anticipated, partly because of the cost of the large scaled-up equipment required, the estimates of the cost of water were revised upward to 35–37 cents per thousand gallons ($114 per acre-foot). This project has now been shelved.

Two surveys were conducted to determine the areas where desalted water might be competitive with conventional supplies in the near future. The survey conducted by Black and Veatch for the Office of Saline Water (1966) found that desalted water might be competitive in 180 cities, only

[17] California Department of Water Resources, Bulletin No. 80-3, March 1966.
[18] Letter to the author from Mr. Robert A. Weese, Superintendent, Water and Sewer Department, Oceanside, California, 8 June 1967.
[19] See Bechtel Corporation (1965).

Table 44.   Costs of Desalting versus Conventional Costs for New Water Supply, Texas

City	Projected 1975 population	Required plant size*	Cost per thousand gallons	
			Desalting	Conventional
	number	*mgd*		
Beeville	18,000	3.3	$0.300	$0.293
Dell City	1,250	0.2	1.442	2.120
El Paso	375,000	10.0	0.545	–
Fort Stockton	8,500	2.2	0.371	0.337
Freer	3,000	0.4	0.556	0.905
Hebbronville	4,000	0.7	0.441	0.448
Italy	1,200	0.2	0.836	0.830
Kingsville	33,000	2.0	0.381	0.356
Port Mansfield	2,000	0.7	0.544	–
Rankin	2,100	0.5	0.505	0.479
Refugio	5,500	0.9	0.369	0.595

Source: Southwest Research Institute (1966), table I, p. 2.
* Based on 1985 water demands.

three of which had populations of 100,000 or more—Tucson, North Miami Beach, and El Paso. The comparative costs were not given, so it is impossible to tell how many cities are really candidates for desalting. The implication seems to be, however, that U.S. applications of desalting will be found in the small- to medium-size range (up to 15 mgd) for municipal and industrial purposes, and not in the large-size plant.

The second survey, carried out by the Southwest Research Institute for the Texas Water Commission,[20] screened all Texas communities of 1,000 or more, and selected thirty-seven for more detailed study. Eleven cities were found where desalting costs were less than or about equal to costs of additions from conventional sources (see table 44). Again, small, isolated cities appear to be the ones where desalting can be economically justified. Since nine of the eleven cities lie in the lower Rio Grande Valley, it might be possible to serve several of them with one large plant. Combining electric power generation, desalting, and the production of ammonia (for fertilizer) in the area has also been suggested.

The lowest desalting cost in table 44 is 30 cents per thousand gallons ($98 per acre-foot). Towns may be able to pay this amount for residential water but it is far above what agriculture pays or could pay for water.

In the longer term, technical innovations such as breeder reactors may drive energy costs quite low. This, in combination with multiple purpose plants, might mean desalted water in the $30 to $50 per acre-foot range. While most agriculture cannot pay this much, there might be a place for such water in the raising of some high-value crops.

[20] Southwest Research Institute (1966).

Weather Modification and Improved Forecasting

Two major reports have dealt with the current state of the art of weather modification.[21] With regard to precipitation, the result appears to be a cautious acceptance of the hypothesis that, under some circumstances, precipitation can be increased 10 to 20 percent. The exact types of clouds that can be successfully seeded are not known with certainty, but clouds must be present in adequate volume. It appears unlikely that current techniques can affect the true desert regions of the world. In fact, the potential for the entire United States has never been assessed in terms of specifying where propitious conditions for increasing precipitation are to be found; what the seasonal patterns of precipitation increases might be; what catchment facilities are available or would be needed to capture the runoff; and finally, what it might cost to produce, capture, store, and distribute the new water supplies.

The most extensive study of the potential of precipitation augmentation is the one carried out by the Bureau of Reclamation's Office of Atmospheric Resources for the Upper Colorado River Basin. "Project Skywater" as it is known (see the Bureau's annual reports of 1967 and 1968) has involved theoretical work and extensive measurement of storm patterns and yields. Of the entire Upper Colorado Basin area of 109,500 square miles, it has been estimated that some 14,200 square miles exhibit conditions propitious for increasing rainfall during winter storms through the method of ground-based seeding with silver iodide crystals (Hurley, 1968). It is anticipated that a 15 percent increase in winter precipitation can be generated, 85 percent of which will find its way into increased stream flows, yielding a total of 1.9 million acre-feet. For a river with an annual flow of 13–15 million acre-feet, this would represent a substantial addition. The operating costs of the program (excluding all development and research costs) have been projected at about $1.50 per acre-foot, a very attractive price if it is achieved.

An extensive program of winter precipitation modification of this type may have profound ecological impacts. Anticipating such possibilities, the Office of Atmospheric Resources sponsored a study of the problems that will require monitoring and analysis as the experiments continue (Cooper and Jolly 1969). The possible problems range from changes in insect life to the possible eradication of large wildlife species.

[21] *Weather and Climate Modification,* Report of the Special Commission on Weather Modification, National Science Foundation 20 December 1965. *Weather and Climate Modification: Problems and Prospects,* vol. 1, *Summary and Recommendations,* vol. 2, *Research and Development,* Final Report of the Panel on Weather and Climate Modification to the Committee on Atmospheric Sciences, Publication No. 1350, National Academy of Sciences, 1966.

Improved weather forecasting or even improved use of weather forecasts might be used to improve irrigation efficiency and the operations of reservoir systems. Current understanding of world weather systems appears to indicate that two weeks is about the maximum period for which forecasts will ever be possible at levels of accuracy equivalent to current 5-day forecasts. Thus weather modification and long-term forecasting must be categorized as uncertain but possible components of future water management systems.

Groundwater Development and Recharge

According to Nace (1967, p. 5), groundwater reservoirs in North America may contain two or three thousand times as much water as would be found in all rivers. He states that "nature's plumbing system has built-in regulating devices that are far larger and far more effective than artificial ones. Surface storage reservoirs viewed in proper scale are mere tinkerings with details of the plumbing system."

Groundwater reservoirs have great advantages for water storage: they do not take up valuable bottomlands; evaporation is nil; and as a rule they do not silt up or wear out. They can be integrated into water resource systems as efficient storage and, under some circumstances, serve to improve water quality.

Groundwater systems may be classified as follows: (1) systems in which natural recharge of the aquifer is high enough to prevent significant lowering of the water table from pumping (e.g., the great coastal aquifer of the southeastern United States); (2) systems where pumping is a "mining" operation because there is no natural recharge and the aquifers are not suited to economic artificial recharge (e.g., the Ogallala formation in the northern High Plains of Texas); (3) systems that have no natural recharge but are suited to economic artificial recharge (e.g., parts of the Ogallala formation in the southern High Plains of Texas).

Generally speaking, rates of natural recharge in the East have been fairly high and water tables have fallen but little. In the West, far greater use has been made of groundwater, particularly for irrigation, and in many cases rates of pumping have far exceeded natural recharge, leading to increased pump lifts, land subsidence, and the migration of salt or brackish water into the aquifers. Overdrafts on groundwater need not be economically inefficient, but the adverse effects of overdrafts on farming and on water quality in some areas indicate that future planning should consider groundwater storage as a component of larger systems. The role of aquifers as water warehouses to be recharged periodically becomes increasingly important as surface storage opportunities are used up.

There has been a great deal of experience with artificial recharge operations on a small scale. Todd (1965) reports that in 1958 California had 276 artificial recharge projects, successfully reinjecting water by the flooding of spreading grounds and recharge pits. Artificial recharge by injection wells in other states has generally proved unsatisfactory and costly.[22]

Aquifers can be used for both seasonal and long-term storage of surface flows and can fit in nicely with the staging of new sources of supply. Importation schemes can take advantage of economies of size and be constructed on a larger scale when aquifers can be used for storage. Hall (1965) poses an interesting example:

Assume that regional demand starts at 1 million acre-feet per year and grows at a rate of 100,000 acre-feet per year. An aqueduct with a capacity of 4 million acre-feet and a 30-year life is built to supply those demands. The present value of all costs is $2.4 billion. At the end of 30 years, demand will have grown to 4 million acre-feet per year and the full capacity of the aqueduct will be devoted to satisfying current demand.

If no storage is available, the aqueduct will have delivered exactly the amount demanded over the 30-year period or 75 million acre-feet. Thus unit costs would be $32 per acre-foot. Construction of a new aqueduct or some alternative action would have to be undertaken starting in year 30.

If inexpensive groundwater storage were available, the full 4 million acre-feet per year could be delivered over the 30-year period—a total of 120 million acre-feet at an average cost of $20 per acre-foot. At the end of 30 years, an inventory of groundwater of 45 million acre-feet would be on hand, making it possible to defer new construction for a period of 10 years.

The example is highly simplified, but it serves to illustrate the possible staging advantages of using ground storage as part of a surface water delivery system.

Descriptions of actual cases of integrated management can be found in Leonard (1964), Snyder (1955), and Smith (1962).

The groundwater storage systems in various regions of the United States should be assessed in terms of their place in an integrated water system. Clear understanding of the potential of this asset will require drawing together knowledge from geology and hydrology (both surface and groundwater) and translating it into an estimate of the economic value of groundwater aquifers.

Saline Water Irrigation

Recent experiments have shown that many plants can thrive in sandy soil when they are irrigated with water that is quite salty, and that under

22 See U.S. Geological Survey Water Supply Papers 1594-D, 1615 A-G, 1819-F.

the right conditions a few crops can be irrigated with seawater (Boyko 1967). Boyko found that certain dune grasses usable for fodder and a particular type of barley can be grown with irrigation water containing 30,000 parts per million of dissolved solids. He also found that barley, rye, Italian millet, alfalfa, ladino clover, field mustard, sugar cane, bermuda grass, and salt grass all have high salt tolerances in sandy soil.

This is a promising field and further advances are likely. Sandy soil conditions, the availability of brackish water, and methods for disposing of percolating brines without contaminating higher-quality ground-water supplies are necessary conditions.[23]

Water Harvesting, Including Phreatophyte Control

Water harvesting is the process of collecting and storing precipitation from land that has been treated to increase the runoff of rainfall and snowmelt. This definition could well include (1) control of salt cedars and other phreatophytes (deep-rooted plants of little or no value that draw heavily on groundwater); (2) management of forest, brush, and alpine snowpack watersheds; (3) reduction of soil moisture losses by intensive soil cover or by treatment methods.

Beattie (1968) has estimated that an additional 9 million acre-feet of water could be obtained from watersheds in the West through known methods of snow fencing and vegetation management at an annual cost of $13 million, or $1.45 per acre-foot. Transport and storage after recovery would increase the delivered cost, but this is still a potentially attractive source. The generation of additional runoff in the alpine areas has, in the Forest Service's experience, cost about $23 per acre-foot, but it is anticipated that large-scale operations and new materials will reduce this to about $8. In the commercial timber zones, it appears possible to increase sustained yields by more than one million acre-feet at an average cost of about $10 per acre-foot (Beattie 1967).

Myers has reported on processes of soil treatment or cover for increasing precipitation recovery. The processes range from simple soil smoothing to soil treatment with sodium salts and various water-repellant materials, including sprayed asphalt, plastic and metal films, rubber sheeting, and aluminum foil. The costs of these treatments are high, ranging from 40 cents to 80 cents per thousand gallons of water har-

[23] Extensive research relating crop response functions to models of salt accumulation in the soil is currently underway at the Hebrew University of Jerusalem, Rehovot, Israel, under the direction of Dr. Dan Yaron.

vested. The unit cost, of course, depends upon the amount of precipitation.

Perhaps the greatest opportunities for large-scale water conservation lie in the control of phreatophytes. T. W. Robinson (1952) estimated that these nonutilitarian water-consuming plants covered about 15 million acres in the seventeen western states and "wasted" 20-25 million acre-feet of water per year. In Committee Print No. 21 (1960) of the Senate Select Committee on National Water Resources, it was estimated that transpiration from phreatophytes was 1.2 million acre-feet in the Lower Colorado Basin alone, while van Hylckama (1966) estimated a total loss of 24 million acre-feet per year in the semiarid zone of the southwestern United States. Much of the loss is from salt cedar (*Tamarix*), which Robinson (1965) has forecast will cover 1.3 million acres by 1970, with consumptive waste of groundwater rising to 5 million acre-feet by 1970.

How much of this water could be saved economically is not known, but Robinson (1952) estimated that 25 percent could probably be saved in Nevada. To date, efforts to suppress phreatophytes have been costly, and the ecological effects of different suppression techniques have not been evaluated. Clearly, *much* additional research is called for by the large water-saving potential.

Costs have been reported for several specific projects undertaken in the Southwest to increase water yields. The Salt Water River Valley Water Users' Association and the U.S. Forest Service have undertaken a cooperative program to increase runoff in the Association's watersheds. Precise figures are not available, but it is estimated (Warskow 1967) that runoff increased by 0.2, 3.0, and 24.0 acre inches per acre per year after eradication of juniper, chaparral, and certain riparian vegetative types respectively. Based on the costs of the treatments, a 20-year life for the cleared areas, and a 5 percent interest rate, the water produced by these three treatments would cost approximately $57, $26, and $1.20 per acre-foot. If the underlying figures are in the right neighborhoods, it would appear that the eradication of certain types of riparian vegetation holds great promise and should be pursued.

The Pecos River Basin Water Salvage Project in New Mexico and Texas is designed to carry out a continuing program of reducing non-beneficial consumptive uses in the Pecos River Basin. It involves clearing vegetation and controlling regrowth. It is estimated (U.S. House of Representatives, 1966) that the chemical treatment of 70,000 acres of phreatophytes at a total project cost of $2.5 million will yield from 105,000 to 140,000 acre-feet annually. If a 20-year life at 5 percent interest is assumed, the cost per acre-foot of this water would be between $1.40 and $1.80 per acre-foot.

Transfers to Higher Valued Uses as an
Alternative to New Supplies

It was noted above that U.S. agriculture consumes 78 million acre-feet of water per year from surface and ground sources and that a 7 percent reduction in the consumptive uses of agriculture would support a 100 percent increase in all other uses in the West. This indicates that the increases in municipal and industrial activity anticipated over the next two decades could, in most regions, be supported by transferring relatively small quantities of water *from* agriculture to these new uses.

Competitive markets have been found to be the most efficient mechanism for allocating most resources because they permit freedom of choice on the part of potential sellers; they increase the "liquidity" of the resources; they provide for new patterns of use in response to changed economic conditions; and they provide for direct compensation to the party surrendering the resource. In the case of water rights, however, it has not proven generally possible to establish markets, and administrative and judicial procedures have had to govern many transfers of water. Many have come to fear that transferring water to higher-valued uses must mean changing uses by fiat without proper compensation to losers. This certainly need not be the case, and such procedures would have no basis in equity or in economic efficiency. By definition, any such transfer that is *economically efficient* will generate enough benefits to compensate the losers directly or to justify compensating them from indirect sources.

The costs of transferring water from agricultural uses to municipal and industrial uses are of three types: the opportunity costs in terms of incomes forgone directly in agriculture and indirectly elsewhere as a result of the water transfer; the costs of the physical transfer system; and the social overhead and other costs involved in population migration. The social costs are difficult to measure and few studies have been made relating to them. The costs of the physical systems that might be needed to transport the water from the point of former agricultural diversion to the new uses differ so widely that no one cost can be said to be typical.[24]

The opportunity costs of the water itself are synonymous with the total net benefits per acre-foot forgone in the process of withdrawing water from agricultural uses. The studies surveyed in chapter 3 showed a wide range of values per acre-foot—from $15 to $32 for low-value crops in

---

[24] For example, Boulder might be able to buy senior rights on Boulder Creek and, by changing the point of diversion, have the water flow directly into existing reservoirs. Denver, on the other hand, might buy Western Slope rights to water that would have to be transported across the mountains.

some regions to over $100 per acre-foot over short periods for a mix of crops in the Texas High Plains (see table 13). The studies of chapter 4 suggested that the likely range would be $10 to $50 per acre-foot and also made it clear that estimates of this kind are extremely sensitive to the degree of factor mobility in the areas adversely affected by the transfer. It would be extremely useful to have complete schedules for each region relating the opportunity costs per acre-foot to the various quantities which might be withdrawn from agriculture. Such studies could be performed using the methods illustrated in chapter 4.

That the quantities of water available at low opportunity costs may be significant, however, can be deduced from Arizona figures. Stults (1966, table 1, p. 137) programmed the reduction in acreage that was likely to result from a falling water table in Pinal County between 1966 and 2006. The results showed a reduction of 130,000 acres and a reduction in water applied of 415,000 acre-feet with a *direct* income loss of $13 per acre-foot. Since Pinal County accounts for only 25 percent of the state's cropped area, three or four times as much water might be available in Arizona at similar direct costs, i.e., 1.2 million to 1.6 million acre-feet.

"Belt-Tightening" as an Alternative to Increased Supply Capacity in Urban Area Drought Protection

Interbasin diversions, desalting, and the development of larger-scale, integrated urban supply systems have all been recommended as forms of urban drought protection in areas that are subject to severe but infrequent droughts. An important alternative that is not openly discussed is simply to do what was done in the Northeast in the exceptionally dry summers of 1964–65: accept the shortages and allocate available water among users. Costs are then borne by the local economies and take the form of income forgone and assets damaged.

The issue is whether or not the long-term average losses are sufficient to warrant investment in standby capacity to prevent infrequent shortage. At present, no one knows the extent of drought-inflicted losses. Until such losses are measured and understood in relation to drought frequency and duration, rational water development policy in the humid areas cannot be determined. A study of the costs of the 1963–66 drought in Massachusetts by Russell, Arey, and Kates (1970) shows per capita annual losses from the drought at $5, $7, and $15 for three towns. Correction for future returns to the investments that were triggered by the drought reduced these figures to $5, $3, and $1, respectively.

Summary of Costs and Quantities of Alternatives to Interbasin Transfers

In this chapter we have attempted to develop some feeling for the wide range of possibilities for the development of additional effective supplies of water, primarily in the West and Southwest. While the exact quantities and costs cannot be known without further extensive investigation, it appears that nearly 60 million acre-feet of water can be con-

Table 45. Alternatives to Interbasin Transfers: Estimated Quantities and Costs

Source	Estimates of quantities available per year	Indicated range of costs per acre-foot
	maf	
Reduction of conveyance losses:[a]		
Colorado Basin	1.5	$2–42
Great Basin	0.6	2–42
Pacific Northwest	3.4	2–42
South Pacific	2.0	2–42
Missouri	1.6	2–42
Evaporation retardation from small ponds and reservoirs	0.5	12–24
Transfers from agriculture:[b]		
Arizona	1.2–1.6	28[c]
Colorado	not known	15–32[c]
Texas High Plains	4.0	81–119[c]
California	0.8	18–106[c]
Additional surface development:		
Western Gulf	11.0	3–19[d]
Central Pacific	21.0	3–41
Weather modification (Upper Colorado Basin)	1.9	1–2[e]
Wastewater reclamation:		
Southern California	0.7	13–32
Desalination	unlimited	100+[f]
Vegetative management and snow fencing	9.0	2–23[g]
Phreatophyte and riparian vegetative control	not known but potentially large	1–57
Minimum total availability	59.2	

[a] These figures are 43 percent of the estimated 1965 loss figures reported in table 1. Phelan (1964, p. 43) found the average project efficiency of a sample of Bureau of Reclamation projects to be 65 percent, and Taylor (1964, p. 35) indicated that project efficiency seldom exceeds 80 percent. We have assumed that average project efficiencies can be raised from 65 to 80 percent, representing a 43 percent *decrease* in the 1965 losses.

[b] Taken from or extrapolated from the area studies of chapter 3.

[c] From table 13, chapter 3. The Texas High Plains figures and the upper range for California represent only short-term costs during the period of substantial capital and labor immobility.

[d] Impoundment costs only.

[e] Cloud seeding costs only.

[f] Cost at plant.

[g] Does not include storage costs.

served or directed toward higher-value uses in the West at costs competitive with those of large-scale, long-distance transfers. A summary of the costs found in the literature plus our estimates of quantities available are given in table 45.

Breakthroughs on evaporation retardation from reservoirs, weather modification, desalination, or phreatophyte control could increase this figure many times. While few of the alternatives present the spectacular image of the large engineering works of the interbasin transfer, several appear to offer substantial amounts of water at costs below those of proposed interbasin transfers. Since the alternative sources are *within* the regions of potential use, much of the available water could be delivered to users at total costs highly competitive with large interbasin transfers.

6

Indirect Costs: The Long-Run Impacts of Expanding Irrigation on Other Regions

The preceding chapter developed measures of the direct construction costs of interbasin transfers, some of the opportunity costs of the water involved, and operating and maintenance costs. In this chapter we examine still another type of cost.

It was argued earlier that most of the water from a large interbasin transfer will have to be used by agriculture. It appears very likely that, even when a project is undertaken to rescue a region with a failing water supply, some of the water will be tapped for the expansion of agriculture along the diversion route. There is nothing inherently wrong in this from an economic viewpoint, but an increase in agricultural output will have direct and indirect impacts on the welfare of other regions through the displacement of production and on the nation as a whole through its effects on the federally financed farm programs. The net benefits of this new agriculture from a national viewpoint will be diminished if the displacement of agricultural production in other regions occurs under conditions that leave land, labor, and capital idle for extended periods of time, and the direct project benefits will be negative if the agriculture can be made profitable only through highly subsidized water prices.

It has been estimated that western farmers served by Bureau of Reclamation projects pay $30 to $135 per acre per year less than the full cost of supplying the water.[1] It thus seems likely that much of the federally sponsored irrigation agriculture could not survive competitively if it had to pay full water costs.

It is the purpose of this chapter to trace likely production displacement effects of irrigation agriculture in the project region and other

[1] See Ruttan (1965) for the method of calculating the cost of supplying water and the prices paid by the farmers.

regions. The evidence will deal with western irrigation lands served by the U.S. Bureau of Reclamation, which is the largest supplier of irrigation water in the country. Whether or not the Bureau would have jurisdiction over new interbasin transfers, the production displacement effects would be in the same direction as the past effects of the reclamation program discussed in this chapter.

This chapter also investigates the costs that new agricultural production creates through the various farm income and price support programs. The budgeted costs of some of these programs reflect the actual economic or resource costs of the program, as is the case with acreage retirement programs which pay just the net income that would have been earned had the land been kept in production. The budgeted costs of price support or loan programs may overstate or understate the real costs of the program, depending upon the method of payment and the use to which the loan commodities are put. Nonetheless, the estimated costs of these programs are presented as a first approximation to real costs.

AGRICULTURAL SUPPLY AND DEMAND RESPONSE

The inelasticity of demand for farm products forces the agricultural sector to hold aggregate output within narrow limits. Retail price and income elasticities of demand for all foods are only about -0.34 and 0.25, respectively; a 10 percent decline in food prices increases consumption by only 3 percent. In contrast, retail price elasticities as high as -2.35 for lamb and -1.60 for veal indicate that consumers must substitute between similar commodities quite readily (Brandow 1961).

Demand measurements over time show that elasticities are greater the longer the time allowance for adjustment. Waugh finds an immediate demand elasticity for cotton of -0.06 and a cumulative elasticity of -0.29 after one year and -1.84 after nine years. Cotton mills will gradually shift from cotton if the competing fibers have a continued price advantage. Likewise, the final consumer will gradually shift from cotton clothing to clothing made from substitutes if the price ratios encourage the shift (Waugh 1964, pp. 57–62).

In summation, increased agricultural production will, in the short run, have strong downward impacts on prices. In the longer term, this will cause shifts in the locus of production and changes in the composition of output as particular areas and crops become unprofitable.

There is much less agreement concerning supply response than there is about the inelasticity of aggregate demand for agricultural commodities. At present the evidence seems to indicate that the aggregate agricultural supply response to changes in prices is inelastic and sluggish. Part of the reason for this is the large agricultural investment in capital inputs with low salvage values. As a result, product prices have to drop considerably to make the marginal value product of these inputs less than their salvage value, a situation which would naturally cause farmers to reduce production. As product prices rise, the prospects for the marginal value product of capital inputs remaining above their cost must be good before farmers will make provision for substantial expansion of their output, thus making expansions of output sluggish. Further contributing to the inelastic response to price change is the fact that, while price changes will cause individual farmers to expand or contract their operations, many of the assets and much of the land transferred remain in agriculture, although in different hands.

In summary, uncertainties and costs of shifting to different crops tend to keep the supply response to price changes inelastic in the short run, but as the time horizon is lengthened the supply response becomes more elastic and large changes occur in the locus and composition of farm output.

IMPACTS OF RECLAMATION PRODUCTION ON THE COMPOSITION AND LOCATION OF U.S. AGRICULTURE

A general decline in cropland acreage harvested and a shift in the distribution of acreage and production among crops and regions has taken place during the past two decades. These shifts undoubtedly have been caused by a number of factors, but an important one has been the increase in reclamation production. There has been a decline in the acreage devoted to grain production, with a good portion of the land formerly used for grains being retired under the wheat and feed grains programs. Some has been converted to soybean production (see table 46). Alfalfa hay has been substituted for other hay varieties with lower feed values, particularly in the northern region.[2] The only major crops to show an increase in acreage, besides sorghum, soybeans, and alfalfa hay, have been sugarbeets and rice, which received higher acreage allotments during the sixties as the result of special circumstances.

The major declines in acreage harvested have occurred in the North and South, the regions with the greatest amount of cropland. The South has experienced the largest absolute and relative declines, with almost one-third (33.8 million acres) of its cropland dropping out of production in the last twenty years. This can be compared with declines of 15 percent (31.1 million acres) in the North and 3 percent (1.2 million acres) in

------

[2] Part of this increase in alfalfa acreage resulted from a change in the Census of Agriculture definition.

Table 46. Changes in U.S. Cropland Harvested by Region between 1944 and 1964

thousand acres

Crop	Recla-mation	West	North	South	United States*
Corn	+246	−610	−11,839	−18,149	−30,598
Sorghum	+64[a]	+113	+2,809	−814	+2,108
Wheat	+152	−510	−6,572	−3,246	−10,328
Oats	−26	−700	−12,964	−2,825	−16,489
Barley	+143	+1,039	−2,894	−34	−1,888
Subtotal (grains)	+579	−668	−31,460	−25,068	−57,195
Alfalfa hay	+713	+1,194	+11,493	+547	+13,234
Other hay[b]	+28	−959	−6,696	+487	−7,168
Potatoes (Irish)	−35	−9	−914	−440	−1,363
Cotton, lint	+369	+812	−48	−5,810	−5,047
Beans, edible dry	+147	−429	−10	−10	−449
Vegetables (excl. all potatoes)	+111	+91	−587	−540	−1,037
Tree fruits, nuts and grapes	+270	+23	−658	−114	−749
Sugarbeets	+436	+575	+232	+22	+830
Rice	+131[a]	+111	+5	+305	+421
Soybeans (1949–64)	n.a.	+1	+12,853	+6,842	+19,696
Total, above crops	+2,749	+742	−25,790	−23,779	−48,827
Total all cropland harvested	+3,145	−1,232	−31,122	−33,804	−66,158

Sources: U.S. Department of Commerce, *Census of Agriculture, 1959* and *1964;* U.S. Department of Agriculture, *Agricultural Statistics, 1951* and *1967;* U.S. Department of the Interior, *Crop Report and Related Data, 1944* and *1964.*

Note: For regional breakdown see figure 14.

* Row totals may not add due to rounding.

n.a. = not available.

[a] Change between 1954 and 1965; sorghum and rice were not reported separately in 1944 and 1949.

[b] Excludes alfalfa, soybean, cowpea, and sorghum hay.

the West, while the cropland acreage served by reclamation irrigation projects has increased by 61 percent (3.1 million acres).

In contrast to the general decline in acreage, production increased for nearly all major crops between 1944 and 1964, because of increasing yields per acre. Within these increases, regional production shifts have occurred (see table 47). The North and South have both experienced net declines in the production of several crops, potatoes being a prime example.

On land receiving reclamation irrigation water, only potatoes and oats declined in acreage harvested between 1944 and 1964. All other crops showed a significant increase in acreage harvested and even greater increases in production. The production of oats, edible dry beans, and pears increased on land served by the Bureau of Reclamation in the seventeen Western States and declined on the nonreclamation lands in

Figure 14. Dotted areas indicate states with reclamation projects.

those *same* states. Similarly, between 1949 and 1964, cotton production doubled on reclamation-served land and dropped by 22 percent (nearly 1.7 million bales) in the nonreclamation portion of these *same* Western States.[3]

In the twenty-year period 1944–64, the Bureau of Reclamation irrigated 3.3 million additional acres of cropland.[4] In terms of land held in retirement, reclamation has probably replaced 5–18 million acres elsewhere. The lower estimate is based on the assumptions that 25 percent of the reclamation production would have existed without reclamation irrigation and that the yields were twice those on retired land. The upper limit is based on the assumptions that 10 percent of the reclamation production would have existed without reclamation irrigation and the yields were six times those on retired land.[5] This means that 8–26 percent of the 66-million-acre decline in cropland harvested during 1944–64 would not have been necessary had reclamation not irrigated additional

[3] The reader can see this by turning to table 53.

[4] Includes cropland not harvested or in soil building crops which adds 120,000 acres to the figure shown in table 46.

[5] In 1964, a little less than half the harvested acreage served by reclamation irrigation received full irrigation service while most of the remainder received supplemental irrigation. This raises the question of how much of the production on land receiving supplemental irrigation can be attributed to reclamation. In some cases the supplemental irrigation makes it possible to grow crops that otherwise could not be grown. In others the supplemental irrigation will just stabilize and increase production. For crops where the latter is true or dry farming is a real alternative, the production of reclamation-served land should be adjusted accordingly. An overall 10 to 25 percent reduction is suggested as a reasonable range for such an adjustment factor.

Table 47.   Changes in U.S. Crop Production by Region between 1944 and 1964

thousands

Crop	Unit	Recla-mation	West	North	South	United States*
Barley	bu.	+18,862	+93,890	−882	+7,765	+100,773
Corn	bu.	+22,436	+7,085	+658,809	−93,185	+572,709
Oats	bu.	+1,432	−18,650	−161,512	−52,553	−232,715
Sorghum	bu.	+5,825ª	+28,013	+146,714	+110,286	+285,013
Wheat	bu.	+13,302	+56,301	+141,575	−12,745	+185,131
Rice	bu.	+15,416ª	+23,337	+443	+77,451	+101,232
Sugarbeets	tons	+8,420	+12,084	+3,804	+472	+16,361
Soybeans	bu.	n.a.	+10	+327,088	+154,840	+481,939
Alfalfa hay	tons	+3,877	+6,603	+27,628	+1,480	+35,711
Cotton lint	bales	+814	+2,222	−8	+680	+2,894
Potatoes	cwt.	+15,273	+26,498	−10,477	−8,075	+7,946
Pears	cwt.	+2,324	+1,939	−591	−1,431	−82
Beans, edible dry	cwt.	+2,834	+796	+2,398	−33	+3,161

Sources: See table 46.

n.a. = not available.

* Row totals may not add due to rounding.

ª Change between 1954 and 1964; sorghum and rice were not reported separately in 1944 and 1949.

acreage during the same period. Furthermore, 8–43 percent of the 40–65 million acres diverted under the annual commodity programs during the 1960s would not have had to be diverted if reclamation had not increased irrigation.

If reclamation continues to increase irrigation service by 165,000 acres per year (the average rate between 1944 and 1964), 2.64 million acres could be added to reclamation's service area from 1965 through 1980. By 1965, the Bureau of Reclamation had already been authorized to bring 3 million additional acres into its service area. The addition of 3 million acres would increase the irrigable service area to 12.6 million acres.[6] Based on past history (1944–64), the projection of a 3-million-acre increase in reclamation irrigation service could cause significant decreases in farm income and increased annual commodity program payments.[7] During 1964–65, production on reclamation irrigated lands was significantly increased for most crops in response to higher prices, changes in acreage allotments, and increased reclamation service. The only exceptions of any importance were sugarbeets and wheat which were cut back under the annual commodity programs (see table 48).

[6] U.S. Department of the Interior, *Federal Reclamation Projects Statistical Appendix to 1965 Crop Report and Related Data* (U.S. Government Printing Office: 1966).

[7] Abel and Rojko (1967) estimate that the United States will have excess productive capacity at least through 1980. In fact to maintain current average prices for grain, over 20 million acres of grain land will have to be kept in retirement in 1980. Heady and Mayer (1967) estimate that 38 million to 78 million acres of cropland will need to be retired through 1980.

Table 48. Cropland Harvested and Pasture on Federal Reclamation Projects, 1964–65[a]

thousand acres

Crop	1964	1965	Change
Barley	501	612	+111
Corn	314	355	+41
Sorghum	146	209	+63
Oats	137	128	−9
Feed grains	1,098	1,304	+206
Silage	286	326	+40
Alfalfa hay	1,868	1,859	−9
Other hay	180	187	+7
Pasture (irrigated)	1,121	1,197	+76
Other forage	39	43	+4
Forage crops	3,493	3,612	+118
Wheat	393	352	−41
Rice	147	157	+10
Other cereals	118	120	+2
Potatoes (Irish)	235	275	+40
Beans, edible dry	301	323	+22
Vegetables	309	349	+40
Cotton (lint)	514	583	+69
Sugarbeets	587	503	−84
Fruit and nuts	384	537	+153
Misc. field crops	63	64	+1
Total	7,643	8,179	+536

Sources: U.S. Department of the Interior, Crop Report and Related Data, 1964, p. 32; 1965, p. 33.

[a] This includes full, supplemental, and temporary service.

A good example of the impact of expanded acreage on farm income is provided by the 1965 potato crop. Potato acreage served by reclamation irrigation increased 40,000 acres during 1964–65. Production increased almost 19 million cwt., accounting for 40 percent of the total U.S. increase in potato production. Approximately $69 million of the $173 million decline in the farm value of potatoes can be attributed to increased production on lands served by reclamation. Net farm incomes fell even more after netting out the cost of producing the added potatoes. This large drop in total farm value of potatoes may be compared with a $2.9 million increase in farm value of potatoes produced on reclamation-served lands.

HIGHER COMMODITY PROGRAM PAYMENTS

The preceding section strongly suggests that the Bureau of Reclamation's irrigation program has a major impact on the volume and location of agricultural production. Here we consider in some detail the impact of reclamation irrigation on the payments made under the annual commodity programs, i.e., the effects of reclamation on costs borne by the general public through federal programs. As stated earlier, the budgeted costs of these programs may not precisely measure the real resource costs involved since some income redistribution toward agriculture is involved, but the estimates presented here have been calculated so as to approximate real costs.

Under the wheat program, producers who comply with the federally established acreages receive certificate payments and price supports. Farmers who plant less than this limit receive additional payments based on the amount of extra cropland not planted (diverted). The feed grain program offers price supports and support payments to farmers who comply with federally established acreages, while diversion payments are made for additional acreage diversion. The 1966 cotton program works in a similar manner with price supports and support payments to farmers meeting acreage requirements and with diversion payments to retire additional land. The principal means of support for sugarbeets is import quotas, but prices are supplemented by Sugar Act payments.

It has been estimated (table 49) that between $110 million and $239 million of the total *annual payments* to farmers under the three major annual agricultural commodity programs (diversion payments plus price support and certificate payments for cotton, wheat, and feed grains) and $19 million in Sugar Act payments to growers of sugarbeets can be attributed to the production on reclamation-served land brought in between 1944 and 1964. Since about 40 percent of the increased production on reclamation irrigated land was on land receiving supplemental service, not all of these payments can be attributed directly to reclamation. A 25-percent reduction in payments is suggested as more than adequate to account for any production that might have occurred without reclamation service. This reduces the annual total payments that could be attributed directly to reclamation irrigation during 1944–64 to the range from $83 million to $179 million.

It should be noted that this analysis of impacts on the annual commodity program costs excludes crops that contributed 58 percent of the 1944–64 increase in reclamation-served acreage. The impact of nearly 2 million additional irrigated acres directly and indirectly displacing other acreage may more than offset the 25 percent reduction for supplemental service. For example, increased fruit and vegetable production in the West may cause fruit and vegetable producers in the North to shift to feed grain production and thus increase annual payments under the feed grain program.

Furthermore price support, acreage retirement, and commodity pur-

Table 49. *Estimated USDA Annual Commodity Program Payments Resulting from Increased Bureau of Reclamation Irrigation during 1944–64*

Crop	Increased reclamation harvested acreage 1944–64	Diversion payments per acre of new acreage under three yield assumptions[d]			Total diversion payments under three yield assumptions			Price support, certificate, and Sugar Act payments[e]
		0.9	0.5	0.3	0.9	0.5	0.3	
	thousand acres	*. . . . . dollars/acre . . . . .*			*. . . . . . . million dollars . . . .*			
Corn	246	44	78	131	10.8	19.2	32.2	1.3
Barley	143	26	47	79	3.7	6.7	11.3	0.3
Sorghum[a]	96	39	71	118	3.7	6.8	11.3	0.6
Wheat	152	16	29	48	2.4	4.4	7.3	2.9
Cotton[b]	327	134	241	401	43.8	78.8	131.1	21.8
Sugarbeets	436	–	–	–	–	–	–	19.0
Subtotal*	1,401	–	–	–	64.4	115.9	193.2	46.0
25% reduction[c]	–	–	–	–	16.1	29.0	48.3	11.5
Total*	–	–	–	–	48.3	86.9	144.9	34.5

144

Procedure for estimating diversion payments per acre

[(Yield on reclamation irrigated land) ÷ (U.S. average yield) × (% diverted yield is of the harvested yield)] × (Average diversion payment per acre) = payment required to retire production equal to that due to reclamation irrigation.

Example of wheat:

$$\frac{(56 \text{ bu.})}{(25.8 \text{ bu.})(0.9)} \ (\$6.41) = \$15.96 \text{ per acre.}$$

e *Procedure for estimating price support and certificate payments*

[(1944–64 increase in reclamation served acreage × 1964 average yield) ÷ (U.S. production)] × (total price support payments for the crop in 1964) = certificate payments arising from increased reclamation irrigation during 1944–64.

Example of wheat:

152,000 acres × 56 bu./acre = 8,512,000 bu.
(8,512,000 bu. ÷ 1,217,792,000 bu.)($410.2 million) = $2,875,386.

Federal Sugar Act payments due to the 1944–64 increase in reclamation irrigation:

$$\$25,568 \times \frac{436,000 \text{ acres}}{587,000 \text{ acres}} = \$18,990.$$

Sources: U.S. Department of the Interior, *Crop Report and Related Data, 1944* and *1964*; U.S. Department of Agriculture, *Agricultural Statistics, 1968*; U.S. Department of Agriculture, *State Estimates of Farm Income, 1949–66* (FIS 207 Supplement), pp. 130–35.

Note: 1964 payments were used for all crops except cotton. 1966 payments were used for cotton since this was the first year of the new program.

*Totals may not add due to rounding.

a 1944 acreage for sorghum grain on reclamation irrigated land was estimated at 50,000 acres based on the rate of increase in sorghum acreage on reclamation-served land during 1954–64.

b Upland cotton only. Excludes the increase in American Egyptian cotton acreage (estimated at 42,000 acres) because American Egyptian was not covered by the upland cotton program. Total diversion and price support payments implied by the figures in the table range from $201 to $468 per acre.

c The 25-percent reduction is to correct the payment estimates for any production that would have occurred without reclamation irrigation.

d The USDA assumes that yields on diverted acreage will be 90 percent of the yields on harvested acreage; others suggest that 50 percent or even 30 percent would be more realistic. Vernon W. Ruttan, "Are Grain Surpluses a Thing of the Past?" Paper presented at the Regional Extension Grain Marketing Conference, Duluth, 18 May 1967, p. 5.

chase programs help control the supply and/or increase prices of many other agricultural commodities. Rice and dairy products are both under price support programs while nonbasic commodities such as edible dry beans and soybeans are put under price support programs if supplies are determined to be in surplus. In addition, fruits, vegetables, meats and other agricultural commodities are purchased with Section 32 funds during periods of oversupply to reduce commercial supplies and hold up prices. Selected commodities are also purchased for sale or donation in foreign countries through Public Law 480. And on top of this, general land retirement programs such as the Soil Bank and the Cropland Adjustment Programs have been used to reduce agricultural production across the board. Thus the impacts of reclamation irrigation on all USDA supply control and price support programs will probably be more than double the estimated impact on the three major commodity programs and Sugar Act payments.

It is instructive to calculate the added annual commodity program payments resulting from each additional acre brought into production by reclamation irrigation. The average annual price support payment for cotton produced on reclamation irrigated land is estimated at almost $67 per acre ($21.8 million ÷ 327,000 acres). The diversion payments necessary to retire cotton production equal to one acre of reclamation irrigated cotton run from $134 to $401 per year, making the total price support and diversion payments arising from an acre of reclamation irrigated cotton between $201 and $468. The actual diversion payments may not be quite as high as the upper limit since acreage allotments may be reduced across the board rather than making excessive diversion payments. Even so, payments under the annual commodity programs resulting from each acre of reclamation cotton are substantial.

The increase in cotton acreage harvested during 1964–65 provides an example of reclamation's impact on the costs of annual commodity program payments. Cotton production under reclamation irrigation increased from 978,000 bales to 1,084,000 bales, and acreage harvested increased by 69,000 acres. Within this total, the acreage of American Egyptian cotton actually declined from 59,000 to 38,000 acres. Therefore, the acreage of upland cotton actually increased by 90,000 acres, which in turn increased USDA cotton diversion and price support payments by an amount in the range of $18.1 million to $42.1 million.[8]

8 The wide range of values stems from a wide range of assumptions regarding the yields on diverted acreage. The USDA assumes that the yield will be 90 percent of that on harvested acreage, but others have suggested that 30 to 50 percent would be more appropriate. The lower value of $18.1 million assumes a cost of $201 per acre and the higher value of $42.1 million assumes a cost of $468 per acre. See table 49.

Similar annual commodity program payments arising from each acre of reclamation production can be calculated for feed grains and wheat from Table 49. Although the annual payments are not as large as for cotton, they will be between a low of $16 per acre for wheat (assuming diverted land yields are 90 percent of the yields on harvested acreage and no change in the total U.S. wheat support payments) and a high of $136 per acre for corn (assuming diverted land yields are 30 percent of the average yields on harvested acreage and a *reduction* in total U.S. corn support payments equal to those made to reclamation corn producers).

In the case of sugarbeets, the cost is transferred to the consumer through higher prices and does not constitute a cost to the USDA. The $44 per acre ($18,990,000 ÷ 436,000 acres) is definitely the lower limit of the annual cost to consumers. If one considers the cost to the consumer as the difference between world and U.S. sugar prices minus transportation and import costs, the annual cost could be almost $200 per acre ($114.8 million ÷ 587,000 acres) of sugarbeets brought into production by reclamation irrigation. (See the section on sugarbeets later in this chapter.)

Another way of showing some of the external effects and inconsistencies between increasing production through reclamation irrigation projects and retiring land under annual and longer term USDA programs is to exhibit USDA land retirement expenditures in reclamation counties. This was done for 171 counties in which more than 1,000 acres were irrigated by reclamation as of 1965. These 171 counties account for most of the 8 million acres receiving reclamation irrigation in 1965. Over 3 million acres were in retirement in these same counties in 1965, 1.9 million acres under annual commodity programs and 1.2 million acres under longer term programs (see table 50). In terms of payments, $11 million was spent through the longer term programs and over $121 million under the annual commodity programs.[9] The 1966 commodity program payments to cotton producers would be much larger due to the new cotton program. The 1966 price support and diversion payments to all cotton producers were over eleven times higher than 1965 payments. Thus payments to 1966 cotton producers alone in these 171 counties were probably in the range of $30 to $40 million.[10]

[9] These payments may be compared with the 3 million acres of cropland the Bureau of Reclamation brought into production during 1944–64 and with the Bureau's cumulated construction appropriations since 1944 of over $4 billion. U.S. Department of the Interior, *Summary Report of the Commissioner of the Bureau of Reclamation 1966 and Statistical Appendix* (U.S. Government Printing Office, 1967).

[10] U.S. Department of Agriculture, *Farm Income State Estimates, 1949–1966* (FIS 207 Supplement) (U.S. Government Printing Office, 1967), pp. 132–34.

Table 50.   *Acreage Retired and USDA Payments to Farmers in Counties
Served by Reclamation Irrigation, 1965*

thousands

Programs	Acres retired	Cost-share and diversion payments	Price support and certificate payments
	(1)	(2)	(3)
Wheat and feed grains	1,795	$35,625	$ 82,866
Cotton	88		2,842
Subtotal (annual programs)	1,883	35,625	85,708
Conservation reserve	1,041	10,070	
Agricultural Conservation Program[a] (permanent cover)	125	803	
Cropland conversion program[b]	13	36	
Subtotal (longer-term programs) *	1,180	10,909	
Total*	3,063	46,534	85,708
Total of columns 2 and 3			$132,242

Source: Compiled from records of USDA, ASCS, by Kenneth G. Ruffing.

* Totals may not add due to rounding.
[a] Data from 1964.
[b] Data available for 1963–64 only.

DIRECT CROP DISPLACEMENT IMPACTS

This section presents more detailed data and analysis concerning the direct displacement impact of reclamation irrigation on cotton, potatoes, sugarbeets, fruits, nuts, vegetables, alfalfa hay, rice, and feed grains in terms of production, income, and acreage adjustments.

Cotton

Reclamation projects have simultaneously added directly to U.S. cotton surplus problems and provided subsidized competition to other cotton-producing regions. The acreage of cotton harvested has declined by two-thirds from the high levels of the twenties, although production has remained fairly stable. Much of the decline in acreage harvested since 1944 occurred in the South, while in the West (California, Arizona, Nevada, and New Mexico) there has been an increase. Since 1949, acreage harvested has declined in all cotton-producing states although the decline has been greater in the South where most states have experienced a 50 percent decline in acreage harvested.

A normative regional study completed in 1966 indicates that, on the assumptions of no annual commodity programs, advanced technology, and complete adjustment to changing cotton prices (other commodity prices remaining constant), 18.6 million bales would be produced at a price of 21 cents per pound.[11] If the price were raised to 30 cents, production would reach 37.8 million bales. At low prices, cotton competes in production primarily with feed grains, but at higher prices it is more profitable than all other crops except tobacco.

The acreage distribution without acreage restrictions and with a price of 21 cents would be roughly the same as it was in 1964 when 14.7 million bales were produced on 13.9 million acres—78 percent in the South, 19 percent in the West, and 3 percent in the North—although the West would increase its share slightly. At 30 cents a pound, the West would produce a smaller percentage of a much larger production total because the South has a much larger capacity to increase production.

Part of the reason the West would increase its share of cotton production at low cotton prices (as it has been doing over the years) is the competitive advantage provided by low-priced reclamation water. Data from an analysis of the costs of producing upland cotton in the United States indicate that Southern California and Southwest Arizona are enabled to stay in production at lower cotton prices only because of the low price they pay for reclamation irrigation water—about $3 per acre-foot. For these regions the private cost of irrigation was about $7 per bale, compared with the average cost of about $20 for the High Plains of Texas, $18 for the San Joaquin Valley, $22 for Southern Arizona, and $30 for the Upper Rio Grande–Trans Pecos areas (Starbird and Hines 1966).

The costs of projects currently underway for providing additional supplies of water to Southern California have been estimated at $65 to $100 per acre-foot for large deliveries from Northern California. If irrigators currently paying approximately $3 per acre-foot for Colorado River water delivered to the Imperial Valley and other districts in Southern California had to pay the average cost of providing new water, their costs of production would be raised substantially, and they would no longer have average returns of $16 per bale. Instead, as shown below,

[11] *Cotton: Supply, Demand and Farm Resource Use,* Southern Cooperative Series Bulletin 110, November 1966. Available from Arkansas Agricultural Experiment Station, University of Arkansas, Fayetteville, Arkansas.

there would be an average loss ranging from $36 to $96 per bale depending on the price of the water and the efficiency with which it is used.

	Water cost and rate of application		
	$3 per acre-foot 2.7 acre-feet/bale	$30 per acre-foot 2 acre-feet/bale	$120 per acre-foot 1 acre-foot/bale
Value per bale	$140	$140	$140
Less average costs	124	176	236
Average net receipts	$ 16	$–36	$–96

The claim that reclamation regions have a cost-efficiency advantage over other areas in producing cotton is not supported by the data shown in table 51. The California-Arizona reclamation-served region has costs

Table 51. Upland Cotton Production: Average Private Costs and Receipts per Pound of Lint, Fourteen Regions, 1964–65

Regions	Direct cost[a]	Total cost
	cents/lb.	cents/lb.
Southeast:		
Southern Piedmont, Clay Hills and Black Belt	23.9	30.5
Coastal Plains	25.8	31.3
South Central:		
Limestone Valley–Sand Mountain	21.4	28.0
Brown Loam	19.7	26.5
Mississippi Delta	18.6	24.0
Northeastern Arkansas	22.1	29.3
Texas–New Mexico:		
Black Prairie	20.5	27.9
Coastal Prairie[b]	17.7	24.9
Lower Rio Grande Valley	23.8	31.2
Rolling and High Plains	20.7	28.3
Upper Rio Grande–Trans Pecos	28.5	36.5
California–Arizona:		
San Joaquin Valley	22.9	30.3
Southern California and Southwest Arizona	19.3	24.8
South Arizona	24.0	30.3
United States	21.2	27.8

Source: I. R. Starbird and B. L. French, *1965 Supplement to Cost of Producing Upland Cotton in the United States, 1964* (1965 supplement to Agricultural Economic Report no. 99) USDA, September 1967, p. 8.

[a] Direct costs are chiefly those expenditures which producers must make annually. They exclude overhead and land costs.

[b] There were no reclamation irrigation projects serving the coastal prairie region.

uniformly higher than the Mississippi Delta, even under conditions of highly subsidized water.

The impact of this low-cost reclamation water on increased cotton production has been felt in many areas of the United States. The acreage of cotton harvested on reclamation-served land increased over 3½ times between 1944 and 1954 and since then has remained fairly constant due to the federally established acreages. In contrast, total acreage harvested in the nonreclamation portion of the West declined between 1949 and 1964, and other major cotton-producing areas also experienced declines. In 1964, the acreage harvested in the South was 50 percent lower than in 1949 and one-third lower than in 1944 (see tables 52 and 53). From the late fifties through 1965 the decline was fairly small, as federally established acreages were not reduced again until 1966.

Some argue that Western cotton does not compete with cotton produced in the South. Yet, in 1961–62, 45 percent of the cotton crop produced in California, Arizona, and New Mexico was shipped directly to southeastern textile mills. In contrast, in 1933 approximately 96 percent of the cotton from the Western region went to California and Texas ports; little was shipped to the southeastern textile mills. Texas and Oklahoma shipped 31 percent of the 4.5 million-bale crop in 1961–62 to southeastern mills. In 1932–33, Texas had shipped less than 1 percent of its crop to southeastern mills (Potter 1965, p. 6).

Since cotton acreage has been controlled through federally established acreages based on historical production, adjustments have taken place in *all* cotton-producing areas rather than in the marginal areas only, as would have been the case if price had been the controlling factor. This means that the United States fails to produce its cotton at the lowest cost and in the most efficient manner.

Assume for the moment that in 1964 the United States produced just enough cotton to meet present demands and that increases in yield would be enough to meet future increases in demand. If cotton were not produced on reclamation land, then 978,000 bales (see table 53) could be produced in other areas by increasing acreage allotments. To meet this production, allotments could be increased by about 1 million acres since the land coming back into cotton production would be less productive and would yield, on the average, about 1 bale per acre (reclamation land yields almost 2 bales per acre). A uniform increase in the allotments based on the 1964 distribution of acreage would give the South about 550,000 more acres and the North 20,000. In the West (including Texas and Oklahoma) acreage would decline by about 85,000 acres despite a 430,000 acre gain in acreage of cotton for land not served by reclamation

Table 52. *U.S. Cotton Acreage Harvested and Production by Regions*

Regions[a]	Harvested acreage (1,000 acres)					Production (1,000 bales)				
	1964	1959	1954	1949	1944	1964	1959	1954	1949	1944
California–Arizona	1,125	1,190	1,318	1,234	401	2,523	2,500	2,301	1,761	449
New Mexico–Nevada	191	190	199	286	104	261	298	293	262	113
West*	1,317	1,380	1,517	1,520	505	2,784	2,798	2,595	2,023	562
Texas–Oklahoma	6,203	6,754	8,417	11,802	8,070	4,191	4,530	3,825	6,117	3,157
South Central	4,502	4,523	6,115	9,010	6,915	5,790	4,832	4,605	5,142	5,330
South Atlantic	1,545	1,576	2,383	3,673	3,074	1,568	1,261	1,489	1,663	2,381
South*	12,250	12,854	16,914	24,485	18,060	11,549	10,624	9,919	12,922	10,869
North	349	384	427	594	397	399	458	407	474	407
Total*	13,915	14,618	18,858	26,599	18,962	14,732	13,880	12,921	15,419	11,838

Source: Census of Agriculture, 1959 and 1964; U.S. Department of the Interior, *Federal Reclamation Projects, 1944, 1949, 1954,* and *Crop Reports and Related Data, 1964.*
* Totals may not add due to rounding.

[a] *South Central* includes the states of Alabama, Arkansas, Kentucky, Louisiana, Mississippi, and Tennessee. *South Atlantic* includes the states of Florida, Georgia, Maryland, North Carolina, South Carolina, and Virginia. *North* includes the states of Illinois and Missouri. See figure 15.

Table 53. *Cotton Acreage Harvested and Production in the Western States*

Regions	Harvested acreage (1,000 acres)					Production (1,000 bales)				
	1964	1959	1954	1949	1944	1964	1959	1954	1949	1944
California–Nevada–Arizona	1,129	1,194	1,320	1,235	401	2,528	2,506	2,304	1,762	449
New Mexico–Texas–Oklahoma	6,391	6,941	8,614	12,087	8,174	4,447	4,822	4,116	6,379	3,270
Total	7,520	8,135	9,934	13,322	8,575	6,975	7,328	6,420	8,141	3,719
Reclamation portion[a]	514	504	514	381	145	978[b]	984	898	487	164
Nonreclamation	7,006	7,631	9,420	12,941	8,430	5,997	6,344	5,522	7,654	3,555

Source: See table 52.

[a] In 1964, 775,000 of these bales were produced on 360,000 acres in California, Arizona, and Nevada, while 203,000 bales came from New Mexico, Texas, and Oklahoma and were produced on 154,000 acres. Also 567,000 bales were produced from land receiving full reclamation irrigation service, 403,000 bales from land with supplemental service and 8,000 bales from land with temporary service.

[b] Only 6 percent (64,000 bales) of the reclamation production was American Egyptian cotton.

irrigation. In terms of annual net income for farmers, the South would gain roughly $27.5 million, the North $1 million and the nonreclamation West $21.5 million, while the reclamation West would lose $50 million.[12]

Potatoes

For potatoes, as for cotton, reclamation production has a very significant direct impact on production and income in other regions. Idaho alone accounts for almost one-fifth of the entire nation's production and nearly 60 percent of the Idaho crop is produced on reclamation irrigated lands. In 1964, the West as a whole accounted for almost 42 percent of U.S. production, and over 53 percent of this production was on land receiving reclamation irrigation water.

Since 1944 the acreage harvested has declined rather drastically in both the North and South while remaining nearly constant in the West (table 54). In both the reclamation and nonreclamation West, higher yields have led to increased production. In contrast, increased yields in other regions have not been enough to offset the acreage decline of the forties. In 1947, Idaho and California had 17.2 percent of U.S. potato production and Maine and New York had 25.5 percent; by 1963, California and Idaho had jumped to 30.6 percent while New York and Maine had only 21.2 percent. (See table 55.)

Idaho ships almost as many potatoes to Chicago as do North Dakota and Minnesota combined. Not far behind as major markets for Idaho potatoes are New York City and Detroit. The third, fourth, and fifth largest markets for California potatoes are Chicago, New York City, and Houston, respectively. On the other hand, very few eastern or midwestern potatoes reach western markets. One reason for the West's competitive position is that the increased demand for processed potatoes appears to have favored the type of potato from the West, and that from Idaho in particular (Hee 1967, p. 9). Again, however, low-priced irrigation water has been a factor.[13]

By lowering potato prices, reclamation irrigation has substantially reduced the incomes of nonreclamation potato farmers. Since demand

[12] The difference between the average return on cotton and the average return on the next best alternative crop was estimated at roughly $50 per acre. Data for this estimate came from: (1) I. R. Starbird and F. K. Hines, *Cost of Producing Upland Cotton in the United States, 1964* (Agricultural Economic Report no. 99), September 1966, and (2) *Cotton: Supply, Demand and Farm Resource Use* (Southern Cooperative Series Bulletin 110), November 1966.

[13] Another reason is the somewhat lower freight rates for long-distance eastbound hauls as compared with westbound hauls of equal length. For example, the 1963 freight rate per cwt. for an average 1,200 mile trip from Maine was $1.25 compared to $0.70 from Idaho (Ulrey 1964).

Table 54. *U.S. (Irish) Potato Acreage Harvested and Production by Regions*

Regions	Harvested acreage (1,000 acres)					Production (1,000 cwt.)				
	1964	1959	1954	1949	1944	1964	1959	1954	1949	1944
South	121	149	176	257	561	16,982	18,522	21,147	21,449	25,057
North	600	622	651	854	1,514	111,844	110,120	105,746	124,930	122,321
West (11 States)	452	430	384	403	461	93,048	95,498	77,219	73,423	66,550
Total*	1,174	1,200	1,211	1,514	2,537	221,874	224,140	204,113	219,802	213,928
Reclamation portion	235	247	206	237	270	49,545[a]	54,985	39,304	35,101	34,272

Source: See table 52.

Note: Production includes total quantity harvested, whether for home use or sale. Acreage in 1944 includes all harvested acreage while in the last four census years acreage was reported only when production was 20 or more bushels.

*Totals may not add due to rounding.

[a] 28.3 million cwt. came from land receiving supplemental reclamation irrigation service while 21.2 million cwt. came from land receiving full reclamation irrigation service. Since a dependable water supply is fairly critical for potato production, the supplemental service may make the difference between producing potatoes or some other crop requiring less water.

Table 55.   *The Distribution of Potato Production: Five Important Producing Areas,*
1947 and 1963

| | Percentage of U.S. total | |
Area	1947	1963
California	9.8	10.9
Idaho	7.4	19.7
Maine	16.8	13.8
New York	8.7	7.4
North Dakota and Minnesota	9.3	10.1
All other	48.0	38.1
Total	100.0	100.0

Source: Ivan W. Ulrey, *Fresh Potato Transportation to Large Markets from Five Major Producing Areas,* Marketing Research Report No. 687, USDA, November 1964, p. 21.

elasticity for potatoes has been estimated at from −0.1 to −0.2, any reduction in price will reduce income (Brandow 1961). For every one million cwt. increase in production, the price will drop at least 4 cents per cwt. if demand elasticity is −0.2. This means income to potato producers would drop by $9.2 million from a one million cwt. increase in reclamation production.[14]

The long-run gain in income to potato producers from no reclamation production would depend on the supply response in other areas. At a higher price more potatoes would be produced in other regions, but in the absence of supply-response data it is difficult to say how much more. If one assumed the elimination of the 68 million cwt. reclamation product and an increase of 30 million cwt. in other areas, this would mean an increase in net farm income to potato producers of roughly $350 million due to higher prices.[15] In addition, net income for nonreclamation farmers would also increase because of the 30 million cwt. increase in their share of potato production. Between 1963 and 1964 potato production declined by 32 million cwt. The inelasticity of potato demand is supported by the corresponding price increase of $1.72 per cwt. The

[14] Using demand elasticity (e) of −0.2, a 1 million cwt. cut in 1965 potato production would have the following estimated impact on United States farm income:

$$1965 \text{ price } (p) = \$2.34/\text{cwt.}$$
$$1965 \text{ production } (q) = 289 \text{ million cwt.}$$
$$\Delta p = \frac{(p)\ (\Delta q)}{(q)\ (e)} = \frac{(\$2.34)\ (-1)}{(289)\ (-0.2)} = \$0.04/\text{cwt.}$$
$$\Delta I = (q + \Delta q)\ (P + \Delta P) - (Pq)$$
$$= (288 \text{ million} \times \$2.38) - (289 \text{ million} \times \$2.34)$$
$$\$685.4 \text{ million} - \$676.2 \text{ million} = \$9.2 \text{ million.}$$

[15] An estimate based on a production cut of 38 million cwt. and a $9.2 million increase in income per million cwt. cut.

impact on farm income was a $357 million increase in the farm value of potatoes.

Sugarbeets

The increase in sugarbeet acreage since 1944 was gradual until the United States made an effort to increase domestic production during the 1962–63 world sugar shortage (table 56). Reclamation-served land contributed 216,000 acres (46 percent) of the substantial increase in production and by 1964 made up 43 percent of the total U.S. acreage harvested, as compared with 28 percent in 1944. In 1964, reclamation production accounted for 45 percent of U.S. production and 51 percent of the production in the seventeen reclamation states—much larger shares than in 1944, when the percentages were only 28 and 33 percent, respectively (table 57).

Table 56. U.S. Sugarbeet Acreage Harvested by Regions

thousand acres

Regions	1964	1959	1954	1949	1944
South (Texas)	22	2	1	1	(a)
North	406	292	276	217	174
West (11 States)	948	618	587	444	373
Total	1,376	912	864	662	546
Reclamation portion	587	371	378	175	151

Source: See table 52.

[a] Less than 500 acres.

Table 57. U.S. Sugarbeet Production by Regions

thousand tons

Regions[a]	1964	1959	1954	1949	1944
North Central	3,081	2,603	1,923	1,502	1,025
West (17 states)	20,120	14,219	11,715	8,443	5,817
West (11 states)	17,171	12,447	10,363	7,545	5,087
Plains	2,949	1,772	1,352	898	730
U.S. total*	23,202	16,822	13,638	9,944	6,841
Reclamation portion	10,361[b]	7,147	6,289	2,817	1,941
Nonreclamation West	9,759	7,072	5,424	5,626	3,876

Source: See table 52.

* Totals may not add due to rounding.

[a] Regions are shown in figure 15. The 17 western states include the West (11 states) and the Plains (6 states).

[b] 5.2 million tons were produced on land receiving full reclamation irrigation service, 5.0 million tons came from land with supplemental service while the remainder came from land with temporary service.

Figure 15. Regions used in Table 58.

The United States could reduce the cost of sugar by cutting back domestic sugar production and importing more. The savings would be substantial as the world price of raw sugar is about 2¢ a pound and the domestic price is over 7¢ a pound. Over the long run the United States could probably obtain an adequate and dependable supply of sugar at a price of 3¢ to 4¢ a pound (D. Gale Johnson 1968, p. 44). Transportation cost and import fees might increase the price by 1¢ to 1.5¢ a pound, but consumers would still save from 3.5¢ to 4¢ a pound in the short run and 1.5¢ to 3¢ a pound in the long run. The saving from substituting imports for reclamation raw sugar (approximately 2,870 million pounds in 1964) could range from $43.1 million at a saving of 1.5¢ per pound to $114.8 million at 4¢ per pound.[16, 17] One difficulty in the way of a quick reversal of sugar policy is that, once reclamation brings land into production and sugarbeets become the basis for reclamation loan repayment, it is almost impossible to reduce reclamation sugar allotments without either bankrupting farmers and reclamation districts or increasing the federal irrigation subsidy.

Vegetables

Only the eleven Western states showed an increase in commercial vegetable acreage over the fifteen years from 1949 to 1964 (see table 58).

[16] Savings would accrue on all sugar if the U.S. set lower sugar prices.
[17] U.S. Department of Agriculture, *Sugar Reports*, August 1966, No. 171, and *Agricultural Statistics, 1966*, pp. 80–96.

Table 58.   U.S. Vegetables, Commercial: Acreage of Principal Crops by Regions
Excluding Potatoes

thousand acres

Regions[a]	1964	1959	1954	1949	Percentage change 1949–64
North Atlantic	397	434	517	526	−25
North Central	779	792	911	901	−14
South Atlantic	633	728	878	673	−6
South Central	110	143	149	146	−25
West (17 states)[b]	1,352	1,395	1,447	1,275	+6
Plains	291	331	482	381	−24
West (11 states)	1,060	1,064	965	894	+19
Total*	3,371	3,491	3,902	3,521	−4
Reclamation portion	325	273	221	220	+48
Nonreclamation West	1,027	1,122	1,226	1,055	−3

Source: Agricultural Statistics, 1951, 1956, 1961, and 1967.

* Totals may not add due to rounding.
[a] See figure 15 for a map of the regions used in this table.
[b] No acreage report for North Dakota.

Each of the other regions experienced reductions ranging from 6 to 25 percent as vegetable production shifted to the West. The total decline in the United States was only 150,000 acres, a 4 percent drop. In 1964, 168,000 acres of the reclamation-served area received full irrigation service, 141,000 acres supplemental service, and 16,000 temporary service. Without this service it is doubtful that many vegetables would be grown on these lands because of the importance in vegetable production of a dependable supply of water. The major vegetables contributing to the 1964 production on reclamation-served lands were lettuce, melons, sweet corn, tomatoes, onions, and carrots.

The shift in production has centered in the reclamation-served lands of the eleven Western states where producers can count on a stable, low-cost supply of water. Between 1949 and 1964 reclamation-served vegetable acreage increased 48 percent (105,000 acres), virtually all of the increase occurring after 1954. The total increase for the seventeen Western states was only 77,000 acres (6 percent). The Plains states, which have only 1 percent of the reclamation-served vegetable production, show a decline of 90,000 acres (24 percent) for 1949–64 and an even larger decline of 191,000 acres for 1954–64. Nonreclamation-served acreage in the eleven Western states has increased by only 61,000 acres since 1949 and has actually been declining since 1954. Thus, increased reclamation-served acreage has been a big factor in increasing the West's share of vegetable acreage and in reducing production in the nonreclamation West and other U.S. regions.

Fruits and Nuts

Like vegetables, fruits and nuts produced on reclamation-served land are primarily in the eleven Western states, less than 0.5 percent of the acreage being in the Plains states. Twenty-one percent (383,000 acres) of the fruits and nuts in the eleven Western states are on reclamation land (see table 59). Reclamation-served land accounted for 9.5 percent of total U.S. fruit and nut acreage in 1964.

Between 1944–64 the acreage of fruits and nuts fell 50 percent in the North and dropped by 6 percent in the South. In contrast to these declines, overall acreage in the West increased by 23,000 acres while the acreage on reclamation-served lands increased 237 percent or 270,000 acres. Hence, acreage in the nonreclamation West must have declined by 247,000 acres, or 13 percent.

Some of the important fruits produced on reclamation-served land are apples, citrus, grapes, and pears. Citrus production on reclamation land, which increased sharply from 3 million to 14 million cwt. between 1944–64, competes directly with the Southeast and the nonreclamation West. Similarly, reclamation apple production, which rose from 5.8 million to 8.7 million cwt. during the same twenty-year period, competes directly with the apples grown in the North.

Pear production on reclamation-served land increased 2.3 million cwt. during 1944–64 while in the eleven Western states the increase was only 1.9 million cwt. (See table 60.) Since all the reclamation production was in these eleven states the nonreclamation West actually had a decline of 385,000 cwt. and an even greater decline of nearly 2.5 million cwt. since 1949. Both the North and South experienced drops in relative and absolute production during the same period. The decline in the non-

Table 59.   *U.S. Fruit and Nut Acreage Harvested by Regions*

thousand acres

Regions	1964	1959	1954	1949	1944
North	640	700	793	1,049	1,298
South	1,725	1,647	1,579	1,835	1,840
West (11 States)	1,886	1,773	1,632	1,833	1,863
Total*	4,251	4,120	4,003	4,716	5,001
Reclamation portion	384[a]	309	254	196	114

Source: See table 52.

* Totals may not add due to rounding.

[a] 255,000 acres received supplemental irrigation service, 118,000 full irrigation service and 11,000 acres temporary service.

Table 60. U.S. Pear Production by Regions

thousand cwt.

Regions	1964	1959	1954	1949	1944
North	1,244	1,126	669	1,271	1,835
South	93	219	264	638	1,524
West (11 States)	12,474	11,981	12,453	11,541	10,535
Total*	13,812	13,326	13,386	13,450	13,894
Reclamation portion	4,410ᵃ	3,303	1,768	1,003	2,086

Source: See table 52.

* Totals may not add due to rounding.

ᵃ 3.4 million cwt. were produced on land receiving supplemental reclamation irrigation while the remaining 1 million cwt. came from land receiving full reclamation irrigation.

reclamation (North, South and nonreclamation West) production since 1949 totaled 3 million cwt., only slightly less than the 3.4 million cwt. increase on reclamation-served land. At 1965 farm prices of $6.50 per cwt., the value of the shift in production would be between $19 and $23 million.

Rice

Rice acreage has been under fairly tight federal controls, and the acreage harvested has fluctuated mostly in response to changes in federal acreage limitations. Even with the limitations, rice production has more than doubled over the last twenty years. Production in the eleven Western States and on reclamation lands is almost exclusively in California's Central Valley. Rice acreage on reclamation-served lands accounts for 43 percent of California's total rice acreage and over 8 percent of the total United States acreage; 10 percent of the total U.S. rice production and 44 percent of California's production (see table 61). The increase in Western rice output has been quite rapid, but the four southern states are the big rice producers.[18]

A transfer of 12 million bushels of rice production from reclamation-served lands to the South would mean a 10 percent increase in rice production for those states. At 1965 prices of $2.22 per bushel, this amount of production would be worth $26.6 million in gross farm income. Using $1.24 per bushel as a rough estimate of the cost of production, the production transfer would be worth $11.8 million in net farm income.

[18] Resource Use Adjustment in Southern Rice Areas (Effects of Price Changes with Unrestricted Rice Acreages), Southern Cooperative Series Bulletin 122, June 1967. Available from Arkansas Agricultural Experiment Station, University of Arkansas, Fayetteville, Arkansas.

Table 61. *U.S. Rice Acreage Harvested and Production by Regions*

Regions	Harvested acreage (1,000 acres)					Production (1,000 bushels)				
	1964	1959	1954	1949	1944	1964	1959	1954	1949	1944
North (Missouri)	5	4	6	n.a.	n.a.	443	276	376	n.a.	n.a.
South[a]	1,467	1,311	2,017	1,515	1,162	127,980	91,217	116,578	67,410	50,529
West (California)	343	302	474	304	232	37,852	29,404	28,122	22,022	14,515
Total*	1,815	1,617	2,498	1,819	1,394	166,276	120,896	145,076	89,432	65,044
Reclamation portion (California)[b]	147	7	16	n.a.	n.a.	16,548	656	1,132	n.a.	n.a.

Source: See table 52.

n.a. = not available.

* Totals may not add due to rounding.

[a] South includes Mississippi, Arkansas, Louisiana, and Texas.

[b] This land receives primarily supplemental reclamation irrigation service. The big acreage increase in 1964 is due to the inclusion of rice acreage on the Central Valley Project in California. These lands, long irrigated under private initiative, now fall under the repayment requirements of Reclamation Law.

Feed and Forage Crops

Taking the nine major feed and forage crops (barley, corn, oats, sorghum, wheat, pasture, silage, other hay, and alfalfa hay) and converting the production to feed units, one obtains a good picture of reclamation's direct contribution to feed and forage production in the last twenty years. Almost 10 percent of the total U.S. increase in feed and forage output has been on reclamation-served land. (See table 62.)

Increased feed production on reclamation land has a fairly direct effect on livestock prices. Brandow finds that prices of hogs and poultry

Table 62.   Changes in the U.S. Production of Major Feed and Forage Crops
by Region between 1944–64

millions of feed unit

Crop	Reclama-tion	United States*	West	North	South
Barley	+830	+4,434	+4,131	−39	+342
Corn	+1,122	+28,635	+354	+32,940	−4,659
Oats	+42	−6,749	−541	−4,684	−1,524
Sorghum	+309[a]	+15,106	+1,485	+7,776	+5,845
Wheat	+838	+11,663	+3,547	+8,919	−803
Alfalfa hay	+4,265	¦ 39,282	+7,263	+30,391	+1,628
Other hay[b]	+104	−11,909	−303	−14,702	+3,096
Silage[c]	+1,970	+23,001	+3,392	+15,522	+4,087
Pasture (irrigated)	+178	n.a.	n.a.	n.a.	n.a.
Total*	+9,658	+103,463	+19,328	+76,123	+8,012

Sources: Production data from sources listed in table 52. Conversion factors from Earl F. Hodges, *Consumption of Feed by Livestock 1940–1959*, USDA Production Research Report no. 79, March 1964; *Livestock-Feed Relationships 1909–1963*, USDA Statistical Bulletin no. 337, November 1963, and *Supplement*, September 1965.

Conversion factors. The following factors were used to convert production to feed units:

Wheat—bu. × 63   Alfalfa hay—tons × 1,100
Barley—bu. × 44   Pasture (irrigated)—acres × 1,600
Corn—bu. × 50   Other hay—tons × 800
Sorghum—bu. × 53   Silage—tons × 400
Oats—bu. × 29

n.a. = not available.
* Totals may not add because of rounding.
[a] Reclamation production figures for sorghum were not available in 1944 and 1949; the 1944 production was estimated at 1.5 million bushels based on the rate of increase in sorghum production on reclamation-served lands during 1954–64 and the quantity of other cereals reported (which included sorghum) in the reclamation statistics for 1944.
[b] Other hay excludes alfalfa, soybean, cowpea, and sorghum hay.
[c] Silage figure includes corn, sorghum, and grass silage. Reclamation 1944 silage production was estimated at 50,000 tons based on other forage crops reported (which included silage) in the reclamation statistics.

are sharply reduced by an increase in the tonnage of concentrated feed (corn, barley, oats, sorghum and wheat). He notes that a 1 percent increase in the quantity of concentrate fed to livestock increases the weight added in cattle feeding about 1.9 percent and total cattle slaughter 0.23 percent. (Brandow 1961, pp. 72–74.)

Concentrate feed prices are quite responsive to changes in quantity. Elasticity of demand is about −0.23 which means that a 1 percent increase in quantity will cause a 4.4 percent drop in prices. Since reclamation has increased total U.S. concentrate production over 1 percent during the last twenty years, prices would be about 4.4 percent lower because of this production if it were not for annual commodity programs. Reclamation's increased production of hay and silage has had an even greater impact than concentrates. In the last twenty years reclamation irrigation has increased U.S. silage production by 5 percent and alfalfa hay production by 6 percent. Since there are no federal programs to control the supply of forage crops, these increases have had direct effects through lower prices and farm income for nonreclamation farmers.

Feed Grains

The feed grains included in this discussion—corn, barley, oats and sorghum—are readily substitutable both in production and consumption. Their demand is derived primarily from the production of livestock and livestock products. Small changes in relative prices bring quick shifts in use by buyers while sustained price changes bring adjustments in production.

Besides the overall decline in acreage, there has been some shifting among feed grains (see table 63). Sorghum and barley acreages have

Table 63.   U.S. Feed Grain Acreage Harvested by Regions

thousand acres

Regions	1964	1959	1954	1949	1944
North	70,392	91,107	92,024	90,721	95,279
South	16,542	25,862	28,433	28,784	38,363
West (11 States)	6,727	8,429	8,117	6,476	6,885
Total*	93,661	125,398	128,574	125,982	140,529
Reclamation portion	1,098[a]	1,207	1,065	697	589

Source: See table 52.

Note: Feed grains include corn, barley, sorghum and oats.

* Totals may not add due to rounding.

[a] 605,000 acres received full reclamation irrigation service, 487,000 acres received supplemental service while the remaining 6,000 acres received temporary service.

Table 64. U.S. Soybean Acreage Harvested by Regions

thousand acres

Regions	1964	1959	1954	1949
North	21,614	16,367	13,569	8,761
South	8,229	5,712	2,874	1,387
West (11 States)	1	1	1	(a)
Total	29,844	22,080	16,444	10,148

Source: See table 52.

a Less than 500 acres.

tended to increase while the acreage of oats has declined sharply. Between 1959 and 1964 feed grain acreages were cut back through the annual feed grain programs in an attempt to raise prices and farm income. Up through 1959, reclamation feed grain acreage had bucked the trend with steady increases.

Before the institution of annual feed grain programs, increased production on reclamation lands put direct pressure on feed grain producers in marginal areas in the Southern and Plains States through lower prices. Even with the feed grain programs, shifts in production continue to take place, particularly increases in soybean acreage harvested in the North and in the South (see table 64). The primary reasons for these acreage shifts appear to be the growing market for soybeans and the decline in acreage used for cotton and grain production. Some of this decline is the result of increased reclamation production.

Alfalfa Hay

Reclamation alfalfa hay acreage increased by 713,000 acres between 1944 and 1964 and production more than doubled (see table 65). The impact of this production was felt in livestock and livestock product markets rather than in the hay markets of the North or South. Since hay cannot be shipped great distances except in dehydrated form it is generally fed to livestock not very far from the local markets. But hay competes on the national markets through the final product. At any given level of livestock prices, the cheaper the hay and feed grains the more livestock and livestock products that will be produced, which in turn drives down livestock prices.

How much the increased alfalfa hay production on reclamation-served land may have contributed to lower livestock and livestock product prices is difficult to determine. The increase of over 4 million tons of

Table 65. *U.S. Alfalfa Hay Acreage Harvested and Production by Regions*

Regions	Harvested acreage (1,000 acres)					Production (1,000 tons)				
	1964	1959	1954	1949	1944	1964	1959	1954	1949	1944
South	1,713	1,593	1,788	1,433	1,166	3,888	3,562	3,011	3,020	2,408
North	20,408	19,015	18,767	10,688	8,915	45,054	39,900	36,792	20,597	17,426
West	6,091	5,499	5,453	4,291	4,897	19,438	16,410	15,112	11,637	12,835
Total*	28,211	26,107	26,008	16,412	14,977	68,381	59,871	54,914	35,254	32,670
Reclamation portion	1,868	1,629	1,483	1,106	1,155	7,708ᵃ	6,289	5,090	3,551	3,831

Source: See table 52.

* Totals may not add due to rounding.

ᵃ 4.1 million tons were produced on lands receiving full reclamation irrigation service, 3.5 million tons on land with supplemental service and the remainder on lands with temporary service.

alfalfa on reclamation-served land between 1949 and 1964 represented 13 percent of the total U.S. increase. In 1964 reclamation-served land produced over 11 percent of the total U.S. production.

Conclusion

There can be little doubt from the data analyzed that reclamation irrigation has had a significant effect on U.S. agriculture. Increased production on reclamation-served land has increased USDA payments, stimulated regional production shifts, and reduced the incomes of non-reclamation farmers. It is estimated that an acre of land irrigated by reclamation is responsible for an increase of $16 to $468 in annual commodity program payments, the amount varying with the commodity, the assumptions made concerning the relative productivity of displaced land, and the effectiveness of the commodity programs. The reclamation impact on crops not under the annual commodity programs ranged from a shift of $19 million to $23 million in gross farm income for pears to an estimated change of $350 million in net farm income for potato farmers. Finally, from 5 million to 17 million acres of cropland have been displaced by the 1944–64 increase in reclamation irrigation. In terms of income forgone this impact would fall within the range of $50 million to $170 million annually.

These impacts of reclamation projects have not been adequately considered in evaluations of project feasibility. Thus two steps are needed: (1) additional research, indicating possible procedures for estimating and including the appropriate related costs in the cost-benefit analysis, and (2) legislative or executive action requiring federal water agencies to include such costs in their project analysis.

Even if the United States had no excess capacity in agriculture (which the numerous land retirement programs remind us is not so), it would not follow that additional federal irrigation is needed. If additional agricultural capacity is desired, the least-cost means of increasing capacity should be selected.

Summary and Conclusions

The primary objectives of this study have been: (1) to assess the economic desirability of large-scale interbasin transfers of water in the western United States by gathering evidence on the value of water and by illuminating the variety of alternatives available to solve the perceived problems of the area; and (2) to emphasize the variety of economic impacts, both beneficial and detrimental, that large transfers can have on the regions they affect directly and on far-removed regions of the nation.

The benefits arising directly and indirectly from new supplies of water, the direct and indirect costs of providing new water by large-scale transfers, and the availability of a variety of alternative water supply developments set limits on the situations in which large-scale transfers should receive further consideration. The preponderance of the evidence indicates that, except for certain sets of circumstances in so-called "rescue operations," the national economic benefits from the use of the water provided would be less than the cost of the transfers. Furthermore, there is evidence that substantial supplies could be obtained from alternative sources at lower costs.

A survey of interbasin transfers has shown that such undertakings are certainly not new to the United States. The feature which does, however, distinguish current proposals from past projects is size—a characteristic which leaps by a factor of ten or more between the largest existing interbasin transfer and typical current proposals. This difference in size, combined with a growing economy and a population whose attention is turned toward economic growth, implies conflict over transfers of water of an intensity not encountered in earlier transfers—conflict between the water importing and exporting regions and between those who would benefit from expanded, subsidized agriculture and those agricultural producers who are pushed out of the market by this new output.

168

Tracing the impacts of water importation is a difficult undertaking in part because of the complex physical relationships among water users in a hydrologic system. Externalities or downstream effects which greatly complicate the analysis of even simple steps such as changing points of water diversion along an existing stream tremendously complicate the task of computing benefits to an importing region or the opportunity costs of water diverted from an exporting region. Beyond the complexities of physical interrelationships among water users lie the market relationships between direct water users and other parties: those who supply inputs to the water users, those who depend upon the water users for inputs, and those who compete against them for markets. An analysis of these relationships is necessary for projects as large as those currently being proposed, particularly since substantial induced unemployment and resource immobility may be connected with such projects. In the analysis of such projects, we have left the happy world of partial equilibrium analysis in which other regions can be assumed to be unaffected.

The analysis of the benefits from additional water has concentrated on the agricultural sector because agricultural uses constitute about 90 percent of total consumptive uses in the West and because direct benefits per acre-foot are lower in agriculture than in most municipal and industrial uses. Evidence on the latter point in the form of prices paid for water, the values of irrigation company shares, and seasonal rental prices for water has been cited in the study. *Direct* benefits to established agriculture were found to range roughly from zero in some irrigation areas to $45 per acre-foot in a small number of areas, but most areas fell in a $10 to $20 per acre-foot range. Total benefits, both to established agriculture and related industries were found to range from $14 to $120 per acre-foot, the latter only under conditions of extreme labor and capital immobility.

Whether such values will increase or decrease in the future depends largely upon the demands placed upon U.S. irrigated agriculture. The authors have concluded that there are ways of increasing agricultural output which would cost substantially less than the expansion of Western irrigated acreage and, further, that it is unlikely that demands for U.S. agricultural products will grow to such an extent that it would become economically justifiable to expand irrigated acreage in the arid areas. The preponderance of evidence at this time seems to indicate a world grain surplus past 1980, with only a slow growth in U.S. exports.

There are many alternative sources from which additional water can be extracted for use in the West. These include reduction of conveyance losses, additional surface development, wastewater reclamation, desalination, vegetative management and phreatophyte control, evaporation retardation, and transfers from agriculture to higher-valued uses. Several of these alternatives promise large additional supplies of water at costs lower than those of large-scale transfers. Cost figures (in 1963–65 dollars) for the major interbasin transfer proposals are based on very preliminary plans, but fall mostly in the range of $50 to $60 per acre-foot. These figures are highly dependent upon electrical power costs and the extent of possible power recovery, and would undoubtedly be affected substantially by the inflation of construction costs in recent years.

A very promising alternative is the reduction of conveyance losses for irrigation water. It has been indicated that as much as 9 million acre-feet per year could be saved in the United States west of the 100th meridian at costs ranging from $2 to $50 per acre-foot. This source would provide about the same amount of water as most of the proposed Columbia–Colorado transfers, most of it at lower costs.

A second source would be continued surface development—a source capable of substantial increase in the Western Gulf and Central Pacific regions. As much as 32 million acre-feet per year might be developed in those regions at impoundment costs at $3 to $41 per acre-foot. Much of this water would require smaller scale transfer systems but much could still compete with large-scale transfers. Naturally, there is possible conflict between reservoir site development and preservation of natural areas for recreation and fish and wildlife preservation. It is not clear that the surface water development costs quoted above properly reflect the site values being forgone in these other uses. (It is known that reservoir sites reserved in the public domain are, in general, assigned no opportunity cost whatsoever, and that in a few cases positive benefits have been counted for the values of the one-time harvesting of timber or taking of minerals prior to inundation, no account being taken of forgone future harvests of these products.) This practice must be changed if water development alternatives are to be honestly assessed and compared.

The control of phreatophytes and streamside vegetation promises to salvage large amounts of water at costs ranging from $1 to $50 or $60 per acre-foot. Chemical and physical controls and manipulation of groundwater levels to deprive the plants of water are the methods currently used, and biological or pathological controls can probably be developed.

Desalting, though highly publicized as a source of water for agriculture, seems to be the least-cost alternative for only isolated urban needs. Costs, both present and prospective, prohibit the use of desalted water in most agricultural applications.

A valuable source of "new" water currently available at very low cost for municipal areas is wastewater reclamation. The current potential

for Southern California is at least 700,000 acre-feet per year, nearly equal-
ling the amount of Colorado River water which Southern California may
ultimately have to give up to other Colorado River users. Los Angeles
is currently producing about 16 mgd of potable reclaimed water which is
recharged to the ground and then pumped by downstream municipal and
industrial users. The full costs of the operation have been $18 per acre-
foot, excluding downstream pumping costs.

A controversial source of water for municipalities and industries and
one that has already been tapped by expanding urban areas in the Southwest is the purchase of agricultural water rights by urban water systems
and industry. The transfers that have taken place so far have been from
relatively low-income agriculture to activities that produce higher incomes. Since such transfers tend to take place gradually over time, the
problems of relocating displaced farm labor and capital are not massive
and are facilitated by the opportunities presented by the expanding
urban area itself. Studies of northeastern Colorado and Tucson, Arizona,
where this process has been taking place quite smoothly for many years,
indicate the ranges of total cost of such transferred water (in terms of all
incomes forgone in agriculture and related sectors) to be $15 to $32 per
acre-foot and $16 to $39 per acre-foot respectively. These costs are considerably less than those of most of the sizable interbasin transfers.

In the cases cited above, rural-urban water transfers are clearly much
cheaper than large-scale interbasin transfers. For example, the Central Arizona Project will cost at least $35 per acre-foot *plus* local delivery works *plus*
the opportunity cost of the water diverted from the Colorado River. Yet the
Central Arizona Project receives strong backing from the people of
Arizona and other western states. This raises the issue of the *incidence*
of benefits and costs implied by different modes of water supply and
related financing arrangements. The federal government will pay for a
large part of the Central Arizona Project while the people of Central
Arizona will have to pay the costs of purchasing agricultural water rights
in any rural-urban water transfers. While the benefits are essentially the
same, the *incidence of costs* is much different, being placed upon the
whole nation in the case of the Central Arizona Project, but upon the
beneficiaries alone in the case of the purchase of agricultural water rights.
Federal subsidies and repayment policies thus have the power of sub-
verting economically rational decisions in this vital area of water supply.

Turning to the short-term and long-term economic impacts of transfer projects, it must be recognized that the proposed projects are quite
large, ranging in estimated total cost from $1.3 billion to $100 billion.
The hypothetical transfer studied in some detail in chapter 4 had a
(1963) cost of $5.7 billion and involved a transfer of 7.5 million acre-feet

per year. Even when spread over several years, such a project would represent a large part of the budget of any federal agency, and the inputs required for the project's construction, both labor and materials, would be large, especially relative to supplies available in the likely construction regions. An analysis of construction period impacts, using a method of analysis developed by Haveman and Krutilla, has indicated that the direct and indirect demands of such a project for material requirements would be felt most in the highly industrial East-Central section of the country, while the direct and indirect labor skills requirements fall very heavily upon the highly skilled and professional categories. It thus seems clear that the act of constructing such projects does not lend much to the solution of chronic regional unemployment problems.

Potential longer-term impacts and benefits have been analyzed in some detail through the application of state input-output models and related calculations. The analysis covered two hypothetical situations: one in which the water delivered by the transfer was applied to the expansion of agricultural acreage in Oregon and another in which the water was used in a rescue operation to prevent the phasing-out of established agriculture and related activities in Southern California. The crucial difference between the two situations is that the expanding area must find markets for its output and attract inputs from other areas and occupations, while the contracting area already has its markets and economic structure established and would experience outward immobility of some of its capital and labor resources. In the former situation, benefits from the transfer project would be confined largely to project-related irrigated agriculture, perhaps extending to some other sectors if agricultural output has been acting as a bottleneck to their expansion. In the case of a contracting region, induced unemployment of capital and labor may pervade the contracting area, depending upon the degrees of "forward linkage" of agriculture to other sectors and the extent of capital and labor immobility. It is the prevention of these income losses, part temporary, part permanent, which a water rescue operation would achieve.

The range of national benefits stemming from the hypothetical Oregon expansion case study was estimated to be from $7 per acre-foot to $65 per acre-foot, depending strongly upon the degree of forward linkage assumed between agriculture and other sectors and upon the extent to which the utilization of otherwise unemployed labor and capacity can be claimed by the project. In the hypothetical Southern California case, the range of national benefits was found to be from $8 per acre-foot to $129 per acre-foot, actual values depending upon the degrees of forward linkage of agriculture to other sectors and the pattern of immobility of labor and capital resources should agriculture be phased out. Figures estimated by others for the state of Arizona indicate that a $15 to $40 per acre-foot range is probably most realistic.

The major point to be learned from the long-term impact studies is that the national benefits stemming from large-scale transfers are crucially dependent upon forward linkages from agriculture and the degree of labor and capital immobility—topics about which little is known. The matter of forward linkages is, in reality, a matter of the extent to which substitute commodities are available for local agricultural outputs. If substitutes can be readily procured from other areas, there will be little dependence of other sectors on local agriculture.

The potential impact of large-scale expansions of irrigated agriculture on other regions is an aspect of water transfers that is usually ignored. The expansion of irrigated acreage displaces, through the market, production in other areas. When the new irrigated acreage is made profitable only by continuing Federal subsidies, this displacement clearly is economically inefficient. Further social costs are incurred if displaced farm labor then migrates to cities, and these costs can offset advantages that may accrue to the nation from keeping people "down on the farm" in irrigated areas.

Substantial evidence of production displacement by western irrigated agriculture has been presented in chapter 6 suggesting that increased reclamation irrigation over the period 1944–64 has displaced millions of acres of farmland in nonreclamation areas: somewhere between 8 and 26 percent of 66-million-acre decline in harvested cropland during 1944–64, depending upon the assumed productivity of the retired lands. For crops such as potatoes, edible dry beans, and sugarbeets, the direct displacement effects are large since reclamation-served lands account for a substantial share of U.S. production—almost 20 percent of potato producttion, over 30 percent of edible dry bean production, and 45 percent of sugarbeet production in 1964.

The real value of the 1944 to 1964 additions to cropland served by the Bureau of Reclamation is called into question by a survey of land retirement in 171 reclamation counties which accounted for most of the 8 million acres receiving reclamation irrigation in 1965. Over 3 million acres were in retirement under federal programs in those counties in 1965. This is just the amount of cropland brought into production by the Bureau of Reclamation in the period 1944–64. It is, of course, true that the retired land is of lower productivity.

An example of the impact of irrigated acreage on national farm income is provided by the 1965 potato crop. Potato acreage served by reclamation irrigation increased 40,000 acres during 1964–65, while irrigation production was up almost 19 million hundredweight. Since this accounted for 40 percent of the total U.S. *increase* in production, approximately $69 million of the $173 million *decline* in farm value of potatoes that year can be attributed to increased production on lands served by reclamation. Farm incomes fell even more, when account is taken of production costs. These losses may be compared with an increase of $2.9 million in the farm value of potatoes produced on the reclamation-served lands themselves.

The increase in irrigated cotton acreage harvested during 1964–65 provides an example of the impact which new irrigated acreage can have on federal farm commodity payments. Upland cotton increased by 90,000 acres. As a result, it is estimated that Department of Agriculture diversion and price support payments increased by an amount falling somewhere in the range of $18 million to $42 million. Additional calculations indicate that cotton price support and acreage diversion programs imply a *total federal cost between $201 and $468 per year per acre of reclamation irrigated cotton.* The price support payments are largely income transfers from the general population to cotton growers and the acreage diversion payments, insofar as they represent the net income which the farmer would have realized from using the land in production, represent the net value of production forgone.

Other large programs of subsidy are related to other irrigated crops. Annual payments attributable to sugarbeets grown on reclamation irrigated land amount to a *minimum* of $11.5 million. If one considers the cost to the consumer to be the difference between the world price and the quota-protected U.S. sugar price minus the difference in transport costs, the annual cost to the consumer, expressed as a cost per acre of irrigated sugarbeets, is nearly $200. Other commodity program payments are estimated to run from a low of $16 per acre for wheat to $136 per acre for corn.

The tremendous conflicts among major federal programs and the very high cost of these conflicts stand out clearly in these examples. The provision of water for agriculture has conflicted directly with attempts to raise the incomes of farmers and of particular regions and has placed large costs on the general taxpayer. These costs are never counted in the project reports which justify irrigation works.

Our conclusions, then, point to a need for more inclusive evaluations in water resource planning and design. Various methodologies which would be useful in that direction have been demonstrated. All alternatives need to be considered for water supply, and the full range of impacts of water projects must be taken into account. To assume that one agency or department can plan without close technical and policy-level coordination with other departments can only lead to a continuation of inconsistencies like those illustrated above.

It is also clear that resolving Western water problems in the *national* interest is highly dependent upon improved repayment policies which will provide a better market test for the outputs produced by federal water projects and eliminate biases in current decisions which occur because of an uneven incidence of benefits and costs among the population.

The research needs uncovered by this study stem first from the general lack of knowledge about regional trade patterns and the degrees to which industries within a region are linked together by mutual isolation from competitive, substitute commodities from other regions. The importance of these linkages to the developmental impacts of water projects and the benefits accruing from them was pointed out in chapter 4.

A second research need is to learn more about the patterns of immobility of resources in a region under major economic change. We should know who can and who cannot move quickly to other areas or jobs and what costs are incurred in making these moves. We should know what characteristics of the area and population determine these responses. What happens to capital equipment of different types and what proportion can be expected to be employed in alternative activities should also be known. We should know more about the social factors, costs, and losses involved in the process of job change or migration. Greater knowledge in these areas can lead us closer to the goal of adequate assessment of the impacts of large-scale projects.

References

Abel, Martin E., and Rojko, Anthony S. 1967. *World food situation: Prospects for world grain production, consumption, and trade*. USDA Foreign Agricultural Economic Report no. 35.

Allen, Robert Loring, and Watson, Donald A. 1965. *The structure of the Oregon economy: An input/output study*. Eugene: Bureau of Business and Economic Research, University of Oregon.

American City Magazine. 1966. *Modern water rates*. New York: Buttenheim Publishing Corporation.

American Society of Agronomy. 1967. *Irrigation of agricultural lands*. Monograph 11. Madison, Wisconsin.

American Society of Civil Engineers, Los Angeles Section. 1967. *Water for the West: Summary of regional water plans*.

Anderson, Raymond L. 1961. The irrigation water rental market: A case study. *Agricultural Economics Research*, vol. 13, no. 2, pp. 54–58.

Arizona Game and Fish Department. 1964. *A summary of the fish and wildlife features of the Pacific Southwest Water Plan, including the Central Arizona Project*.

Bagley, Jay M. March 1965. Effects of competition on efficiency of water use. *Journal of the Irrigation and Drainage Division, Proceedings of the American Society of Civil Engineers*, vol. 91, IR1, pp. 69–77.

Bathen, R. E.; Cunningham, P. R.; and Mayben, W. R. 1967. A new water resource for the Great Plains. Paper presented at Annual Meeting, Mid-West Electric Consumers, Omaha, Nebraska, December 1967. Denver: R. W. Bech and Associates.

Baumol, William J. 1958. *Economic theory and operations analysis*. Englewood Cliffs, N.J.: Prentice-Hall.

Beattie, Byron. 1967. Increased water yields and improved timing of streamflow through manipulation of forest vegetation and snowpack management. Paper

177

presented at the International Conference on Water for Peace, Washington, D.C., May 1967.

———. 1968. Harvesting the National Forest water crop. Paper presented at 36th Annual Convention of National Reclamation Association, Honolulu, Hawaii, November 1967. U.S. Forest Service.

Bechtel Corporation. 1965. *Engineering and economic feasibility study for a combination nuclear power and desalting plant: Summary.* Study sponsored jointly by the Metropolitan Water District of Southern California, U.S. Department of the Interior, Office of Saline Water, U.S. Atomic Energy Commission. Available from Clearinghouse for Federal Scientific and Technical Information, National Bureau of Standards, U.S. Department of Commerce, Springfield, Va.

Berry, Brian J. L. 1967. *Strategies, models, and economic theories of development in rural regions.* USDA Agricultural Economic Report no. 127.

Bittinger, M. W. 1964. The problem of integrating ground-water and surface water use. *Ground Water*, vol. 2, no. 3.

Blaney, H. F., and Criddle, W. D. 1962. *Determining consumptive use and irrigation water requirements.* USDA Technical Bulletin no. 1275.

Borton, Glen T., and Brown, Herbert. 1967. The commercialization of southern agriculture. Paper presented at a symposium on Research to Aid the Commercialization of Southern Agriculture, Atlanta, Georgia, March 1967.

Boyko, Hugo. 1967. Salt-water agriculture. *Science*, June 1967, pp. 89–96.

Brandow, G. E. 1961. *Interrelations among demands for farm products and implications for control of market supply.* Bulletin 680, Pennsylvania State University.

Brown, Gardner M., Jr. 1964. Distribution of benefits and costs: A case study of the San Joaquin Valley–Southern California Aqueduct System. Doctoral dissertation, University of California, Berkeley.

Brown, Gardner M., Jr., and McGuire, C. B. 1967. A socially optimum pricing policy for a public water agency. *Water Resources Research,* vol. 3, no. 1, pp. 33–43.

Brown, Lester R. 1966. The world food/population problem: An overview. Remarks at the Conference on Alternatives for Balancing Future World Food Production and Needs sponsored by Iowa State University Center for Agricultural and Economic Adjustment, Ames, Iowa, November 1966.

———. 1968. New directions for world agriculture. *Foreign Agriculture*, March 25, 1968, pp. 8–10.

———. 1970. *Seeds of change: The green revolution and development in the 1970's.* New York: Praeger.

California, Department of Water Resources. 1957. *The California Water Plan.* Bulletin no. 3. Sacramento.

———. 1965. *The California State Water Project in 1965, Appendix C: Statistics.* Bulletin no. 132–65.

———. 1966. *Reclamation of water from wastes: Coachella Valley.* Bulletin no. 80–3.

———. 1966. *Implementation of the California Water Plan.* Bulletin no. 160–66.

Carter, H. O., and Ireri, Dunstan. 1967. An input-output model for the Southern California economy.

Cooper, Charles F., and Jolly, William C. 1969. *Ecological effects of weather modification: A problem analysis.* Ann Arbor: School of Natural Resources, University of Michigan.

County Sanitation Districts of Los Angeles County, California. July 1963. *A plan for water re-use.*

Dore, Stanley M. 1962. New York City's water supply system. New York City Board of Water Supply.

Dortignac, E. J. 1966. Criteria for water yield improvement of forest and range land. Paper given at 21st Annual Meeting, Soil Conservation Society of America, Albuquerque, N.M., August 1966.

Dunn, William G. 1965. Statement on modified Snake–Colorado project (Dunn Plan). Statement prepared for presentation before Subcommittee on Irrigation and Reclamation, Committee on Interior and Insular Affairs, U.S. House of Representatives.

Erie, L. J.; French, Orrin F.; and Harris, Karl. 1965. *Consumptive use of water by crops in Arizona.* Technical Bulletin no. 169. Tucson: Agricultural Experiment Station, University of Arizona.

Federal Water Pollution Control Administration (*see* U.S. Department of the Interior).

Fellows, Sidney M., et al. 1967. *Potential direct economic loss due to system agricultural water deficiencies.* Interim report. Department of Water Resources, State of California.

Flack, John Ernest. 1965. *Water rights transfers: An engineering approach.* Report EEP-15. Institute in Engineering-Economic Systems, Stanford University.

Fullerton, Herbert H. 1965. Transfer restrictions and misallocation of irrigation water. Master's thesis, Utah State University.

Gardner, B. Delworth, and Fullerton, Herbert H. 1968. Transfer restrictions and the misallocation of irrigation water. *American Journal of Agricultural Economics,* vol. 50, no. 3, pp. 556–71.

Goss, James W., and Young, Robert A. 1967. Organization and pricing policy of major water-distributing organizations in central Arizona. File Report 67–5. Department of Agricultural Economics, University of Arizona.

Grant, Warren R. 1967. A model for estimating cost of government export programs for rice. *Agricultural Economics Research,* vol. 19, no. 3, pp. 73–80.

Grubb, Herbert W. January 1966. *Importance of irrigation water to the economy of the Texas High Plains.* Texas Water Development Board Report no. 11.

———. October 1966. A note on returns to water, southern High Plains. *The Cross Section* (monthly publication of the High Plains Underground Water Conservation District No. 1), vol. 13, no. 5.

Hall, Warren A. 1965. The Pacific Southwest Water Plan and regional planning for water resources. A final report to the Legislature by the University of California. Water Resources Center, University of California, April 1965.

Hanson, Harry G. 1956. Public Health Service interest and program in reservoir evaporation control research. Paper delivered at First International Conference on Reservoir Evaporation Control, San Antonio, Texas, April 1956. Southwest Research Institute, San Antonio.

Hartman, L. M. 1965. On the political economy of inter-state water transfers. In *Water resources and economic development of the West.* Report no. 14, Conference Proceedings of the Committee on the Economics of Water Resources Development of the Western Agricultural Economics Research Council, Berkeley, California.

Hartman, L. M., and Anderson, R. L. 1962. Estimating the value of irrigation water from farm sales data in northeastern Colorado. *Journal of Farm Economics,* vol. 44, no. 1, pp. 207–213.

Hartman, L. M., and Seastone, D. A. 1965. Efficiency criteria for market transfers of water. *Water Resources Research,* vol. 1, no. 2, pp. 165–71.

————. 1966. Regional economic interdependencies and water use. In Allen V. Kneese and Stephen C. Smith (Eds.), *Water research.* Baltimore: The Johns Hopkins Press for Resources for the Future.

————. 1970. *Water transfers: Economic efficiency and alternative institutions.* Baltimore: The Johns Hopkins Press for Resources for the Future.

Haveman, Robert H., and Krutilla, John V. 1968. *Unemployment, idle capacity, and the evaluation of public expenditures: National and regional analysis.* Baltimore: The Johns Hopkins Press for Resources for the Future.

Heady, Earl O., and Dillon, John L. 1961. *Agricultural production functions.* Ames: Iowa State University Press.

Heady, Earl O., and Mayer, Leo V. 1967. *Food needs and U.S. agriculture in 1980.* Technical papers, vol. 1. Washington, D.C.: National Advisory Commission on Food and Fiber.

Hee, Olman. July 1967. *Demand and price analysis for potatoes.* USDA Technical Bulletin no. 1380.

Hirschleifer, Jack; DeHaven, James C.; and Milliman, Jerome W. 1960. *Water supply: Economics, technology, and policy.* Chicago: University of Chicago Press.

Hirschleifer, Jack, and Milliman, Jerome W. 1967. Urban water supply: A second look. *American Economic Review,* vol. 57, no. 2, pp. 169–78.

Hodges, Earl F. 1963. *Livestock-feed relationships, 1909–1963.* USDA Statistical Bulletin no. 337.

————. 1964. *Consumption of feed by livestock, 1940–1959.* USDA Production Research Report no. 79.

————. 1965. *Supplement for 1965 to livestock-feed relationships, 1909–1963.* USDA Statistical Bulletin no. 337.

Hogg, Howard C., and Larson, Arnold B. 1968. An iterative linear programming procedure for estimating patterns of agricultural land use. *Agricultural Economics Research,* vol. 20, no. 1, pp. 17–24.

Houston, Clyde E., and Shade, Richard O. 1966. *Irrigation return-water systems.* California Agricultural Experiment Station Extension Service Circular 542.

Howe, Charles W. 1968. Water resources and regional economic growth in the United States, 1950–1960. *Southern Economic Journal,* April 1968.

Hurley, Patrick A. December 1968. Augmenting Colorado River by weather modification. *Journal of the Irrigation and Drainage Division, Proceedings of the American Society of Civil Engineers*, vol. 94, IR4, pp. 363–80.

Idaho, Department of Agricultural Information. 1962. *Agricultural Science*, vol. 47, no. 2.

Jacobs, James Jerome. 1968. An economic supply function for the diversion of irrigation water to Tucson. Master's thesis, Department of Agricultural Economics, University of Arizona.

Johnson, D. Gale. 1968. Sugar program–costs and benefits. *Foreign trade and agricultural policy*. Technical papers, vol. 6. Washington, D.C.: National Advisory Commission on Food and Fiber.

Johnson, Richard L. 1966. An investigation of methods for estimating marginal values of irrigation water. Master's thesis, Utah State University, Logan, Utah.

Jones, Douglas M. 1967. Selected data relating to resources, costs, and returns on irrigated crop farms in Yuma County, Arizona. File Report 67–4, Department of Agricultural Economics, University of Arizona.

Kierans, Thomas W. 1964. Grand replenishment and Northern Development Canal. Brochure. Sudbury, Ontario.

Kirk, Dudley. 1968. World population: Hope ahead. *Standard Today* (Winter 1968), Series I, no. 22.

Krutilla, John V. 1967. Conservation reconsidered. *American Economic Review*, September 1967, pp. 777–86.

———. 1968a. The value of wildlife resources. Paper given before the National Capital Chapter of the Wildlife Management Society, Washington, D.C.

———. 1968b. Balancing extractive industries with wildlife habitat. *Transactions of the Thirty-Third North American Wildlife and Natural Resources Conference, March 11, 12, 13, 1968*. Wildlife Management Institute, Washington, D.C.

Krutilla, John V., and Eckstein, Otto. 1958. *Multiple purpose river development*. Baltimore: The Johns Hopkins Press for Resources for the Future.

Kuiper, E. 1966. Canadian water export. *The Engineering Journal* (Montreal, Canada), vol. 49, no. 7, pp. 13–18.

Lauritzen, C. W. 1967. Water storage: Seepage, evaporation, and management. Paper presented at Symposium on Water Supplies for Arid Regions, Committee on Desert and Arid Zones Research, American Association for the Advancement of Science, Tucson, Arizona, May 1967.

Lave, Lester B. 1963. The value of better weather information to the raisin industry. *Econometrica*, vol. 31, no. 1–2.

Lee, F. C., and Stern, D. 1965. A feasibility study of mainland shelf undersea aqueduct. Report to the U.S. Department of the Interior, National Engineering Science Company, Pasadena, California.

Leonard, Robert L. 1964. *Integrated management of ground and surface water in relation to water importation*. Giannini Foundation of Agricultural Economics Research Report no. 279, University of California, Berkeley.

Leven, Charles L. 1961. Regional income and product accounts: Construction and application. In Werner Hochwald (Ed.), *Design of regional accounts.* Baltimore: The Johns Hopkins Press for Resources for the Future.

Löf, George O. G., and Hardison, Clayton. 1966. Storage requirements for water in the United States. *Water Resources Research*, vol. 2, no. 3, pp. 323–354.

Lofting, E. M., and McGauhey, P. H. 1963. *Economic evaluation of water: Part III, An interindustry analysis of the California water economy.* Contribution no. 67, Water Resources Center, University of California, Berkeley.

Maass, Arthur. 1966. Benefit-cost analysis: Its relevance to public investment decisions. *Quarterly Journal of Economics*, vol. 80, pp. 208–226.

Marglin, Stephen A. 1962. Objectives of water resource development: A general statement. In Maass et al., *Design of water resource systems.* Cambridge: Harvard University Press.

————. 1967. *Public investment criteria.* Cambridge: MIT Press.

Martin, William E., and Bower, Leonard G. 1966. Patterns of water use in the Arizona economy. *Arizona Review*, vol. 15, no. 12, pp. 1–6.

Martin, William E., and Carter, Harold O. 1962. *A California interindustry analysis emphasizing agriculture: Part I, The input-output model and results.* Giannini Foundation of Agricultural Economics Research Report no. 250, University of California, Berkeley.

McCammon, L. B., and Lee, F. C. 1966. Undersea aqueduct system. *Journal of American Water Works Association*, vol. 58, no. 7.

McGuinness, C. L. 1963. *The role of groundwater in the national water situation.* U.S. Geological Survey Water-Supply Paper 1800.

Mohring, Herbert D., and Harwitz, Mitchell. 1962. *Highway benefits: An analytical framework.* Evanston: Northwestern University Press.

Moore, Charles V., and Hedges, Trimble R. 1963. *Economics of on-farm irrigation water availability and costs, and related farm adjustments: Vol. 2, Farm size in relation to resource use, earnings, and adjustments on the San Joaquin Valley Eastside.* California Agricultural Experiment Station, Giannini Foundation of Agricultural Economics Research Report no. 263, University of California, Berkeley.

Musick, J. T.: Grimes, D. W.; and Herron, G. M. 1963. *Water management, consumptive use, and nitrogen fertilization of irrigated winter wheat in western Kansas.* U.S. Department of Agriculture Production Research Report no. 75. Agricultural Research Service in cooperation with Kansas Agricultural Experiment Station.

Myers, Lloyd E. 1967a. New water supplies from precipitation harvesting. Paper presented to the International Conference on Water for Peace, Washington, D.C., May 1967.

————. 1967b. Precipitation runoff inducement: Vegetation management and water harvesting. Paper given at the Symposium on Water Supplies for Arid Regions, Committee on Desert and Arid Zones Research, American Association for the Advancement of Science, Tucson, Arizona, May 1967.

Nace, Raymond L. 1967. Are we running out of water? U.S. Geological Survey Circular no. 536. Washington, D. C.

Nadeau, Remi A. 1950. *The water seekers.* Garden City, N.Y.: Doubleday.

Nations, Louis Ray. 1966. Livestock water problems in the year 2000. Paper given at the 21st Annual Meeting, Soil Conservation Society of America, Albuquerque, N.M., August 1966.

Nelson, Samuel B. 1963. Snake–Colorado Project: A plan to transport surplus Columbia River Basin water to the arid Pacific southwest. Department of Water and Power, City of Los Angeles.

New York, City of, Board of Water Supply. 1967. *61st Annual report, 1966.*

Norwood, G. 1963. Alaska water resources, a strategic national asset. Paper presented at Seminar on Continental Use of Arctic Flowing Water. State of Washington Water Research Center, Pullman, Washington. Wenatchee, Washington: Wenatchee Daily World.

Office of Saline Water (*see* U.S. Department of the Interior).

Parsons, The Ralph M. Company. *NAWAPA: North American Water and Power Alliance.* Brochure 606–2934–19. Los Angeles (no date).

———. 1964. *Engineering,* vol. I of *North American Water and Power Alliance: Conceptual study.* Reference no. 606–2934–001. Los Angeles.

Pavelis, George A. 1965. Irrigation policy and long-term growth functions. *Agricultural Economics Research,* vol. 17, no. 2, pp. 50–60.

Peterson, Arthur W. *Economic development of the Columbia Basin Project compared with a neighboring dryland area.* EM 2601. Pullman, Washington: Washington State University.

Phelan, John T. 1964. Research progress and future needs in farm use of irrigation water. In *Research on water,* ASA Special Publication Series no. 4. Madison, Wisconsin: Soil Science Society of America.

Pirkey, F. Z. 1963. Water for all (with diagrams and maps).

Potter, J. R. 1965. *The traffic pattern of American raw cotton shipments, season 1961–62.* USDA Marketing Research Report no. 705.

Robinson, T. W. 1952. Phreatophytes and their relation to water in western United States. *Transactions,* American Geophysical Union, vol. 33, no. 1, February 1952.

———. 1965. Introduction, spread, and areal extent of saltcedar (*Tamarix*) in the western United States. Geological Survey Professional Paper 491–A, Washington, D.C.

Roefs, T. C.; Nodohara, Koso; and Fellows, Sidney M. 1967. *Potential direct economic loss due to system agricultural water deficiencies.* Preliminary interim report, Department of Water Resources, State of California.

Russell, Clifford R.; Arey, David; and Kates, Robert. 1970. *Drought and water supply: Implications of the Massachusetts experience for municipal planning.* Baltimore: The Johns Hopkins Press for Resources for the Future.

Ruttan, Vernon W. 1965. *The economic demand for irrigated acreage: New methodology and some preliminary projections, 1954–1980.* Baltimore: The Johns Hopkins Press for Resources for the Future.

———. 1967. Are grain surpluses a thing of the past? Paper presented at the Regional Grain Marketing Conference, Duluth, May 18, 1967.

Smith, Lewis G. 1968. Western States water augmentation concept. Rev. ed. Denver, Colorado.

Smith, Stephen C. 1962. *The public district in integrating ground and surface water management: A case study in Santa Clara County.* Giannini Foundation of Agricultural Economics Research Report no. 252, University of California, Berkeley.

Smith, Stephen C., and Brewer, Michael F. 1961. *California's man-made rivers: History and plans for water transfer.* Berkeley: Division of Agricultural Sciences, University of California.

Snyder, J. Herbert. 1955. *Ground water in California: The experience of Antelope Valley.* Giannini Foundation of Agricultural Economics Ground Water Study no. 2, University of California, Berkeley.

Socha, Max K. 1965. Construction of the second Los Angeles Aqueduct. *Journal of the American Water Works Association,* June 1965, pp. 699–706.

Soil Science Society of America. 1964. *Research on water: A symposium on problems and progress.* Madison, Wisconsin.

Southwest Research Institute. 1966. The potential contribution of desalting to future water supply in Texas. Report prepared for the Texas Water Development Board and U.S. Office of Saline Water. San Antonio, Texas.

Starbird, I. R., and French, B. L. 1967. *1965 Supplement to costs of producing upland cotton in the United States, 1964.* USDA Agricultural Economic Report no. 99.

Starbird, I. R., and Hines, F. K. 1966. *Cost of producing upland cotton in the United States, 1964.* USDA Agricultural Economic Report no. 99.

Stetson, T. M. 1964. Review of Pacific Southwest Water Plan. Consulting Engineer Report to Six-Agency Committee, Los Angeles, California.

Stoyer, Ray L. 1967. The development of "total use" water management at Santee, California. Paper presented at the International Conference on Water for Peace, Washington, D.C., May 1967.

Stults, Harold M. 1966. Predicting farmer response to a falling water table: An Arizona case study. In *Water resources and economic development of the West,* Report no. 15, Conference Proceedings, Committee on the Economics of Water Resources Development of the Western Agricultural Economics Research Council, Las Vegas, Nevada, December 1966.

Taylor, Gary C. 1964. Economic planning of water supply with particular reference to water conveyance. Doctoral thesis, University of California, Berkeley.
————. 1967. *Economic Planning of water supply systems.* Giannini Foundation of Agricultural Economics Research Report no. 291, University of California, Berkeley.

Texas Water Development Board. 1968. *The Texas Water Plan.* Austin, Texas.

Tiebout, Charles M. 1957. Regional and inter-regional input-output models. *Southern Economic Journal,* October 1957, pp. 140–47.

Tinney, E. R. 1967. Engineering Aspects [of NAWAPA]. *Bulletin of the Atomic Scientist,* September 1967, pp. 21–25.

Todd, David K. 1965. Economics of ground water recharge. *Journal of the Hydraulics Division, Proceedings of the American Society of Civil Engineers,* July 1965, pp. 249–70.

Tolley, G. S. 1959. Reclamation influence on the rest of agriculture. *Land Economics,* vol. 35, May 1959, pp. 176–180.

Tolley, G. S., and Hartman, L. M. 1960. Inter-area relations in agricultural supply. *Journal of Farm Economics*, vol. 42, May 1960, pp. 453–73.

Ulrey, Ivan W. 1964. *Fresh potato transportation to large markets from five major producing areas.* USDA Marketing Research Report no. 687.

U.S. Congress. 1968. Colorado River Basin Project Act. PL 90-537, 90th Congress, September 30, 1968.

U.S. Department of Agriculture. *Agricultural statistics.* Annual.

———. 1966. *Sugar reports.* No. 171.

———. November 1966. *Cotton: Supply, demand, and farm resource use.* Southern Cooperative Series Bulletin no. 110.

———. 1967. *State estimates of farm income, 1949–66.* FIS 207 Supplement.

U.S. Department of Commerce. *Census of agriculture, 1959* and *1964.* Vol. II.

———. 1967. *Census of agriculture, 1964.* Vol. I, part 47 (Oregon) and part 48 (California).

U.S. Department of the Interior. 1963. *Pacific Southwest Water Plan: Report and Appendix.* August 1963.

———. 1967. *Summary report of the Commissioner of the Bureau of Reclamation, 1966, and statistical appendix.*

U.S. Department of the Interior, Bureau of Reclamation. 1950. Interim report on reconnaissance of California section, United Western Investigation. December 22, 1950.

———. 1966. The Southwest Idaho Development Project. Project Planning Report, Region 1, Boise, Idaho.

———. May 1968. Progress report on West Texas and Eastern New Mexico Import Project Investigation.

———. 1968. Reconnaissance report—augmentation of the Colorado River by desalting sea water.

U.S. Department of the Interior, Federal Water Pollution Control Administration. 1967. *Santee Recreation Project, Santee, California, final report.* Water Pollution Control Research Series, WP-20-7. Publication office, FWPCA, Cincinnati, Ohio 45226.

U.S. Department of the Interior, Office of Saline Water. 1966. *Results of a preliminary survey of candidate communities for saline water demineralization applications.* Research and Development Progress Report no. 162.

U.S. Geological Survey. 1968. *Estimated use of water in the United States, 1965.* Circular no. 556.

U.S. Geological Survey. Water Supply Papers: (1594-D) *Induced recharge of an artesian glacial-drift aquifer at Kalamazoo, Michigan* by J. E. Reed, Morris Deutsch, and S. W. Wiitala 1966; (1615 A through H) *Artificial recharge of ground water in the Grand Prairie region, Arkansas,* 1963 through 1966; and (1819-F) *Recharge studies on the High Plains in northern Lea County, New Mexico,* by J. S. Havens, 1966.

U.S. House of Representatives. 1967. Hearings before the Subcommittee on Irrigation and Reclamation of the Committee on Interior and Insular Affairs, March 13–17, 1967. Serial no. 90–5.

U.S. House of Representatives. 1966. Hearings before the Subcommittee on Public Works Appropriations. 89th Cong., 1st sess. Committee Print, Part 2.

U.S. Senate, Committee on Interior and Insular Affairs. 1958. *Control of evaporation losses.* Committee Print no. 1. 85th Cong., 2d sess.

U.S. Senate, Select Committee on National Water Resources. 1960a. *The impact of new technologies on integrated multiple-purpose water development.* Committee Print no. 31. 86th Cong., 2d sess.

———. 1960b. *Water resources activities in the United States: Water supply and demand.* Committee Print no. 32. 86th Cong., 2d sess.

U.S. Senate, Subcommittee on Western Water Development of the Committee on Public Works. 1964. *Western water development.* Committee Print.

United States Water Resources Council. 1969. Procedures for evaluation of water and related land resource projects. Report to the Water Resources Council by the Special Task Force. Draft no. 3. Washington, D.C.

Upchurch, M. L. 1966. The capacity of the United States to supply food for developing countries. Paper presented at the Conference on Alternatives for Balancing Future World Food Production and Needs, sponsored by Center for Agricultural and Economic Adjustment, Iowa State University, Ames, Iowa, November 1966.

Van Hylckama, T. E. A. 1966. Effect of soil salinity on the loss of water from vegetated and fallow soil. *Proceedings of the Wageningen Symposium,* International Association of Scientific Hydrology, June 1966, pp. 635–44.

Wadleigh, Cecil H. 1964. Fitting modern agriculture to water supply. In *Research on water.* Special Publication Series no. 4. Madison, Wisc.: Soil Science Society of America.

Walker, A. L., et al. 1966. *The economic significance of Columbia Basin Project development.* Bulletin 669, Washington State University, Pullman, Washington.

Warnick, C. C. 1969. Historical background and philosophical basis of regional water transfer. In William G. McGinnies and Bram J. Goldman (Eds.), *Arid lands in perspective.* Tucson: University of Arizona Press and American Association for the Advancement of Science.

Warskow, William L. 1967. The Salt River Valley Water Users' Association Watershed Rehabilitation Program: A progress report. Paper presented at the Range Weed Research Meeting, Las Cruces, N.M., August 1967.

Washington, State of, Water Research Center. 1967. *An initial study of the water resources of the state of Washington: Digest.* Report No. 2. Pullman, Washington.

Waugh, Frederick V. 1964. *Demand and price analysis: Some examples from agriculture.* USDA Technical Bulletin no. 1316.

Whittlesey, Norman. 1959. Economics of irrigation: Uncompahgre Project. Master's thesis, Colorado State University.

Wineland, J. A., and Lucas, C. V. 1963. Economic comparisons of canal linings for the California Aqueduct. In *Proceedings of the Seepage Symposium,* Phoenix, Arizona, February 19–21, 1963. USDA—ARS 41–90.

Wollman, Nathaniel, et al. 1962. *The value of water in alternative uses with special application to water use in the San Juan and Rio Grande Basins of New Mexico.* Albuquerque: University of New Mexico Press.

Wollman, Nathaniel, and Bonem, Gilbert W. 1971. *The outlook for water: Quality, quantity, and national growth.* Baltimore: The Johns Hopkins Press for Resources for the Future.

Yaron, Dan. 1966. *Economic criteria for water resource development and allocation.* Rehovat, Israel: Department of Agricultural Economics, Hebrew University of Jerusalem.

Young, Robert A., and Martin, William E. 1967. The economics of Arizona's water pollution. *Arizona Review*, vol. 16, no. 3, pp. 9–18.

Zusman, Pinhas, and Hoch, Irving. 1965. *Resources and capital requirement matrices for the California economy.* Giannini Foundation for Agricultural Economics Research Report no. 284, University of California, Berkeley.

Index

Abel, Martin E., 54, 141n
Adams Tunnel, 9
Agriculture: changes in acreage and production (1944–64), 138–41; commodity program payments, USDA, 143–48; displacement caused by reclamation irrigation, 173; as greatest consumer of water, 3, 36, 41, 112, 169; high consumptive uses and conveyance losses for irrigated, 3; low benefits per acre-foot in relation to municipal and industrial uses, 169; varieties of government support programs, 32–33; withdrawn acreage, 55
Agricultural Census, 138n, 139; 1964 for Oregon, 63
Alfalfa hay, 165–67
All-American Canal, 78, 79, 106, 116
Anderson, Raymond L., 40
Arey, David, 133
Arizona: "ability to pay" for water, 41–42; direct benefits of water, 48; estimated income losses from decreased water, 94–95; Public Service Company, 36n; pumping costs, 37; southern region's private costs of irrigation per cotton bale, 149; value

added per acre-foot of water intake for different agricultural sectors, 52–53
Ashokan Reservoir, New York, 8

Bagley, Jay M., 112
Beattie, Byron, 130
Beck Plan, 13
Benefit-cost relationships: direct and secondary, 19–20; measurement of direct benefits, 21–26, 37–48; measurement of secondary benefits and costs, 26–33, 48–55
Benefits and costs of water, 105–7; of alternatives to interbasin transfers, 134–35; of interbasin transfers in California, 107–8, 111; of interbasin transfers in Western interstate cases, 108–11; of supplying water in relation to prices paid by farmers, 136. See also Incidence of benefits and costs
Big Thompson River, 9
Bittinger, M. W., 25
Blaney, H. F., 79n, 113
Bonem, Gilbert W., 119–22
Bonneville Dam, 109
Boulder, Colorado, 132n

189

Incidence of benefits and costs, 20, 171, 175; Oregon, 74–77; rescue operations such as Southern California, 86, 93
Income losses stemming from loss of agricultural water, 49–50
Inelasticity of demand for farm products, 137–38
Inflation of costs for construction and equipment, 111
Input-output-labor requirements model: for analyzing construction period impacts, 96–104; concentration of industrial demands in East-Central industrial belt, 103, 104; concentration of skilled personnel, 100, 103, 104; expenditures for machinery and construction vs. direct labor, 100–102, 104
Input-output models for states, 58–59; California application, 80–94; Oregon application, 61–74
Interbasin transfer projects: cost estimates, 105–10; impacts, 56–104 passim; proposed, 11–17; scope, 4, 56
Inyo Basin, 107

Jackson, Henry M., Senator, 10–11, 11n
Jacobs, James Jerome, 95
James Bay watershed, 17, 110
Johnson, Richard L., 46
Jones, Douglas M., 79

Kaiser Steel, 37n
Kates, Robert, 133
Kelso, Maurice M., 51
Kern County Water Agency (KCWA), 37–38
Keswick Dam, 7
Keynsian multiplier effects, 57n, 58n
Kierans, Thomas W., 13, 17n, 110
Klamath River irrigation project, 63
Krutilla, John V., 27n, 74, 77n, 96–104 passim, 106n, 172

Labor: assumption of full employment and mobility, 26–27; pattern of income losses, 90–92; pattern of mobility, 27–28, 32, 87, 90; unemployment caused by phase-out of agricultural acreage, 86–90
Lake Havasu, 16, 108
Lake Huron, 110
Lake Mead: evaporation rate, 118; as part of Columbia-Colorado diversion project, 59, 108, 109; as part of Snake-Colorado diversion project, 108; as part of Western Water Project, 109
Land, pattern of income losses to, 90–92
Laycock, Arleigh, 6, 6n
Liard River, 109–10
Linkages: between agriculture and industries, 57; California case, 50; dependence of impacts of water withdrawals on, 86; dependence of national benefits for rescue operations on, 92–94, 172–73; Oregon cases, 64–77, 172; Southern California, 80–86, 172
Los Angeles: Aqueduct, 6; County Sanitation Districts, water reclamation system, 120n, 123–24, 171; Department of Water and Power, 108; Second Los Angeles Aqueduct, 107
Lower Colorado River Basin: Project, 16; proposed diversions, 14; transpiration from phreatophytes, 131

McGuire, C. B., 37
Mackenzie River, 110
McNary Dam, 108–9
Madera Irrigation District, California, 37
Marginal value of water: Arizona, 41–44; California (KCWA districts), 38–40; Colorado, 40–41; Texas, 44–45; Utah, 46–47
Martin, William E., 37, 41, 41n, 42, 50, 52–53, 94–95
Metropolitan Water Districts (MWD), Los Angeles, Orange, and San Bernadino counties, 6, 8, 106–8, 123
Mexico, 4, 17, 110

THE JOHNS HOPKINS PRESS
Designed by Arlene J. Sheer
Composed in Baskerville text and display
by Montotype Composition Company

Printed on 60 lb. Perkins and Squier, R
by Universal Lithographers, Inc.
Bound in Riverside Linen RL-3320
by L. H. Jenkins, Inc.